Contents

I0892403

Troubling Minds

TROUBLING MINDS

The Cultural Politics of Genius
in the United States
1840–1890

Gustavus Stadler

University of Minnesota Press
Minneapolis • London

Parts of chapter 4 were originally published in "Louisa May Alcott's Queer Geniuses," *American Literature* 71, no. 4 (1999): 657–77; reprinted with permission from Duke University Press.

Copyright 2006 by the Regents of the University of Minnesota

All rights reserved. No part of this publication may be reproduced, stored in a retrieval system, or transmitted, in any form or by any means, electronic, mechanical, photocopying, recording, or otherwise, without the prior written permission of the publisher.

Published by the University of Minnesota Press
111 Third Avenue South, Suite 290
Minneapolis, MN 55401-2520
http://www.upress.umn.edu

Library of Congress Cataloging-in-Publication Data

Stadler, Gustavus.
Troubling minds : the cultural politics of genius in the United States, 1840–1890 / Gustavus Stadler.
p. cm.
Includes bibliographical references and index.
ISBN 13: 978-0-8166-4225-0 (hc), 978-0-8166-4226-7 (pb)
ISBN 10: 0-8166-4225-7 (alk. paper), 0-8166-4226-5 (pbk. : alk. paper)
1. American prose literature—19th century—History and criticism. 2. Genius in literature. 3. Race in literature. 4. United States—Intellectual life—19th century. 5. Politics and culture—United States—History—19th century. I. Title.
PS368.S73 2006
810.9'353—dc22

2005035150

Printed in the United States of America on acid-free paper

The University of Minnesota is an equal-opportunity educator and employer.

12 11 10 09 08 07 06 10 9 8 7 6 5 4 3 2 1

For Anna

Acknowledgments

It has been my great fortune to enjoy a wealth of intellectual, personal, and professional generosity during the writing of this book.

Although this project was only getting started when I completed graduate school, its foundations lie very much in the impact of my mentors there: Cathy Davidson, Jan Radway, Eve Kosofsky Sedgwick, and especially Michael Moon. Thomas Sherratt's pedagogy was also a vital source of sustenance during these years.

Since then, a number of scholars of nineteenth-century Anglo-American literature and culture have been generous with support, suggestions, and criticism. I especially thank Christopher Castiglia, Julia Stern, Meredith McGill, Jonathan Freedman, Sara Blair, Maurice Wallace, Ann Cvetkovich, and Eric Lott.

Specific chapters of this book have benefited tremendously from the insights of Rachel Adams, Kim Benston, Florence Dore, Kendall Johnson, David Kazanjian, Anna McCarthy, José Muñoz, Bethany Schneider, Theresa Tensuan, Jen Travis, Patty White, and Tina Zwarg. Dana Nelson and Chris Castiglia provided indispensably acute readings. For their feedback, thanks also to the New York University Faculty Working Group in Queer Studies, the Tri-College Faculty Working Group in American Studies, the New York University Performance Studies Colloquium, the Haverford Literature Colloquium, the New York Americanists' Group, and the graduate students and faculty of the Department of English and American Literature at the Universidad Federal de Santa Catarina in Florianopolis, Brazil.

For their camaraderie and support during these years, thanks also to Renu Bora, Adam Frank, Joseba Gabelando, Maude Hines, Carrie McClaren, Diane McKay, Hank Okazaki, John Plotz, Mark Simpson, Gillian Silverman, Helen Thompson, and Ben Weaver.

Haverford College and the National Endowment for the Humanities provided vital financial support for this project.

The stewardship of Richard Morrison, the book's editor at the University of Minnesota Press, has been extraordinarily wise and attentive, and working with him and the Press has been downright pleasurable.

My students at Haverford College and Bryn Mawr College are likely unaware of how much I have learned from them. For their insight at formative stages of this book's composition, especial thanks to Miriam Achtenberg, Tamar Adler, Debra Auspitz, Stephanie Flournoy, Brendan Lanctot, Lauren LeBlanc, Iain Pollack, Jenny Sawyer, Ivan Weiss, and Isaac Zaur. Thanks also to my two superb research assistants, Shannon Carson and David Fask.

A happy wealth of individuals has made the greater Tri-College community still greater: Cristina Beltran, Kim Benston, Matthew Budman, Israel Burshatin, Billy Galperin, Lisa Jane Graham, Rob Haley, Laurie Kain Hart, Carol Henry, the late Brad High, Jenny Horne, Saleha Jilani, Kendall Johnson, Jonathan Kahana, Libby Kleine, Ken Koltun-Fromm, Jim Krippner, John Lardas, Baki Mani, Laura McGrane, Anne McGuire, Jerry Miller, Lynn Mountwell, Jennifer Patico, Jim Ransom, Bethel Saler, Bethany Schneider, Cynthia Schneider, Ulrich Schoenherr, David Sedley, Julie Summerfield, Theresa Tensuan, Kate Thomas, Sharon Ullman, Patty White, and Judy Young. Tina Zwarg and Raji Mohan have been amazing friends and comrades in and out of the workplace, and I continue to be inspired by their brilliance in matters literary, political, pedagogical, and personal.

For such close comradeship of such extraordinary duration, José Muñoz and Marina Rustow deserve special mention—or medals. Brian Selsky's thinking, writing, and conversation helped convince me to take this topic seriously while I was writing a dissertation on something else; it deeply saddens me to memorialize rather than directly thank him here.

I also wish to express my deep gratitude to a diaspora of friends whose geniuses, of many sorts, provided vital nourishment during the writing of this book: Michael Cobb, Ann Cvetkovich, Florence Dore, Jennifer Doyle, Lisa Duggan, Jonathan Flatley, Robert Frankel,

Elizabeth Hutchinson, David Kazanjian, Amy King, Pamela M. Lee, and John Vincent.

My family's deep resources of love and support deserve infinitely more credit than I could ever give here, and for far more than only this book, but I must nonetheless thank Evalyn, Tuck, Frances, and Priscilla Stadler.

To Anna McCarthy, burning genius, and my partner in joys and adventures of every kind, I dedicate this book with a fervor I can only express directly: thank you for the unabashed excess of your love for orange tabbies and *Hunky Dory,* for letting me watch you think and write, for grabbing me before I could pull an "Amy March" on this project, for reminding me to breathe, for every single thing you are. Thank you, in other words, for the fire.

INTRODUCTION

"This Unclassified Condition"

"In short, he's a man of genius?"
"Yes, call it genius."
—Henry James, *Roderick Hudson*

Here is a partial list of some people and phenomena that authors and critics associated with the category of genius in the mid-nineteenth-century United States: the "Swedish Nightingale," Jenny Lind; Benjamin Lundy's newspaper, *The Genius of Universal Abolition*; the actress Fanny Kemble; Jean-Jacques Rousseau; Frederick Douglass; the teenaged chess player Paul Murphy; Madame de Staël; P. T. Barnum; the "Young American" poet Cornelius Matthews; George Sand; and Toussaint L'Ouverture. What did *genius* mean, in the face of such diversity? Then as now, the term was associated with the accomplishments of individuals perceived to be exceptional—persons become "figures" distinguished for the originality and historical significance of their work in the arts, politics, or sciences. Then as now, the term also implied a *question* of judgment, a provocation to readers, writers, and critics to articulate their ideas about what made aesthetic or intellectual labor *valuable,* for whom, within what situation. Lately, however, many people regard use of the term *genius* as politically naïve, superficial, or ridiculous: the post-1968 insistence of Marxist literary theorist Pierre Macherey that "genius is a topic by nature uninteresting" finds affirmation in the mawkishness of recent Hollywood films such as *Shine, A Beautiful Mind,* and *Baby Geniuses,* and recent books on the subject by academics like Peter Kivy and Harold

Bloom do little to resurrect interest in the category among either intellectuals or a more general literary readership.[1] In short, a term that the intellectual world of the nineteenth-century United States regarded as a provocation worthy of extended theorization, discussion, and revision is now at best outmoded, at worst shamed into obscurity by the superego of a critique that remains panicked by the conservatism it has so effectively critiqued.[2]

This neglect is astounding given the extent to which books and journals of the nineteenth century debate the characteristics of the category, rival theories of its origins, and, perhaps most of all, attribution of its mantle to particular live, dead, and fictional persons. Taken together, these modes of discussion constitute the *discourse* of genius, and more broadly of cultural value and cultural politics, in the nineteenth-century United States. Within this discourse, the concept assumed a number of typical forms: that of the "great" man whose life and words were seen to crystallize a nation or period of history; that of the innate, unlearned talents of an artist, performer, writer, or orator; that of the irreducible originality of an idea, work of art, or collective self-conception; that of the irreducible essence of an idea, work of art, or collective self-conception. The category was also a key concept through which writers and critics sought to identify "essentially American" cultural producers. The history of genius as a core concept in Western thought is long and diverse, but after the blossoming of eighteenth-century aesthetic philosophy, the concept became increasingly associated with the principles of fine art and aesthetic taste, naming (as Kant put it) "an innate mental aptitude through which nature gives the rule to art," even when that art was political oratory or theatrical performance.[3] Recent books by Andrew Elfenbein and Barbara Will have captured the genealogical complexity of this modern conception of genius within different critical, cultural, and historical contexts from those operative in this study, and from one another's.[4]

This book examines the encounter between ideas of aesthetic genius and the United States' sense of itself as "modern" as this developed between 1840 and 1890. I describe this notion of modernity as it appears along two avenues of historical change: shifts in the scale of "culture," and in the role culture was imagined to play in individuals' lives; and, second, notions of whiteness and blackness as they shifted, and remained static, in response to slavery, abolitionism, and emancipation. My argument, at its broadest, is that discussions and representations of genius during this era reflect changing understandings of cultural and intellectual labor—changing understandings, that is, of such labor's importance and in the way it is important. As the book proceeds through these five decades, we see in the discourse of genius an increasing demand for writers and other cultural practitioners to perform emotional work for a citizenry made up of cultural consumers. The genius figure becomes more integral to the everyday life of the individual American (always presumptively middle-class and white) as culture becomes a fundamental area of self-definition (what Bourdieu would call "distinction"), rather than simply of taste or diversion. The geniuses' labor is to fortify middle-class men and women by taking upon their own minds and bodies the troubling, potentially shattering phenomena associated with modernity. And although, as we shall see, the category of genius repeatedly focused the attempts of certain writers to articulate alternate visions of the nation—in particular, offering a wedge with which to trouble basic suppositions about relationships among labor, race, gender, and "freedom"—the term was ultimately most useful for rendering, on a mass scale, the consumption of aesthetic culture as a necessary and vital part of the "freedom" known as good citizenship.

From the 1840s through the 1880s, the discourse of genius operated for authors, critics, and an increasingly self-consciously "literary" readership as a forerunner of the modern concept of *culture*.[5] As my opening list illustrates, by the mid-nineteenth century in the United States, genius was carrying its aesthetic origins into the quotidian realms of politics, mass culture, and commerce: realms the German and British Romantics had defined genius *against*.[6] Like culture, genius was a category that referred to both "the best that has been thought and said" (in the famous Arnoldian phrase) and the proto-anthropological notion of a collective *essence*. During this period, when *modernity* had arrived but *modernism* had not, genius served the useful theoretical and performative function of delineating an "ambivalent conceptual, psychological, and historical space between the individual and social collectivity," to borrow Susan Hegeman's formulation.[7] But over the course of these five volatile decades of U.S. history, the representative capacities of genius gradually shifted: toward collectivities other than the nation, and toward an increasingly detailed, psychologized, and sexualized notion of the individual genius: the genius as pathological subject.

The chapters of this book explore a series of instances in this cultural history, in which writers' use of the keyword "genius" reflected and shaped changes in, as well as resistances to, the dominant understanding of the relationship between the cultural field and politics.

Throughout these decades, genius was a term through which a range of authors and intellectuals projected their understanding of what made their own work important, and to whom. Both the category and the discourse surrounding it provided these men and women with a syntax for representing the value of their work and existence, and for casting that value as aesthetic, political, historical, or some combination of the three. A great deal of recent criticism has treated genius skeptically if not with outright hostility, seeing its effects as what I have called a "projection" essentially mystifying the political, economic, and historical factors shaping authorship, or cultural production more generally. In a range of fields, the category of authorship has generated much powerful critique in recent decades. But such criticism generally ignores the term's place in the texture of this different time, when it was a speech act in the lingua franca of an intellectual life coming to grips with both grave national crisis and vast transformations in the way literature and other culture was produced, distributed, and consumed. If, as scholars such as Meredith McGill and Lora Romero have shown, authorship is an attribution that can nurture reflexive suppositions in scholarly accounts of nineteenth-century literary culture, the discourse of genius can provide a framework for understanding idealisms *as* historical formations—ones located, moreover, in particular political and cultural networks.[8]

As Pierre Bourdieu reminds us, "It is within history that the principle of freedom from history resides."[9] Although genius does very often signify a fantasy of transcendence, in this specific historical and national situation, it does so in ways that repeatedly undermine the confidence in the individual will that grounds the ideology of American nationalism. In particular, as it circulates in the new mass-scale cultural field, it becomes increasingly associated with a surprisingly diverse combination of people marked as alienated from the individualism fortified by ideologies of race, gender, and class in such forms as "free labor": fugitive slaves, female performers, and queer flaneurs—cultural figures whose symbolic value is so conflated with their bodies and internal "essences" that they can hardly be understood to work at all.[10] Sharing an etymology with the word *genie,* genius is a concept that invites consideration of the generative effects of possession by *alterity*—by other people, by people imagined as "other," by temporalities and histories unassimilable to the dominant "common sense" of the present. Moreover, genius and genius figures invite affective and psychic attachments that overflow their "representative" significance. They can produce an excessive level of fascination—intellectual, erotic, or both—with the potential to disrupt their "use value" in any single symbolic economy, such as that of a nation. This surplus is, essentially, the quality that led historian Richard Hofstadter, in his 1962 book *Anti-Intellectualism in American Life,* to refer to the "suspicion of genius" rooted in the "canons" of American capitalism.[11]

This view of genius as *troubling* is firmly established in long-running accounts of national identity, such as the practical, results-oriented culture that Hofstadter elsewhere discusses as giving rise to a "paranoid" political style.[12] Yet these accounts elide another history: the *promiscuity* of genius as a discourse crossing a variety of social categories in unexpected, unpredictable ways. Both unsettling qualities of genius—its anti-practicality and its invasive excess—are evident in an "Editor's Study" column for *Harper's* in 1886, in which William Dean Howells praised the newly published *Personal Memoirs of Ulysses S. Grant:*

> [Grant's book is] a great piece of literature, because great literature is nothing more nor less than the clear expression of minds that have something great in them, whether religion, or beauty, or deep experience. . . All the conditions here, then, are favorable to supposing a case of "genius." Yet who would trifle with that great heir of fame, that plain, grand, manly soul, by speaking of "genius" and him together?[13]

Howells's comments are characteristic of the ongoing suspicion and fascination surrounding the notion of genius in American literary and intellectual culture, but they also reflect a cultural elite's increasing sense of the category as both superficial and obfuscatory. Indeed, these remarks may constitute a foundational moment for the now often reflexive habit of putting the term in "scare quotes"—here an attempt to stave off the rest of the paragraph from infection by a case of genius. Howells discusses genius in pathological terms, describing it as a mode of "speaking" that renders the clarity and efficacy of a "grand, manly soul" surprisingly vulnerable. A discursive mode more akin to gossip than sound literary criticism, to "speak of" genius is to give shape to a spectral companion whose unnecessary presence sullies the great man's manliness.[14] To associate a good man with what Henry James's novel *The Tragic Muse* was to call four years later "this unclassified condition" is to besmirch him.[15]

In the lens of recent literary theory, genius can be seen as a form of fetishism that "links a self-evident character with a cloud of associations whose principle of coherence resists analysis," as Nancy Armstrong and Leonard Tennenhouse have described the modern notion of the author. But the concept also offers the benefit of keeping within the purview of analysis the processes that Bourdieu calls the "fact of belief in the work of art and of the social conditions which produce that belief," a focus that, for Bourdieu, permits an "escape from the usual choice between celebratory effusions and the reductive analysis which . . . destroys the work of art as such."[16] When Bourdieu refers to the author as the "apparent producer" of culture, his phrase enables analysis less concerned with revealing a truth lurking underneath ideology—something of the order of, say, "an author is really just a laborer"—than with suggesting that we pay greater attention to the processes by which cultural production *becomes apparent,* in particular forms, within a "circle of belief."[17] *Troubling Minds* is a genealogy of the forms genius assumed within the practice of this belief during a volatile half-century of U.S. history.

Bourdieu's framework shifts attention from the "production of value" to the "production of belief in value," a process that traverses multiple "regimes of value," in Arjun Appadurai's phrase, from money to aesthetics to state power.[18] If genius is a central form of this belief, the category's shape in the United States has been deeply imbued with the symbolic weight of national representativeness—a form that the faces on state-issued print culture such as currency and postage stamps maintain. But the history that has allowed figures as different in profession, sexuality, gender, and race as Andy Warhol, Elvis Presley, Amelia Earhart, and Langston Hughes simultaneously to occupy this position of national iconicity is a delayed echo of processes that, in the nation's most powerful literary circles, brought greater attention and detail to notions of *difference.*

Over the course of the mid- to late-nineteenth century, representations of genius increasingly focused on forms of exemplary otherness exemplifying a historical trajectory Robert Weimann has called the "diminishing social representativeness of art . . . exemplified in the antagonism between the status of the artist and the role of the politician."[19]

The starting point of the present study is the political, cultural, and economic context that initially brought on this crisis, or (as Weimann puts it) "erosion," of representativeness. Indeed, each of the first three chapters, which examine antebellum authors and texts, unfolds in a similar context of historical transformations in political ideology, political economy, and, because of the intensification of the crisis over slavery, political geography. Historian Charles Sellers has called the period from 1815 to 1846 the occasion of a "market revolution" that "crystallized a politics that has ever since muffled the contradiction between capitalism and democracy in a mythology of consensual and democratic enterprise." By the 1840s, Sellers writes, no constituency in the nation offered any significant challenge to "bourgeois hegemony."[20] The cultural marketplace grew rapidly around this time, as a number of scholars have shown, its expansion enabled by advances in technologies of production and distribution, increasing literacy rates, and the growth of a middle-class quotidian, reserving significant portions of space and time for routine leisure.[21]

At the same time, the tenor of political ideology, in its hegemonic forms, was shifting in ways that ultimately shaped the politics of representation within the expanded cultural sphere. Recent works by scholars such as McGill and Jay Grossman have brought a greater level of historical and cultural specificity to the shift in dominance from republicanism to liberalism, a transition that U.S. historians for many years portrayed as culminating in Andrew Jackson's election to the presidency at the end of the 1820s. McGill and Grossman show that in the 1840s certain aspects of the shift were still underway, and that the persistence of republican ideals was particularly apparent in the literary public sphere, where notions of authorship and intellectual property resisted the otherwise increasingly widespread tide of possessive individualism.[22] The ongoing influence of republican notions of public virtue, most apparent in the political and literary worlds of the eighteenth century, sustained what Michael Warner has called a "principle of negativity" toward the individual presence in the public sphere, a fundamental assumption that "[w]hat you say will carry force not because of who you are but despite who you are. Implicit in this principle is a utopian universality that would allow people to transcend the given realities of their bodies and their status."[23]

Although literary and intellectual histories are never the tidy narratives scholars generally attempt to make them seem, it is, I think, possible to identify the 1840s as a key period of transition in the Euro-American bourgeoisie's broad view of the cultural significance of literature, from a constitutively civic frame to a private, interiorized one. In the antebellum United States, the economic trends pinpointed in Sellers's *The Market Revolution* were crucially formative factors in this overall change in the scale through which the writing and reading of published texts was conceived. The expansion of the publishing industry both diversified the types of books available to consumers and made it more difficult to view these books as luxury items distinct from the spectrum of consumer goods on the market. For decades now, Walter Benjamin has been considered the major theorist of the interlocking, transnational trends in economics and aesthetics that produced the affective texture of a modern cultural marketplace around this time. As Benjamin explains in his *Arcades Project*: "Around the middle of the century, the conditions of artistic production underwent a change. This change consisted in the fact that for the first time the form of the commodity imposed itself decisively on the work of art and the form of the masses on its public" (23). Simultaneously, as Benjamin remarks, cultural marketplaces became oriented increasingly by the notion of a "mass" audience, a generalized, abstract entity to which no individual reader actually belonged (as Raymond Williams reminds us with his crisp formulation, "There are in fact no masses. There are only ways of seeing people as masses").[24] Because more people were reading, and were reading within a market-driven process of selecting, via acts of "taste," texts of particular interest, the viability of the nonparticular, representative individual that had framed the literary sphere within republican political ideology diminished. Critics such as Warner, Lauren Berlant, Ann Cvetkovich, and Jonathan Elmer have described how the mass scale of the production and consumption of culture incurred ambivalent, even dissonant, responses in Anglo-American subject-citizens because, as Warner puts it, "Where consumer capitalism makes available an endlessly differentiable subject, the subject of the public sphere proper cannot be differentiated."[25] As cultural production under modern capitalism brought more forms of difference into representation, the mythos of the undifferentiated, abstract, national, civic-public sphere became more difficult to sustain through the notion of national representativeness.

Where latter-day critics working in the wake of Benjamin and the Frankfurt School have generally looked to developments in capitalism to account for these historical processes, the American cultural discourse of genius in the 1840s and 1850s demonstrates the central, dynamic role that slavery and race played in them, and illuminating this role is among this book's central projects. One of the new cultural forms introduced in the aftermath of the "market revolution" was the fugitive slave narrative, a genre that exemplified the significant role played by abolitionism in the new cultural modernity.[26] Along with the rising attention the literary public was paying to music produced by slaves, this genre marks the incipience of a belief among northeastern white intellectuals that such a thing as black or black American culture existed. The possibility of attributing genius to people of African descent caused intellectuals of European origins to consider their own bodies as racialized, as white, in newly concrete ways. Many of the period texts examined in this book struggle to represent the white body of the genius figure while maintaining genius's potential for abstraction as a universally representative symbol. Indeed, this struggle sparked what I call (in chapter 2) a "cosmopolitan whiteness" that, well before the more widely studied cosmopolitanisms of the postbellum years, looked to snowy Northern Europe for genius unsullied by a political sphere shared with the slave South.

Indeed, the impact of slavery and racial politics on genius discourse in the antebellum semirepublic of letters demonstrates the difficulty of sustaining the conventional depiction of the powerful northeastern intellectual circles of this period as resolutely in search of some stabilizing, nationally representative, homegrown genius figure.[27] Such presumptions guide even some of the most trenchant ideological critique of recent decades. For instance, Sacvan Bercovitch contrasts the model of genius described in New England literature with that articulated in the work of Romantic and post-Romantic European writers such as Carlyle, Nietzsche, Byron, and Goethe. In the latter, he writes, the genius rejects society, and announces himself the adversary of "everything from which he is alienated—history, the common laws, the representative men and women that constitute social normality." In contrast, "the very concept of 'Americanus,' from Mather through Emerson, advances a mode of personal identity designed as a compensatory replacement for (rather than an alternative to) the ugly course of actual events."[28] Assigning the "representative man" an American essence excludes some important strands of that category's intellectual history.[29] But more significantly, eliding antebellum cosmopolitanism from cultural history also erases the consistently formative role whiteness has played *across* various articulations of genius and cultural politics in the United States. For even if this international sensibility might qualify, from some vantage points, as the sort of critical "alienation" Bercovitch calls absent, it nonetheless constitutes another instance in the long history of U.S. cultural authorities' insistence that the nation's culture is specifically *not African,* an especially charged position at a time when more Africans had crossed the Atlantic than Europeans.[30] Indeed, to look to Europe during this era is to participate in the same "theatrical" work that Ralph Ellison described as giving rise to blackface minstrelsy in the mid-nineteenth century, a response to "a profound doubt in the [American] white man's mind as to the authenticity of his own image of himself."[31]

Moreover, in a cultural sphere of a mass scale, authors and intellectuals increasingly saw themselves as economically undifferentiated from their readers, with whom they participated in the cultural marketplace, as laborers in a literary *profession* subsuming an older, vocational model of authorship.[32] Within this process of realignment and market formation, genius became less explicitly tied to rhetorics of publicity and nation. Instead, it took on greater significance as a symbolic medium for representing a troubled model of the individual, a self whose struggle to maintain coherence registered through newly intricate social discourses, such as that of sexuality, which emerged at roughly the same time as the modern "culture concept." Throughout the nineteenth century, the notion of genius was closely linked to what Bourdieu has identified as the nineteenth-century bourgeoisie's belief in the "aesthetic disposition" of the individual, allowing the middle class to employ participation in the cultural field as a form of "distinction" in which rigid lines of race and class upheld a degree of fluidity in gender.[33]

But in the later decades of the century, genius became closely tied to ways of conceiving of interiority and intimacy, the languages of which were emerging from scientific fields such as psychology and sexology. Ultimately, as a discursive keyword, genius allows us to see the contemporaneous emergence of the discourses of sexuality and of culture as both epistemologically and genealogically congruous.[34]

In the years after Matthew Arnold published *Culture and Anarchy,* and the most powerful literary men in the United States consolidated institutionally in a cluster of magazines and publishing houses one critic has dubbed the "*Atlantic* group," genius discourse reflects changing ideas about cultural production and consumption as practices. It appears as part of a world in which thinking about, evaluating, and speaking to others about "artistic and intellectual activities" were matters of deeply personal stakes, subject to a range of pathologizations through which the later century represented and regulated the intimate regions of the self.[35] Culture was the site of new institutions and professions in which the bourgeoisie were both laborers and consumers.

Relatedly, what brings authors as apparently incompatible as Louisa May Alcott and Henry James together in my final two chapters is how their representations of genius dramatize the intensely urgent stakes of an individual's relationship to culture, a matter inextricable from her ability to stay healthy and to form intimate bonds with others. This common focus is evident in two texts that I do not discuss in the chapters themselves. In James's *The American* (1877), a fellow expatriate brags to the protagonist, Christopher Newman, of his "happy formula" of caring more for "reality" than for the paintings in the Louvre "with an assurance which the numerous class of persons suffering from an overdose of 'culture' might have envied him."[36] Despite Alcott's alienation and exclusion from the *Atlantic* group over the course of the 1860s, a more drawn-out use of similar metaphors makes up the opening sentences of a relatively obscure tale of hers from 1868 (the same year *Little Women* appeared), "Psyche's Art":[37]

> Once upon a time there raged in a certain city one of those fashionable epidemics which occasionally attack our youthful population. It wasn't the music mania, nor gymnastic convulsions, nor that wide-spread malady, croquet. Neither was it one of the new

> dances which, like a tarantula-bite, set every one a-twirling, nor stage madness, nor yet that American lecturing influenza which yearly sweeps over the land. No, it was a new disease called the Art fever, and it attacked the young women of the community with great violence.
>
> Nothing but time could cure it, and it ran its course to the dismay, amusement, or edification of the beholders, for its victims did all manner of queer things in their delirium.[38]

A midcentury term like "Lindmania," a journalistic term for the eruption of genius-celebrity around Jenny Lind (the subject of chapter 2 of this book), anticipates some of this, but Alcott's language is a far more pathology-oriented satire of the fashionability and ephemerality of aesthetic preoccupations running rampant through the once healthy bodies of young, middle-class women and men. The epidemiological rhetoric ("lecturing influenza," "Art fever," "delirium," etc.) directly connects the pursuit of Arnoldian ideals with contemporary discourses of physical and mental illness. Indeed, by centering the story around a protagonist named Psyche, Alcott implies that her own aim is to rescue the mind from the dangerous, dissipative threats that she associates with genius.

In the latter decades of nineteenth-century U.S. cultural production, one more rarely encounters the nation as an explicit framework of evaluation; a rare exception is James's *The Bostonians,* which ultimately marks the passing of the notion that genius's basis lies in "great" national questions.[39] Instead, genius is portrayed in a range of variations also evident in "Psyche's Art." The figures with whom it is associated give shape to threats to individual bodies and minds: illness, intoxication, psychic trauma, and madness. One particularly notable aspect of this mode in Alcott's and James's fiction is the way these disruptive forces figure erotically, outside the lines of conventional, marriage-driven plots, a *queering* of genius that crosses these authors' work. More broadly, the preoccupation with these threats made genius an important trope for negotiating a shift in the epistemology of individual difference—a shift in which a range of increasingly distinct, professionalized human sciences positioned the most significant, self-making traits as invisible, repressed. Taxonomies and categories ranging from homosexuality to newly variegated notions of ethnic whiteness reflected a growing assumption that, at some depth, everyone was different.[40]

Yet genius is also a reparative figure for both of these late-century writers, speaking to their own senses of personal, sexual, and literary alienation and suggesting a politicized hierarchy of difference underlying the strains of pluralism emergent in the age. This latter strain of genius discourse is also the legacy of some earlier forms (seen in the antebellum chapters), where writers such as Margaret Fuller and William Wells Brown used the notion of genius to demarcate the limits of conventional collective categories, such as nation, race, and gender, as frames of self-understanding.

The profligate dispersion of genius as a category of cultural discourse, and the term's ability to signify both representativeness and exceptionality in the nineteenth century, makes the task of selecting representative writers particularly challenging. Melville, Hawthorne, Whitman, and Poe are not here, though some readers will likely sense the shadow presence of the latter two men in particular. Elizabeth Peabody, who put together the remarkable volume of *Aesthetic Papers* in the 1840s, appears only in the refracted form of Miss Birdseye, a character in *The Bostonians* in whom many of James's contemporaries claimed to recognize Peabody. Recently revitalized writings by female novelists such as Elizabeth Stoddard and Elizabeth Stuart Phelps, whose work was far more formally bound up with Romantic and proto-modernist aesthetics than was that of their contemporary Louisa May Alcott, are also unfortunately absent. The most Wildean of antebellum literary men, Nathaniel Willis, pops up repeatedly, but I offer no truly sustained discussion of his literary writing. What ultimately governs this book's criteria for inclusion, in a study of a truly inexhaustible topic, is an engagement with genius that generates patterns of resolution, confusion, arousal, fascination, empowerment, shame, or other affective charge of an intensity imperiling either the purity of aesthetics or the neatness of fit of aesthetic value with national symbology. Even this criterion leaves a surfeit of material, but readers will, I hope, find my selections a useful sequence from which to see broader patterns and to launch their own inquiries into the vocabulary, syntax, and politics of culture in the nineteenth century.

My first chapter, "The Geography of Genius in Emerson, Fuller, and Douglass," shows how theories and iterations of genius by three leading antebellum intellectuals in the mid-1840s registered the economic and political tides of the slavery crisis and the "market revolution" as deeply transformative. The annexation of Texas and the war with Mexico made slavery a political issue indelibly linked to the question of national geography. In 1845, Frederick Douglass, as part of an overall effort by the William Lloyd Garrison–led American Anti-Slavery Society to increase the presence of abolitionism in the cultural public sphere, published his *Narrative of Frederick Douglass, an American Slave, Written by Himself.* Juxtaposed with contemporaneous writings by Margaret Fuller and Ralph Waldo Emerson, this text (and Douglass's reception) depict the challenges that race, slavery, and the rapidly expanding cultural marketplace posed to the symbolic wholeness of national genius. All three writers show a preoccupation with cultural practices conceived on a local scale, in the eye-level spaces of everyday life. Across their work, genius is a concept increasingly given shape through particular bodies able to navigate ideal *and* particular spaces.

I argue that these shifts in the spatial scale upon which leading intellectuals represent exceptional figures of cultural authority demonstrate the deep structural role that slavery and blackness were playing for Fuller's and Emerson's comprehensive concepts of the "uses" (to employ one of Emerson's favored terms) of intellectual and literary work. In particular, the portrayal of genius's scale in writings by Emerson and Fuller in the mid-1840s bears the marks of Douglass's visibility to these authors as a cohabitant of the abstract space of literature as well as the material-symbolic space of the nation. Both Emerson (in his journals) and Fuller (in one of the earliest reviews of the *Narrative*) depict Douglass as worthy of being called a genius to the extent that he proves himself a capable cultural agent *outside* the antislavery movement. In a surprising way, this parallels Douglass's own experience of the mid-1840s, in which he found the abolitionist movement a form of constraint on the representativeness of his figure.

Douglass's *Narrative* was published to represent Southern slavery and its author's humanity, but by 1845 Douglass had encountered the bind of representativeness as a cultural form: its demand that the effects of changing conditions—temporal, spatial, and so on—be eviscerated in the service of symbolic continuity. Within the strategies of Garrison's American Anti-Slavery Society, it seemed, Douglass was always to remain the materialized referent of Northern whites' imagination of Southern slavery, still "a chattel, a thing." Douglass's *Narrative* issues a critique of this problem in a manner that anticipates and in some ways exceeds the more explicit critique in his later memoir, *My Bondage and My Freedom,* the preface of which announces him a "representative American man." In particular, Douglass portrays the activities around Colonel Lloyd's "Great House Farm," in the famous "sorrow songs" section, as an everyday routine of cultural production, oriented in relation to a "greatness" whose symbolic force exceeds its ideological content. Traveling to and from the Great House Farm makes the everyday space of labor, stolen from slaves' "creative activity" as laborers, a liminal yet embodied space of cultural production. Parallel tendencies emerge in both Emerson's and Fuller's writing: in Emerson's work on "Representative Men," a new preoccupation with the body of the genius analogous to the physical strain put by cultural and geographical expansion on the lecturing intellectual's body; in Fuller's *New-York Tribune* writings, a concern for the local, everyday spaces of metropolitan life as making available an iconography of history and present-day politics.

The second chapter, "Cosmopolitan Whiteness: Writing Jenny Lind," examines the critical response to Jenny Lind's 1850 tour of the United States, and features the first in a series of female figures represented in the form of genius. Throughout the decades with which this book is concerned, these figures are burdened with the demands of not just symbolizing certain qualities but embodying processes of mediation themselves; Henry James's female performing geniuses from *The Bostonians* and *The Tragic Muse,* Verena Tarrant and Miriam Rooth, may be seen as the pinnacle of this convention in the face of an incipient modernism. But my examination of William Wells Brown's writing in chapter 3 establishes the continuity between these highly aestheticized figures and the "tragic mulatta" tradition, the mixed-race heroine that Brown, in the novel *Clotel; or, The President's Daughter,* based on his encounter with the female slave known as the "fancy girl" when he began working as assistant to a slave trader.

Across the period under examination, a range of intellectuals and authors make use of these female genius figures; questions of sexual virtue prove apt metaphors for the relationship between their own work and modern capitalism, and to address the assumption that the one needs to be kept *pure* from the other's advances. Repeatedly, these writers position femininity and whiteness as outside the commercial economy and the object of a threat whose nature is both sexual and commercial. But some of the instances I examine reframe this trope critically, challenging the exclusion of their labor from the economy by portraying genius as the victim in a cultural melodrama based in particular politics of race, class, and gender.

Chapter 2 argues that midcentury cultural authorities' fashioning of the singer Jenny Lind as a genius responds to many of the national crises already outlined (in chapter 1). Just as Margaret Fuller used the category genius to denationalize Frederick Douglass, widely read authors and critics like Parke Godwin, Henry Tuckerman, and John Sullivan Dwight apply the term to Lind when she tours the States in 1850, in an apparently cosmopolitan embrace of an international star. Originating in the North and embodying the "Anglo-Saxon race," Lind's genius allows critics to avoid discussion of Americanness when the nation's racially constituted crisis is becoming more embattled. At the same time, championing Lind becomes a response to the increasing presence of blackness in the nation's popular culture—particularly in the form of minstrelsy—and to an increasing anxiety that the most legitimate, successful, "native" U.S. representational practices are the products of slaves and slavery. Critics repeatedly emphasize Lind's whiteness, her Nordic origins, and the contrast between her performance style and the "sensual" nature of "Southern" female singers, largely Italians. The rhetoric of genius becomes a way of separating art from a national context, and lodging it in a cosmopolitan conception of taste. This rhetoric demonstrates an emergent model of culture, familiar from the present day, that sees national particularity as a confining force in the practice of taste; it also suggests the basis of an increasingly visible cultural hierarchy in antebellum racial politics. Dwight and Godwin, especially, can be seen as using Lind's genius to construct a nationally conceived realm of cultural value of interest to a wide, white, middle-class audience through the heterogeneous treatments of nation and gender.

In the criticism emerging out of Jenny Lind's tour of the United States, genius was a cosmopolitan concept that warded off national-racial crisis while inviting an expanded breadth of the Northern white middle class to participate in the consumption of "serious" aesthetic culture. Such criticism maintained the basic precepts of Kantian and Emersonian theories of genius, by which genius named a form of freedom unsullied by the materialism and repetitiveness of life in a rapidly expanding market economy. But this criticism simultaneously attempted to distribute such principles in the expanded *cultural* market by constructing the reception of genius in newly personalized, interiorized, gendered, and sexualized terms.

The third chapter, "Stages of Genius: The Traveling Productions of William Wells Brown," examines the late antebellum relations among genius, sex, and commerce from the perspective of a literary and political figure born on the other side of the national-racial crisis, in Southern slavery. In the 1850s, the market in culture and the market in slaves were both expanding at unprecedented rates. William Wells Brown, a fugitive slave author-activist-intellectual who spent five years in Europe during this period, was acutely attentive to the literary market as a "regime of value."[41] But his response is quite different from the Lind critics, or the much-quoted, phobic comment by Hawthorne about "women scribblers." His experience of living as a commodity and actually working in the slave market emerges, when he becomes an author, in his concept of genius as a dialectic between theoretically opposed notions of economic and cultural value.

In the first half of this chapter, I look at Brown's accounts of this time, concentrating in particular on the role played by the "fancy girl" figure—the pale-skinned female slave of mixed racial descent—in Brown's understanding of his own status as a cultural laborer. As the "fancy girl" is an educated, genteel, sexual laborer, her labor is unconventional, and its visibility problematic, in ways that help us understand how the author's own body is affected as it is trafficked across the economies of first slavery and then literary culture. And, as we see in the chapter's second half, unlike Hawthorne and some others, Brown's response to modern commercial expansion is a dynamic one; in the memoir of his cosmopolitan travels, genius signifies a mode of cultural practice: a facility for movement and observation that links the experience of the fugitive slave with that of the cosmopolitan man of culture. In *The American Fugitive: Sketches of People and Places Abroad,* he rejects an older, organicist notion of genius as linked with land-rootedness; his sense of the inadequacy of this ideal appears most pithily in his description of encountering a haggard Thomas Carlyle on a crowded London omnibus. Elsewhere in the book, he sketches the man he calls the "greatest genius I met in Europe," the light-skinned African (of indeterminate national origin) Joseph Jenkins, who works as a Shakespearean actor, musician, minister, street sweeper, and pamphleteer, and whom Brown encounters serially in his rambles through London.

During and after the Civil War, Brown's work manifests resistance to the way interiorized, richly gendered, and sexualized models of genius continue to be underwritten by whiteness. This writing responds to political currents coinciding with the advent of a more detailed, extensive identification of literary and aesthetic consumption with individual psychological health. Indeed, what both Brown and the Lind critics mark as the affective-psychological dimensions of audience and reader relations to genius pervade later century responses to the spread of Arnoldian notions of culture—a process in which the discussion of aesthetic taste spread, as Jonathan Freedman has put it, "out of the starry realms of German philosophy and into the life-practices and institutions of the middle classes."[42] In the postbellum texts examined in my last two chapters, genius discourse reflects the growing integration of aesthetic concerns not only with bourgeois everyday life, but with bourgeois conceptions of interiority and intimacy.

In spite of their common backgrounds in the elite intellectual circles of antebellum Boston, Cambridge, and Concord, Louisa May Alcott and Henry James have come to represent opposite poles of the literary field—the popular girls' companion and the modernist visionary, with James himself known to many as the "master" who solved the "problem" of American genius's relegation to the shadow of Europe, once and for all. Many readers are familiar with the struggles of Alcott's life—initially financial, later centered around the constraint she felt by the genre of children's literature. Genius was a topic Alcott wrote about in multiple fictions, in multiple genres, and yet it repeatedly appears couched in disavowal, a category from which she or her fictional stand-in (e.g., Jo March, who "did not think herself a genius by any means") is immune. At the same time, however, talking about genius, or *to* genius, is repeatedly portrayed as a highly erotic interchange between a same-sex couple. I argue that Alcott here fashions a form of what Eve Sedgwick calls "queer performativity," repeatedly depicting genius in terms of theatrically self-negating forms of shame and arousal. In such texts as *Little Women* and the roughly contemporaneous thriller "The Freak of a Genius," Alcott formulates a burdened, feminine (though not always female) whiteness whose inflammation in the eros of same-sex relations she associates with literary productivity. In its relational model of genius, Alcott's writing demonstrates the persistence of antebellum sentimental-affective dynamics in the diversifying postbellum literary field, but also takes up the transformation of these dynamics by newly therapeutic ways of imagining interiority and its narration.

Analogous concerns drive my reading of two Henry James novels of the 1880s, *The Bostonians* and *The Tragic Muse.* As a sequence, these novels demonstrate James's ambivalent attempt to rid himself of the spectral influence of antebellum culture by shaming it in the former novel and then returning to a similar theme, in an entirely European setting, in the latter. That common theme is genius, and female performing genius in particular. But what links the novels more than simply the sensations surrounding Verena Tarrant and Miriam Rooth is that both books focus on these performing genius figures' *production* by other characters: Olive Chancellor and Gabriel Nash. For, like Alcott, James portrays the notion of genius as a form of relation—and often a *queer* relation, as we see in *The Tragic Muse,* in Nash's formative influence on both Miriam and Nick Dormer.

In chapter 5, "It's the Treatment!" I examine these issues within the frame of changing ideas about racialized and sexualized bodily "difference"—a transformation becoming visible in notions of *culture* influenced by anthropology and ethnography. We see the spectacle of difference becoming a form of universalization, particularly as we see both Miriam Rooth's and Olive Chancellor's integration (at the end of *The Bostonians*) into the realm of esteemed cultural production. We see, in particular, queerness and Jewishness fashioned as particularly culturally capitalized and modern forms of exceptionality, within this developing understanding of culture—forms of genius that are "hybrid" in the racial-corporeal and interior-psychological bases ascribed to them. James, I argue, is powerfully fascinated by this modern sense of culture, particularly as he prepares to reinvent himself as a playwright. But I also argue that, through Nash especially, he is somewhat bitterly attuned to the different ways queer genius and Jewish genius manifest the relationship of whiteness to work, and I suggest his resentful suspicion that his queerness is less acceptable to a wide audience than Jewishness because of its tendency to look like it is not *really* working.

At one point in the writing of this book, I considered naming it after a bizarre volume of biographical essays from the early twentieth century called *Some Queer People,* because I thought (and still think) that both the powerful historical-contemporary signifier *queer* and the indeterminacy of quantity and quality in *some* suited the performativity of this “unclassified condition,” as James called it (and because the book included as its unlikely [for its time] representatives of American culture Margaret Fuller and Edgar Allan Poe).[43] For a long time, I thought it would be called *Freaks of Genius,* after the Alcott story “The Freak of a Genius” (discussed at length in chapter 4), because I thought (and still think) the remarkably multivalent word *freak* an apt synonym for the instability that has made genius the focus of so much emotional, erotic, cultural, national, and intellectual investment. I then settled, for a time, on *Suspicious Minds,* which conjured an image of suspect American genius—the second coming of Elvis Presley, whose hit version of the song was recorded live in Las Vegas. But ultimately the phrase encapsulates not genius itself so much as a characteristic of *thinking* about genius that enlivened the term’s uses in a body of nineteenth-century U.S. literature, as a form of cultural comment and critique. Ultimately what all these titles and my scuttling of them suggest is what I have tried to preserve at least in part: the very opaque yet volatile quality of genius’s performance in that role. If that phrase’s referent threatened to overwhelm its function as the title of a book in nineteenth-century U.S. literary and cultural studies, it nonetheless came close to encapsulating what I have tried to convey with *Troubling Minds.*[44]

CHAPTER 1

The Geography of Genius in Emerson, Fuller, and Douglass

Ralph Waldo Emerson is the central palimpsest of genius in American literature. He wrote about the term copiously, and critics have portrayed him as a genius, in a wide variety of ways, since the publication of his first book in 1836. One of Emerson's most famous sentences concerning genius comes from the essay "Experience," published in 1844: "the true romance which the world exists to realize, will be the transformation of genius into practical power."[1] What is "practical power"? The phrase certainly anticipates the title of an essay written the following year, "The Uses of Great Men." This language would seem to exhort its readers to take up the view that genius's significance lies not in theory but in practice—in what it does (or what people do with it), rather than what it is (or what people think about it). For a nation that considers *The Autobiography of Benjamin Franklin* one of its founding texts, the phrase "practical power" has an immediately nationalist tenor. Genius matters insofar as it fits a characteristically American preoccupation with utility.

But there is a slightly different way of looking at this phrase. To the extent that genius was an important term to a range of antebellum intellectuals, the notion of genius as "practical power" offers a way to forestall the overly simple oppositions (of ideal and material, mind and body, writing and speech, of literariness and historicity, to name a few) in which this nationalist trope is situated. As widely known and celebrated cultural figures, Emerson, Frederick Douglass, and Margaret Fuller "used" genius as a tool for intellectual inquiry and for understanding their experiences of everyday life as intellectuals, experiences made very different by, among other factors, race and gender. Thinking, speaking, and writing about genius was the productive venue of varied, often uneven encounters between the general and the specific, the timeless and the quotidian, that I want to look at in this chapter—encounters that position genius's "practical power" as a facet of intellectuals' everyday *practice* in a sense akin to what Michel de Certeau describes when he urges critical attention toward "ways of operating or doing things" and "ways of using [things, words, and concepts]," a field that humanistic inquiry typically subordinates to "the obscure background of social activity."[2] Following this logic, Emerson's title "The Uses of Great Men" reminds us that the "great man" is a category that different people think, speak, and read about, with specific aims and effects, in specific spatial and temporal contexts.[3] The quotidian here should not be equated with the ground-level truth or "reality" lying "behind" or "beneath" the flimsy idealism of belief in genius; de Certeau helps us to see the very idealism located in that quotidian, and accepting its presence there need not be equated with its deflation or "demystification." In this broader frame, "practical power" is not an assertion of a reductive, clichéd version of Americanness, nor does the sentence from which the phrase is culled simply serve as a truism affirming Emerson's status as a protopragmatist, a reading popular among Emersonians of the late twentieth century.

The discourse of genius provided antebellum intellectuals a site, vocabulary, and syntax to discuss both people in the abstract and specific people with bodies. Analogously, it provided a frame for discussing the ideal and concrete spaces in which these people lived, moved, and worked. Emerson speaks to this use of genius when he writes, in "The Use of Great Men," "Genius is the naturalist or geographer of the supersensible regions, and draws their map" (622). Where is this genius while he draws (for Emerson, genius is presumptively male)? Is he sitting or standing? What "region" is he in? What state? What would his "map" look like? A poem? A piece of legislation? An actual map? Such questions would strike many Emerson scholars as ludicrously literal-minded, superfluous to the series's critical engagement with Carlyle, Coleridge, Cousin, and New England's Puritan legacy. Yet the very fact that such questions can be articulated attests to a difference in Emerson's model of genius as it has developed since an early essay like "The American

Scholar." There, the imagined genius embodied his nation by subsuming space with his authority: "if the single man plant himself indominatably *[sic]* on his instincts, and ther[e] abide, the huge world will come round to him" (70). In "The Uses of Great Men," however, Emerson carves out a swath of space in which he places genius, providing a local vantage point from which to negotiate and to represent space.[4] Emerson's confidence in the possibility of an omniscient overview has been shaken; "Viewed from any high point, this city of New York, yonder city of London, the Western civilization, would seem a bundle of insanities," he writes (627). He portrays his "great men" as contending with a spatial realm that, however generalized, is different from them in scale, and requires a map to be negotiated. He writes further on in the same essay: "This is the key to the power of the greatest men,—their spirit diffuses itself. A new quality of mind travels by night and by day, in concentric circles from its origin, and publishes itself by unknown methods" (631). The men may not move, but their "spirit" does, in a manner that resembles simultaneously the model of historical consciousness in Emerson's essay "Circles" and a topography of literary publication and distribution.

Emerson did not name the nationality of this genius-geographer, but the figure's emergence in the United States of the mid-1840s seems timely. As a mode of representation, geography in the United States was subject to the volatility of a decade in which war, forced removals, and purchases brought 800 million new acres of land into the government's possession.[5] These events became still more problematic for U.S. nationalism as they were increasingly tied to the debate over the status of newly minted states as "free" or "slave." Although Emerson's "regions" are "supersensible," the category of region was gaining new currency in U.S. politics, particularly as sections of the nation became more differentiated by their views on the disposition of newly acquired territories, and on the slavery question more generally.[6]

Emerson's work on representative men coincided with the loud nationalist clarion call for an authentically American literature embodied by a single, representative author, a call issued by the New York literati who referred to themselves as "Young America."[7] Yet the substantial, highly vexed changes in physical, political, and cultural geography challenged the viability of the notion of a singular American genius, a representative individual who could claim spiritual and cultural kinship with the nation as a whole. Emerson's spatial rhetoric may seem at first a reaction formation dissipating contemporary ideological and material conflict into a highly abstract medium in which great men float while their ideas diffuse themselves, requiring no labor to be produced or distributed—a socially efficacious abstraction of space we might identify with the concept of culture as it would be articulated in coming decades by Matthew Arnold and others.[8] But the fact that these geniuses "publish" also suggests that Emerson is encountering difficulty maintaining the distance between this ideal sphere and the everyday world in which he wrote and lectured—that is, in which he worked. It is clear that, after 1844, the year in which Emerson delivered his first "Address on the Anniversary of the Emancipation of the British West Indies," slavery became a more prominent part of his everyday intellectual life and a more frequent sounding board for his ideas. Yet a broader sense of spatial scale, shaped by slavery politics, was at the same time impacting his understanding of how physical bodies carried, distributed, and were marked by cultural knowledge.

The broad focus of this chapter is the influence of slavery, slavery politics, and emergent black culture on the status of the body in the antebellum national discourse of exceptional intellectual achievement. These excerpts from Emerson's writing illustrate a more general shift in ideas about genius as the United States's expanding spatial scale became a political issue inseparable from the status of people of African origins in the nation. Around 1845, the writing and careers of Frederick Douglass and Margaret Fuller, as well as Emerson, display a preoccupation with the practice of culture on a local scale, in the eye-level spaces of everyday life. Concomitantly, genius is a concept they represent as figures able to navigate ideal and particular spaces. These shifts in the spatial scale upon which leading intellectuals portray exceptional figures of cultural authority demonstrate the deep structural role slavery and blackness were playing for antebellum concepts of the uses of intellectual and literary work.

In particular, the portrayal of genius's scale in writing by Emerson and Fuller in the mid-1840s bears the marks of Frederick Douglass's visibility to them as a cohabitant of the abstract and material spaces of culture and nation. The rhetoric of genius provided a syntax for their responses to Douglass's new eminence.

With these responses, two of the nation's leading intellectuals, Yankee New Englanders sympathetic (to varying degrees) to reform, reframed their understanding of their own work and its reach. Douglass was a figure of fascination for Fuller and Emerson partly because he succeeded, despite the ever-present particularity of his body's blackness, at addressing a constituency imagined as broader than abolitionists, a constituency more general and more defined by cultural interests and tastes than by a political or moral position on slavery. This dynamic uncertainty around what, precisely, Douglass represented as a public figure was heightened by Douglass himself, who in 1845 raised such questions in his *Narrative of the Life of Frederick Douglass, an American Slave, Written by Himself.* Although both Fuller and Emerson depict abolitionism as a category out of which Douglass emerges into a more idealized realm, they do so in ways that suggest quite different levels of attunement to the tensions and contradictions characterizing Douglass's position as "representative" of slavery, antislavery, literature, and black literature.

The second and third sections of the current chapter examine how Fuller and Emerson "read" Douglass in a sense that encompasses both his text and his body—a comprehensive sense of presence for which "genius" and "greatness" are common names in antebellum culture. By the early 1840s, after only a few years of work in antislavery lecturing, Douglass had a reputation as a powerful orator throughout the Northeast. Given Douglass's indelible public prominence, we may ask, what aspects of his work and writing did Fuller and Emerson choose to see, and which did they choose not to?

The responses of Emerson and Fuller to Douglass took place in the context of culture's expanding material reach, its new scale of production, consumption, and distribution from the 1840s onward.[9] Emerson's language describing genius as an idealized authorship that "publishes itself by unknown methods" was written at a time of extraordinary expansion and diversification in the nation's commercial publishing. It was also the period in which Emerson had begun lecturing regularly in the thriving network of local lyceums across the Northern states.[10] Fuller, Emerson's longtime intellectual confidante and collaborator, had left Transcendentalist New England at the invitation of Horace Greeley to become literary editor of the *New-York Tribune*. The *Tribune* published daily, weekly, and national editions; by 1850, its circulation had reached a scale that scholars have estimated at anywhere between sixty thousand and one million.[11] Traversing these routes of circulation meant cohabiting with Douglass in imagined and real ways: in the abstract space of literary culture, in its particular market networks, and in the particular spaces in which northeastern intellectuals wrote, spoke, and lived. Such traverse also demanded that they consider how accommodating these real and imagined spaces were for activist politics. And indeed, both Emerson and Fuller manifest a desire to pull Douglass out of the context of antislavery politics in order to fully indulge their fascination with him as a genius figure. Nonetheless, sketching this encounter reveals three antebellum writers using the tropes of genius and greatness to reframe their understanding of their own work under the pressure of new challenges in the negotiation of local and (inter)national space.

From Great House to Great Britain

The Narrative of the Life of Frederick Douglass, an American Slave, Written by Himself, Douglass's first published story of his life in and flight from slavery, famously aligns his intellectual development with his physical and tactical acumen in resisting slavery's power. Douglass's readers have typically made the escape from the South with which the book culminates, the publication of the *Narrative* itself, and Douglass's realization of himself as a free individual stand together in a metonymic chain.[12] Both Douglass's personal history and the publication of the *Narrative* in 1845 would suggest a substantial fit with Emerson's figural constructions of spatial negotiation in "The Uses of Great Men." Movement "by night and by day" in "concentric circles" resonates with the literal and figurative journeys of fugitive slaves. Moreover, the *Narrative* resonates with Emerson's assertion that genius "publishes itself by unknown methods" when it suppresses the details of Douglass's escape from bondage, an escape that brought him to Massachussetts where he commenced his career as a soon-to-be-published antislavery activist-intellectual.

Did Douglass, as an aspiring authority in both culture and politics, hope to enter into the same abstract and real spaces as Emerson's genius-"geographer"? I want to look at how the 1845 *Narrative* itself constructs a model of greatness and space, a model that illuminates the transformation taking place in Emerson's and Fuller's writings on genius, the transformative shift away from imagining the "great man"'s cultural work as taking place in homogenous, disembodied space and time. In other words, I want to reverse the once-reflexive tendency of scholars to read Douglass through Emerson, and read Emerson (with Fuller) through the epistemology and phenomenology of genius in Douglass's most canonical text.

The *Narrative,* of course, offers no theory of genius per se; at best, it figured, for sympathetic white readers such as Fuller, as a performative literary speech act instantiating the possibility that Douglass or other black authors might warrant consideration within the same generalized, abstract space of cultural evaluation that produced writers of genius. But the "greatness" of the "representative man" figure that fascinated both Emerson and Fuller has a significant parallel in the fashioning of the Great House in Douglass's text. Indeed, the spatialized model of greatness in Douglass's account of the Great House Farm resounds powerfully with the attunement to national crises of space and spatial scale in Emerson's increasingly detailed exploration of genius. Moreover, when Fuller reviewed the book for the *Tribune,* it was from this passage that she elected to include a generous portion.

Douglass's description of the Lloyd property, in the *Narrative*'s second chapter, lays a political map of the nation over the grounds of the plantation:

> The home plantation of Colonel Lloyd wore the appearance of a country village. All the mechanical operations for all the farms were performed here. The shoemaking and mending, the blacksmithing, cartwrighting, coopering, weaving, and grain-grinding, were all performed by slaves on the home plantation. The whole place wore a business-like aspect very unlike the neighboring farms. The number of houses, too, conspired to give it advantage over the neighboring farms. It was called by the slaves the *Great House Farm.* Few privileges were esteemed higher, by the slaves of the out-farms, than being selected to do errands at the Great House Farm. It was associated in their minds with greatness. A representative could not be prouder of his election to a seat in the American Congress, than a slave on one of the out-farms would be of his election to do errands at the Great House Farm. They regarded it as evidence of great confidence reposed in them by their overseers; and it was on this account, as well as the constant

> desire to be out of the field from under the driver's lash, that they esteemed it a high privilege, one worth careful living for. He was called the smartest and most trusty fellow, who had this honor conferred upon him most frequently. The competitors for this office sought as diligently to please their overseers, as the office-seekers in the political parties seek to please and deceive the people. The same traits of character might be seen in Colonel Lloyd's slaves, as are seen in the slaves of the political parties.[13]

Douglass describes the Great House Farm as essentially a federal capital, a metropole that concentrates political and cultural authority in symbolic yet material civic edifices very like the U.S. House of Representatives and the White House—federal institutions he mocks by extending the textual-metaphoric reach of slavery to encompass them. Elsewhere in the *Narrative,* he refers to the Great House Farm as the "seat of government" for Lloyd's expansive operation; in *My Bondage and My Freedom* (1855), he calls the plantation "a little nation of its own, having its own language, its own rules, regulations and customs" (160).

How are we to understand Douglass's use of the term "great" here, the category that Emerson was simultaneously using to construct a model of representative genius? The word in itself connotes spatiality in a manner that genius, in itself, does not; indeed, at this same time the latter term had become an identifying signifier of the imperial project of "Great" Britain, where Douglass would travel three months after publishing the *Narrative.* Douglass's use of the term originates in the slaves' ground-level view of the farm, in the symbolics of its verticality over the expansive horizontal grounds of the plantation. It serves as the physical and symbolic destination of slaves esteemed enough (by both overseers and other slaves) to be sent on "errands." To be sent on such an errand, in this text's resignification of the "Puritan errand" narrative of nation-founding, is to be conferred with freedom in a literal and limited sense; mobility between the outer and central farms puts physical distance between the slaves and "the driver's lash." Rhetorically, greatness is here a sarcastic pun. In a poignant sense, what is really great about the Great House Farm is that the necessity of having a centralized locus of power for the large-scale spatial greatness of the plantation creates a liminal but material space the traverse of which provides a respite from the slaveowner's exercise of surveillance and physical violence in enforcing his power. By making movement a necessary part of plantation life, the great scale of a plantation with a Great House Farm allows a temporary experience of this negatively defined freedom.

Douglass does not specify the nature of these "errands," but the passage has associated them with the trips that members of Congress—the elect(ed) great men of a particular moment in the nation's history—make between their local districts and the District of Columbia. Like elected federal legislators, the slaves Douglass describes act out with their bodies a symbolically simultaneous, immediate relationship between metropolitan capital and the confederated outer reaches of the collective space. In the case of the Lloyd plantation and many others, this relation mirrored that between the skilled labor that slaves were performing at the plantation's center and the unskilled labor of its outer reaches.[14] The travel itself is a particular sort of labor, likely consisting in trafficking information, carrying not only physical loads, but language in the form of communiqués between spatially separated areas of the plantation. These slaves' labor is not directly tied to the plantation's production process, nor is it part of the reproduction of that process (as could be said of the labor of the artisan slaves who work on the Great House Farm). In their patterns of movement, the "elect" slaves on errands begin to take on the characteristics of a class of mental laborers, becoming "representatives" in a manner that both mimics and ironizes the enactment of republican ideals in such historically concrete institutions as the U.S. House of Representatives.[15]

The Great House Farm passage portrays the "elect" producing this space of counterhegemonic culture as they engage in plantation-bound activities of production; they revalue their slave labor, with its particular spatial dimension, into the production of an alternative material and abstract space for something nameable, at least from Douglass's present, authorial vantage point, as slave culture. For the respite from the "driver's lash" is also a respite from constrictions on the slaves' generation of culture and performance. The errands provide a situation in which the slaves can sing songs whose lyrics sound empty, banal, and virtually antifigurative, but which, in the liminal space of the woods, resonate affectively and tactically in a manner that inverts the sound of the same music as heard by defenders of the institution.

Although Douglass's passage ultimately arrives at the point I have described, on its way it portrays both the existence of this slave culture and his own relationship to it as he writes:

> Into all of their songs they would manage to weave something of the Great House Farm. Especially would they do this, when leaving home. They would then sing most exultingly the following words—
>
> I am going away to the Great House Farm!
> O, yea! O, yea! O!
>
> This they would sing as a chorus to words which to many would seem unmeaning jargon, but which, nevertheless, were full of meaning to themselves. I have sometimes thought that the mere hearing of those songs would do more to impress some minds with the horrible character of slavery, than the reading of whole volumes of philosophy on the subject could do.
>
> I did not, when a slave, understand the deep meaning of those rude and apparently incoherent songs. I was myself within the circle; so that I neither saw nor heard as those without might see or hear. They told a tale of woe which was then altogether beyond my feeble comprehension; they were tones loud, long, and deep; they breathed prayer and complaint of souls boiling over with the bitterest anguish. Every tone was a testimony against slavery, and a prayer to God for deliverance from chains. The hearing of those wild notes always depressed my spirit, and filled me with ineffable sadness. I have frequently found myself in tears while hearing them. The mere recurrence to these songs, even now, afflicts me; and while I am writing these lines, an expression of feeling has already found its way down my cheek. . . .
>
> I have often been utterly astonished, since I came to the north, to find persons who could speak of the singing, among slaves, as evidence of their contentment and happiness. It is impossible to conceive of a greater mistake. Slaves sing most when they are most unhappy. The songs of the slave represent the sorrows of his heart; and he is relieved by them, only as an aching heart is relieved by its tears. At least such is my experience. (23–24)

In this extraordinarily dense passage, Douglass positions himself as both subject and object of slavery, both analyst and analysand, by differentiating between two forms of signification, located in the spaces both "inside" and "without" the "circle" of song.[16] At the moment of writing, Douglass is outside, in a position from which he can "understand the deep meaning" of the music: the position of interpreter, critic, ethnographer, the sort of subject likely to be familiar with "whole volumes of philosophy." Much like his implied readers, he now sits, reflects on, and analyzes "those songs"—a distancing phrase he employs six times in a single paragraph. In his past, Douglass could not understand the songs sung by the "elect" slaves, whom he portrays here as the critical intellectual class able to articulate signs to those "without." The stakes of Douglass's passage are high: correct interpretation of these signs as slave culture, and as requiring interpretation rather than (to borrow George Frederickson's term) "romantic racialist" projection is, for him, a vital aspect of the abolitionist project. He insists that the relationship between the present of reading/writing and the past of slavery/singing is not immediate; rather, it is mediated by time and space, making any assumption of representational transparency problematic. Thus the opacity of the passage fashions what a neopragmatist critic might call "the unrepresentable" as a critical tool in a specific historical context with specific political stakes.[17] Indeed, he has put his present self in a position analogous to that of the Great House Farm in the passage, assuming the tone and perspective of cultural authority only to illustrate how the material over which he is displaying authority performs in a manner he *lacks* the authority to describe, much as the "elect" slaves' cultural practice remains impervious to the authority of their master in the Great House, Colonel Lloyd.

That Fuller, along with a number of other early reviewers of the *Narrative,* included excerpts from this passage in their reviews (Fuller including what I have quoted in its entirety) suggests a budding interest among some white readers in the opacity (to whites) of slave music, its status as a code requiring interpretation. It is also possible that Douglass, with this passage, was addressing in a submerged fashion the crisis of representation that he describes in his account of working with Garrisonian abolitionists in his next memoir, *My Bondage and My Freedom* (1855).

Douglass's account of his increasing discomfort with his role among the Garrisonians has been discussed by a number of critics, but they are worth revisiting briefly, because they illustrate the burden of being a representative both politically and in the material space and time of the cultural marketplace. Douglass describes the objectifying propensity of his framing in the Garrisonian mise-en-scène: "I was generally introduced as a 'chattel'—a 'thing'—a piece of southern 'property'—the chairman assuring the audience that it could speak" (366). Soon after, he recounts the psychological and physiological discomfort resulting from the tiresomeness of playing this role again and again on the abolitionist lecture circuit:

> During the first three or four months, my speeches were almost exclusively made up of narrations of my own personal experience as a slave. "Let us have the facts," said the people. So also said Friend George Foster, who always wished to pin me down to my simple narrative. "Give us the facts," said Collins, "we will take care of the philosophy." Just here arose some embarrassment. It was impossible for me to repeat the same old story month after month, and to keep up my interest in it. "Tell your story, Frederick," would whisper my then revered friend, William Lloyd Garrison, as I stepped up on the platform. I could not always obey, for I was now reading and thinking. New views of the subject were presented to my mind. It did not entirely satisfy me to narrate wrongs; I felt like denouncing them.[18]

These rallies attempt to re-create the present of Douglass's slave experience, which the *Narrative*'s "sorrow songs" passage represents as irrevocably lost. Moreover, they attempt to re-create it again and again, to create a present that spans the many instances of re-presentation that, across wide swaths of space, make up a long lecture tour. It is especially notable that, in the passage quoted, Douglass distances himself not only from his activities alongside Garrison on these tours, but from the *Narrative* itself. The "sorrow song" passage, I want to suggest, is a section of that earlier text that manifests the basic conflict between Douglass's understanding of the particularity of representation and Garrison's.

Just after publication of the *Narrative,* under threat of recapture as a result of his having used real names in the text, Douglass once again significantly broadened the geographical expanse of his experience, and boarded a ship for Great Britain, where he spent the following two years.[19] The journey was symbolically rich, delivering him to the land most Americans still regarded as the home of the highest precincts of literary culture. In Britain, James McCune Smith wrote in his introduction to the original edition of *My Bondage and My Freedom,* Douglass traveled "not only as an equal, but as a recognized man of genius. . . . There are joys on the earth, and, to the wayfaring fugitive from American slavery or American caste, this is one of them."[20] Smith also called Douglass a "representative man," assimilating him into the form of public and historical iconicity now made widely known by the publication of Emerson's book on the topic in 1850. Such assertions were in their time dogged by the continuing battles Douglass and other fugitives were forced to fight on an everyday basis, as when Douglass was asked to ride in the lower hold of the ship sailing from New York to Liverpool (a request the ship's captain withdrew following the intervention of a group of passengers).[21]

Now I want to suggest some ways that the vexed nature of mobility that Douglass both wrote and experienced manifested itself, in a refracted form, in the grain of the most basic assumptions structuring the representative genius figure in Emerson's work. This is not to suggest that Emerson read Douglass in the manner that I have been reading him; indeed, I know of no evidence suggesting that Emerson ever read Douglass.[22] But the two did address audiences in the same particular and abstract spaces, and both were responding in their writing to these spaces' effect on the enunciation of categories such as "man of genius." I want now to examine how this proximity made Douglass "look" to both Emerson and Fuller, and how the shape of Douglass's appearance as a cultural laborer in turn inflected their understandings of their own status as intellectuals.

GREAT MEN WALKING

By late summer of 1845, Frederick Douglass had gone from a life as a Maryland slave to one as an internationally recognized "man of genius." How Emerson had viewed this emergence is largely a matter of interpreting phantom shapes and silences in Emerson's public and private writings. There is but a single mention of Douglass in Emerson's writing that I know of, in an 1844 journal, and, as I noted, no documentary evidence that Emerson read Douglass. Although in recent years critics have generated a more multifaceted picture of Emerson's politics, including his opposition to slavery, only Christina Zwarg has given substantial attention to his (non)-relationship to Douglass.[23] My aim is to read Emerson through Douglass not to gauge the former's politics per se, but to identify the ways that genius discourse was, in both these men's work, a site for exploring the politics of cultural work, embodiment, and space.

The reference to Douglass occurs in a journal entry from 1844, a year in which Emerson had begun work on the "Representative Men" project in earnest, and had delivered his first public antislavery oration, the "Address on the Anniversary of Emancipation in the British West Indies, August 1, 1844":

> Ideas only save races. If the black man is feeble & not important to the existing races, not on a par with the best race, the black man must serve & be sold & be exterminated. But if the black man carries in his bosom an indispensable element of a new & coming civilization, for the sake of that element no wrong nor strength nor circumstance can hurt him, he will survive & play his part. So now it seems to me that the arrival of such men as Toussaint, if he is pure blood, or of Douglas *[sic]* if he is pure blood, outweighs all the English & American humanity. The Antislavery of the whole world is but dust in the balance, a poor squeamishness & nervousness[;] the might & the right is here. Here is the Anti-Slave. Here is Man; & if you have man, black or white is an insignificance.[24]

The extraordinary language of this passage, with its dramatic resignation to the possibility of the "black man" being "sold & . . . exterminated," would suggest an Emerson who, in 1844, while endorsing abolition publically, was still far from taking up the cause with the vehemence he would exhibit in his address on "The Fugitive Slave Law" in 1852, or in his later support for John Brown. Still, the argumentative vein of the passage, which essentially indicts "Antislavery" far more strongly than it indicts slavery, resonates with what we have seen in Douglass's account of his difficulties among the most powerful wing of New England abolitionists. Both men, that is, see abolition, at least in its contemporary form, as a possible obstacle to the potential of "the black man" to emerge fully into genius status. Reform efforts in the interest of "humanity," whether American or English, are historically feeble in contrast to the acts of men like Douglass and Toussaint, whose works, connected to an "idea" and a "race" rather than to a politically vexed nation of the present, seem a possible harbinger of a "new and coming civilization." Emerson suggests that without the mediation of abolitionism, Douglass might actually have more of a chance of emerging as a genius than a white man, who presumably would carry the limiting signification of his nationality, unlike the transnational category of "Black Man." Still more paradoxically, the passage suggests that it is necessary that these great men, who have the potential to prove the "insignificance" of skin color, be of "pure blood."

The reference to English abolitionism amid these conceptual and rhetorical tensions attests to the broader way that whiteness was proving problematic for Emerson's efforts to think and write about representative men in an American context—a problem that eventually led him to include no U.S. figures in his orations or book. The "American Scholar" Emerson had envisioned in 1837 had remained an abstraction, and the absence of such a figure within the historical present continued to vex him periodically. This struggle is evident in a journal entry from earlier in 1844, in which he runs through a series of names of famous American men that reads like a list of might-have-been's:

> But in America I grieve to miss the strong black blood of the English race: ours is a pale diluted stream. What a company of brilliant young persons I have seen with so much expectation! The sort is very good, but none is good enough of his sort. Everyone an imperfect specimen, respectable not valid. Irving thin, & Channing thin, & Bryant & Dana[,] Prescott & Bancroft. . . There is Webster, but he cannot do what he would; he cannot do Webster. Then the youth, as I said, are all promising failures. No writing is here[,] no redundant strength, but declamation, straining, correctness, & all other symptoms of debility.[25]

On its surface, this rhetoric is even more convoluted than the entry on Douglass; in a striking reshuffling of racial signifiers, Emerson credits the English with a racial "strength" based in the blackness of their blood, foreshadowing the spirit of Anglo-Saxonism he would adopt in one of his next books, *English Traits* (1856). He implies that there is a problem at the core of American whiteness, indicated in what he sees as its inability to manifest itself with the density of "strong black blood" (I take "black" here to refer on its surface to the heartiness of blood-based British "black pudding," or the meaning of the word in a phrase like "black with rage"), and to appear instead as a "pale diluted stream." Surely this entry formed a background for the subsequent one on Douglass and Toussaint, in which their blackness figured to such a significant degree that it exterminated itself as a racial formation.

But perhaps the most telling aspect of Emerson's mention of Douglass is contained not in the comments but in his transformation of them into a section of his "Address on the Anniversary of West Indian Emancipation." For in this speech, Emerson did not simply call on Douglass to eviscerate his blackness; he eviscerated Douglass himself, excising his name (though not Toussaint's) from the speech. Perhaps the motivation for this was the specificity of the occasion, for which Toussaint's name was central, of course. But another plausible explanation lies in the fact that Douglass—not the name, but the embodied person—was present at the same Concord antislavery rally for which Emerson had prepared his oration. Douglass was a formidable, dynamic, and physically striking speaker, but when he appeared in person he was not all that "black"; indeed, his *Narrative* begins by discussing the childhood rumor that his owner was his father. In other words, Emerson's journal entry placed a demand on Douglass's body that their shared space of cultural authority, their everyday life as cultural laborers, betrayed. Indeed, Douglass's physical presence as a participant in the occasion, and the spectacle of his relatively light-skinned visage, would have highlighted not only the contradictory nature of Emerson's representation of race, but the more general lack of consonance between "color" as a figure for racial formation and the physical color of human skin, for which the terms "black" and "white" have functioned for centuries as remarkably imprecise, but ideologically efficacious, signifiers.

Although there is probably no way to confirm the hypothesis that Douglass's presence was the reason Emerson elided him in the "West Indian" address, Emerson's engagement with the topic of genius in the "Representative Men" project does display a persistent struggle in attempting to reconcile particular formations of embodiment with the idealized, symbolic "figure" of the great man. Thus, homoerotically charged spectacles of unnamed but hyper-embodied "great men" appear repeatedly in "The Uses of Great Men." That Douglass would have helped push Emerson in this direction is likely, given the public sensation surrounding the former's personal presence as an orator, which would have become a private sensation had Emerson attended Douglass's 1844 Concord address. As Robert Fanuzzi has shown, Douglass's strategy in the face of his constriction and objectification by the Garrisonians was not so much to attempt self-disembodiment (a process that, at least in oratorical and performance culture, seems largely a lost cause) as to reconstitute himself as a powerful physical presence of the different, neoclassical sort associated with the Revolutionary era.[26] Accounts of Douglass's appearances at lectures are full of allusions to his handsomeness and manly bearing. There is a persistent erotic charge to descriptions of him by both men and women, a potentially scandalous rhetoric that could find a useful mode of disavowal in the rhetoric of genius and great men.[27]

At certain points in "The Uses of Great Men," Emerson seems markedly determined to avow the eroticism he describes in the great man's "power of performance." This power emerges from his statuesque masculinity. "The people," he writes, "delight in a man. Here is a head and a trunk! What a front! What eyes! Atlantean shoulders, and the whole carriage heroic, with equal inward force to guide the great machine!" He insists that intellectual power displays itself in a virtually physical form: "We go to the gymnasium and the swimming-school to see the power and beauty of the body; there is the like pleasure, and a higher benefit, from witnessing intellectual feats of all kinds. . . . as these acts expose the invisible organs and members of the mind, which respond, member for member, to the parts of the body." Indeed, Emerson casts the spectacle of this titillating mental striptease in erectile terms: "When this wakes, a man seems to multiply ten times or a thousand times his force" (622). A bit further on, he portrays this impression from the first person: "I admire great men of all classes, those who stand for facts, and for thoughts; I like rough and smooth. . . . I like a master standing firm on legs of iron, well-born, handsome, eloquent, loaded with advantages, drawing all men by fascination into tributaries and supporters of his power. Sword and staff, or talents sword-like or staff-like, carry on the work of the world" (625). An intense measure of scopophilia propels this writing, a highly aroused, homoerotic gaze that challenges any overly hasty reading of the famous "transparent eyeball" figure as an exemplary instance of a definitive Emersonian association between vision and disembodiment.[28]

Rather than idealizing this erotic energy, I want to particularize it by suggesting it might be located in the "power of performance"—or "practical power"—of contemporary cultural labor, as situated in spaces such as the lyceum. Over the course of the 1840s, the lyceum became an increasingly frequent venue for both Emerson and Douglass; at least three thousand existed by the beginning of the decade. As lyceums across the nation began to host speakers traveling greater distances, the format shifted from group discussion toward the straightforward lecture, with a single speaker, elevated above the crowd, the focus of the audience's individual and collective gazes, much as in Emerson's description of his great men. In the early 1840s, Concord's lyceum banned antislavery orations but soon reversed this policy.[29] Douglass's fame increased in the wake of such decisions, as the antebellum cultural marketplace diversified. His emergence in this context must have attracted more attention from Emerson than the latter's journals and writings reflect. The lyceum was both a physical and abstract space that brought Emerson and Douglass together, making them competitors in the same cultural market, and subject to debate by civic leaders in the same terms concerning their value for culture. Mary Cayton has argued that lyceums helped transform the very meaning of culture by aligning it more strongly with "the conspicuous consumption of performances of people who were nationally and internationally defined as intellectuals."[30] In such a view, the body at the lectern is treated as a commodity; the value of attendance hinges on the very fact of coincident, physical presence with him or her as much as on the content of the address. Particularly as group discussion of the meeting-hall style became less common, the speaker's body played an increasingly central role in his or her success before an audience.[31]

Douglass's emergence within this space of genius production would have registered for Emerson as feelings in and toward his own forty-two-year-old body as it climbed onto stages as far west as Cincinnati, worn from the travel that the lifetime Concord resident repeatedly attested to hating. The expanded scale of speaking tours would, in other words, have brought the scale at which he imagined his own ability to embody the ideals of the great man down to the level, quite literally, of his (as of Douglass's) body. Certainly this is true of a remark like the following from his journal in 1845: "A great man will not make haste or run, no not though he should be late at the Thursday lecture."[32] One can read this pronouncement as a maxim meant to speak to no specific occasion, but it must be acknowledged that such an assumption strains hard against the raw materiality and relevance, on a personal scale, of the situation depicted.

Both the 1845 remark and those we have seen from the lecture on "The Uses of Great Men" restore Emerson's body as a presence in his writing. The attention to the body of the representative genius figure in "The Uses of Great Men" suggests excitement and anxiety in Emerson's experience of his own body's new significance in the national cultural field. This sensual and affective charge brings Emerson's consideration of representativeness, however different and more broadly scaled than Douglass's, back to the local grounding of the everyday in which Douglass based his depiction of the Great House Farm.

This reading will, I hope, point to the limits of arguments that linguistic indeterminacy is the core characteristic of Emerson's engagement with material aspects of history, such as the violent power relations of slavery. Although he is not idealizing the materiality of space, he is also not critiquing the idea that real spaces exist as an ideological manipulation of language. Or, better, he does not see the world as ultimately dictated by the poles of idealism and materiality. And to make these poles the upshot of any interpretation of his writing seriously limits our ability to attend to the intensely variegated, linguistically unsteady, yet historically dense qualities of his texts. Emerson's work at this time is not eviscerating real space but attempting to articulate, amid the expansion and diversification of national space, actual spatial situations in which he might articulate his transcendent notion of genius and greatness. He needs to negotiate real space to most effectively establish enunciative grounds for declaring his desire that it disappear. At a certain point in "The Uses of Great Men," this project becomes particularly evident:

> I go to a convention of philanthropists. Do what I can, I cannot keep my eyes off the clock. But if there should appear in the company some gentle soul who knows little of persons or parties, of Carolina or Cuba, but who announces a law that disposes these particulars, and so certifies me of the equity which checkmates every false player, bankrupts every self-seeker, and apprises me of my independence on any conditions of country, or time, or human body, that man liberates me; I forget the clock. (625)

Emerson imagines a "gentle soul" who "disposes [the] particulars" of space, propelling him to "forget the clock" that ticks off the particular measure of time in which his trip to a convention hall, South

Carolina (where his friend, the white abolitionist Samuel Hoar, had recently been arrested by slaveholders), Cuba (bandied about for years as an object of expansionist desire), falsity, egotism, and misconceived philanthropy all thrive. But, crucially, this apparent fantasy of spacelessness and timelessness is itself grounded in space and time; just as Emerson calls for his great man to take him away from the distant, historically specific places and issues increasingly proliferating in the conversations and reading material of Concord, he also substitutes his own particular space to situate this process of "liberat[ion]": the public lecture hall or lyceum, the increasingly common space of conventions, debates, and orations in the antebellum era.[33] It is this space specifically in which he can "forget the clock"; it is this literal space that provides the grounds for the experience of symbolic spacelessness and timelessness he so desires. Emerson's theory of the great man does not abandon the vicissitudes of the present, wholesale; rather, it imagines a practical route of escape within the routines of his antebellum audience's everyday life.

MORE ABOUT SONGS AND BUILDINGS

Margaret Fuller first gained her formidable intellectual reputation in New England as the nation's greatest reader of German Romantic literature, and as the translator of Eckermann's *Conversations with Goethe* (1836).[34] She became a central member of the Transcendentalist circle, establishing a particularly close relationship with Emerson and a correspondence with him that reached its intellectual height while Emerson was writing his *Essays: Second Series,* as Christina Zwarg has shown. Beginning in 1839, she offered a series of intellectual "Conversations" for women in Boston, a study group "designed to encourage women in self-expression and independent thinking." From 1840 to 1844, she served as the editor of the Transcendentalists' journal, the *Dial.* But her career is also distinguished by her move from Boston to New York to take up a position at Greeley's daily, the *New-York Tribune.* In accepting Greeley's offer, she integrated her authorial labor into the contemporary networks of literary modernity, reaching between thirty and one hundred times as many readers as she had while editing the *Dial* in Boston. As Judith Mattson Bean and Joel Meyerson have put it, "Fuller's nineteenth-century reputation was based primarily upon her praxis, an integration of theory with practice."[35] Situated at the *Tribune,* Fuller displayed a concern for the impact of culture and its major forms, such as genius, in everyday contexts. She wrote to an unidentified friend in early 1845:

> I am pleased with your sympathy about the *Tribune,* for I do not find much among my old friends. They think I ought to produce something excellent, while I am satisfied to aid in the great work of popular education. I have never regarded literature merely as a collection of exquisite products, but rather as a means of mutual interpretation. Feeling that many are reached and to some degree helped, the thoughts of every day seem worth noting, though in a form that does not inspire me.[36]

However uninspired she was by the "form" of her work for the *Tribune,* in pursuing her notion of literature "as a means of mutual interpretation," she used her position to produce writing on topics as various as those covered in the daily as a whole. Although her primary role at the paper was to review books, she also wrote what amounted to investigative features, as when she reported on a visit to a women's asylum, and trenchant political opinion pieces, in which she articulated adamant opposition to the Mexican War. Her book reviews leaned toward works by authors regarded as in some way serious literary practitioners, and covered a strikingly international range: Emerson, Balzac, Sand, Hawthorne, and others.[37] She reviewed concerts occasionally, and repeatedly made references to her wanderings through local streets.

How Frederick Douglass the public figure looked to Margaret Fuller in 1845 is far more apparent than in the case of her longtime confidante and associate Emerson. Fuller read and reviewed the *Narrative* in her position as literary editor and prolific contributor to the *New-York Tribune,* staging an encounter between two major antebellum activist cultural figures who never knew each other personally.[38] Fuller's review of the *Narrative* is the first sign we have of a major white literary-intellectual figure in the United States acknowledging the possibility of black literary culture's existence. As Zwarg puts it in her meditation on this encounter, "Fuller was one of the earliest intellectuals in this country to understand the cost of [the] radical critical division" between "the experience, memories, and events of male and female, white and black Americans."[39] What is also striking about Fuller's reading of Douglass is that, in considering him a possible "genius" among a group of internationally reknowned black authors, she reproduces the "sorrow song" passage—Douglass's own portrayal of cultural production in the interstitial times and spaces of everyday routine.

When we look at Fuller as a practicing antebellum intellectual, it is clear that she produced writing at a rate that, like the *Tribune*'s circulation, was fully in synch with the modernity of the cultural marketplace and the demands it placed on an expanding class of professional mental laborers. Fuller's move from Boston to New York meant immersing herself more fully in the volatility of this diverse, contemporary realm of letters, as the latter city was supplanting the former as the national center of publishing. This shift was one factor of many involved with New York's ascension to the position of the nation's most important metropolis. According to Peter Buckley, the period between 1820 and 1860 in New York "encompassed the highest decennial rate of urbanization ever experienced by an American city: an almost ninefold increase in population."[40] The city had become the preeminent hub in the United States for the circulation of goods, capital, and culture, particularly after the digging of the Erie Canal increased shipping access to the West. At the same time, New York became increasingly tied to international economic and cultural traffic, earning its moniker as the "Empire City"; indeed, in more recent times Kristen Silva Gruesz has referred to it as a "border city," a geographical locus traversed by people and culture of an extraordinarily international nature.[41] Fuller's relatively brief stay in New York preceded a trip to Europe in 1846 (she traveled the Atlantic with Douglass in the same steamship, and recounted the story of his encounter with racist passengers in a *Tribune* column); the trip led her to become involved with the revolutionary risorgimento movement in Italy. Thus New York served for her as a kind of entry point into a far more cosmopolitan milieu than she had habituated in New England.

I mention these biographical details not only as background for my reading of Douglass and genius more generally, but to suggest that the trajectory of Fuller's career manifests early signs of a broad shift in U.S. intellectuals' notion of culture that is traceable in her discussions of genius. As the comments on "mutual interpretation" and "the thoughts of every day" in her letter suggest, Fuller was coming to see her vocation as immersed in the quotidian, and as based in the processes of that quotidian rather than in a set of aesthetic or moral principles that existed in their own untouchable, transhistorical sanctum. As a number of scholars have shown, and as is clear from reading, say, Emerson's essay "Culture," in the first half of the nineteenth century, the word generally referred to a process of development (often expressed in the phrase "self culture") enabled by contact with this sanctum. Fuller was contributing to the articulation of the much wider sense of "culture" conceived as, in Raymond Williams's words, "the body of intellectual and imaginative work, in which, in a detailed way, human thought and experience are variously recorded."[42] It is especially notable that Fuller's conception of this "body" was one that had never been as shaped by nationalism as that of some of her peers among northeastern intellectuals, Emerson included. Over the course of her career, Fuller became gradually less bound by nation, in her movement, in her thought, and in her concept of the object of her writing: thus her description by Ross Posnock as "a striking precedent for the type of 'impure' and anti-organic, radically deracinated intellectual," a "type" he associates with the twentieth-century Algerian intellectual-revolutionary Frantz Fanon.[43]

Posnock's somewhat offhand association is worth considering more deeply, given the striking forthrightness with which Fuller condemned both British and American imperialism. Although she does not draw any direct comparison between the subalternity of American slaves and that of, say, the people of India, she does approach Douglass as part of a wider class of men of color dispersed internationally in a manner spurred by colonialism. Unlike Emerson, who submitted Douglass to a test of "pure" blackness, Fuller embraced his mixed background, basing her response less substantially in such categories as nation and race than other white reviewers.

Her attitude toward his blackness was substantially different from Emerson's. Douglass failed the test of "pure" blackness that Emerson constructed in his journal as the criterion for black genius. Fuller, on the other hand, strongly embraced Douglass's "mixed" background; indeed, in her review of the *Narrative,* she celebrates racial hybridity as an icon of cultural sophistication, a figure for culture itself.[44] As a fugitive slave and a black person, Douglass offered Fuller a receptive screen on which to project ideals about intellectual work and its social contexts. Douglass offered Fuller a model of an embodied, geographically mobile intellectual figure who could be stripped out of conventional contexts, localized via his body's experience of shifting contexts, and culturally emancipated onto a broader, more international scale. This was, in effect, what Fuller wanted for the United States and how she imagined the path of its national progress. In the year that saw the beginning of the Mexican War, which she strongly opposed as an act of imperialist aggression, she was particularly invested in this notion of a nationally constituted principle of cosmopolitanism. She belittled national symbols in a brief, poignant opinion piece published almost exactly a year after her review of the *Narrative:* "Our Stars have lighted us only to the ancient heathen—the vulgar path of national aggrandizement; and our Eagle, like the Roman, loves better to snatch its prey from the field than to soar to the purer regions near the source of light."[45]

The review itself returns us to the Great House Farm and the "sorrow songs" passage, which she appended in its entirety to her text. Fuller thus performs on the surface of the *Tribune* a kind of cross-racial joining of bodies. The review enacts the racial "amalgamation" that she embraced elsewhere and constructs a mini-canon of authors of hybrid Euro-African backgrounds who are worthy of recognition.[46] Although Fuller begins the front-page review by citing Douglass's bravery in using the real names of places and people from the plantations of his youth, the general trajectory of the text is (as in Emerson and, in a different way, Douglass himself) away from Douglass's work for Garrisonian abolition and toward world literature:

> The Cross of the Legion of Honor has just been conferred in France on Dumas and Souliè, both celebrated in the paths of light literature. Dumas, whose father was a General in the French Army, is a Mulatto; Souliè, a Quadroon. He went from New-Orleans, where, though to the eye a white man, yet, as known to have African blood in his veins, he could never have enjoyed the privileges due to a human being. Leaving the Land of Freedom, he found himself free to develop the powers that God had given.

Over the course of the piece, she constructs a model of a diasporic "mixed" authorship. She depicts the wide span between local and global concerns that her career as a whole was coming to embody, and that was also felt less directly in Douglass's and Emerson's spatialized discourse of greatness.

The trajectory in Fuller's piece, however, also replaces politics with genius. But again this trajectory is grounded in an appreciation of the mediated Douglass appearing in the genre of slave narrative. Fuller conveys a condescending romantic racialism, but also signals a sense of the constraint that the form of Douglass's book places on him. She writes: "Considered merely as a narrative, we have never read one more simple, true, coherent, and warm with genuine feeling. It is an excellent piece of writing, and on that score to be prized as a specimen of the powers of the Black Race, which prejudice persists in disputing."[47] Bracketing "mere" narrative, she anticipates Douglass's own comment in *My Bondage and My Freedom* that he wished not to "narrate wrongs" but to "[denounce] them." Her critique is not abolitionist, but having bestowed Douglass with the exceptional qualities that she eventually names genius actually allows her to be more attentive to his mediation by cultural and historical factors. Genius also acts in this critical fashion by allowing her to construct her mini-canon of Dumas, Souliè, and Douglass across genre. The achievements of such men, she implicitly assures us, are limited to the genre of "light literature," a phrase that suggests a pun on racial rhetoric. Such a qualification prefaces her further use of the conventional language of race, as she notes the "peculiar element" certain thinkers have attributed to "the African race. . . . indicated in their lowest estate by a talent for melody, a ready skill at imitation and adaptation, an almost indestructible elasticity of nature."[48] It is this last quality, she writes, that "if it could be assimilated with those imported among us from Europe, would give to genius a development, and to the energies of character a balance and harmony, beyond what has heretofore been seen in the history of the world."

Calling musicality an inherent racial trait of people of African descent is one of the longest-running forms of romantic racialism associated with New World slavery and its legacy. Fuller's comments about Douglass in this vein come off as a clumsy, racist attempt to say that everyday culture (now sometimes called "folk" or "popular") is as important as the work conventionally associated with genius. They recall comments she made about black music in the *Dial* in 1842, in a piece displaying a nervous mixture of seriousness and insouciance:

> Our only national melody, Yankee Doodle, is shrewdly suspected to be a scion from British art. All symptoms of invention are confined to the African race, who, like the German literati, are

> relieved by their position from the cares of government. "Jump Jim Crow," is a native dance to this country, and which we plead guilty to seeing with pleasure, not on the stage, where we have not seen it, but as danced by children of an ebon hue in the street. Such of the African melodies as we have heard are beautiful. But the Caucasian race have yet their rail-roads to make.[49]

It is tempting to understand this as Fuller's variation on present-day clichés like the phrase "white men can't jump," or the "white people are so lame" stand-up comedy routine, happily spoken by white people as a momentary, privileged act of disidentification from whiteness. A more historical companion for her line about originality, blackness, and national culture is Theodore Parker's comment in his essay "The American Scholar" that slave narratives constitute the only legitimately native form of literature. More exceptional is Fuller's comparison of the "African race" and "German literati." Although this remark is clearly offhand, it again performs the work Fuller has been doing to place the everyday and the sacral work of genius on a spectrum of cultural significance. The remark also specifically anticipates the space that Fuller makes in her review for the "sorrow songs" section of Douglass's *Narrative,* and suggests a pretext for her interest in the Great House Farm section as well.[50]

The locale described in this excerpt, Colonel Lloyd's plantation, is distant from Fuller's New York in nearly every way imaginable.[51] Yet Douglass's mode of representing it is to describe the production of culture (and, indeed, of cultural criticism) in movement, that of the everyday though privileged routines of "representatives," through material spaces. Fuller's *Tribune* writings share an interest in the everyday, eye-level scale and the work of orientation performed within that scale by figures of genius. As a "geographer," Douglass depicted a central pseudo-metropole organizing this mobility in both physical and symbolic ways. Fuller writes from a New York whose spaces she repeatedly attempts to materialize, not just because she is writing work institutionally and materially classified as journalism, or because she wants to have a more direct effect on the world, but to align herself with trends she sees as refining and modernizing the shape of culture as a practice. She is particularly interested in how localizing her own practice may actually broaden the scale on which her audience reads.

It may be overreaching to say that Fuller's response to Douglass, which unlike Emerson's is a *reading* of Douglass, culminates with her putting herself in the position of the quasi-intellectual class of slaves traveling to and from the Great House Farm. But it is not overreaching to see the similarities of these models of knowledge production and distribution as indicative of a theoretical kinship in these contemporary thinkers' models of intellectuals as mediators of the relationship between meaning on a local, particular scale and meaning on a national or wider, general scale. Douglass in some senses constructed this model and then refused to occupy it himself, saying he was no longer "in the circle," a performative gesture whose content is betrayed by the fact that it takes place in the middle of a book-length account of his life as a slave.

Fuller does not read Douglass's text at this level of sophistication; although she is clearly powerfully engaged by it, she is still concerned to maintain its status among exemplars of light literature. But she does read this sort of split into a great-man figure who, for Emerson, had also served as a conduit for thinking about contemporary intellectuals: Napoleon. In a review of J. T. Headley's book *Napoleon and His Marshals,* written half a year later than the Douglass piece, Fuller takes the position of urban intellectual ethnographer to examine the great man as a cultural form in the present. In the article, broad scales separating spaces and genres converge around the figure of the great man Napoleon, who registers a kind of radical historical alterity that Douglass's representation could not approximate.

This piece best exemplifies Fuller's use of the city as a text and pre-text in her *Tribune* writing—her attunement not only to the plethora of topics the city presented her to write about, but to the changes its physical spaces offered for the mode of her writing. She assumes a flaneurial position of authorship in contextualizing this review, describing the book first in the form it takes as an advertisement on a Manhattan street near the *Tribune* office, setting aside another placard advertising a book about Christ's apostles. In other words, she brings attention to how the micro scale of the city street performs dramatic alterations in macro conceptions of historical, geographical, and cultural scale.

> As we pass the old Brick Chapel our eye is sometimes arrested by placards that hang side by side. On one is advertised "the Lives of the Apostles," on the other "Napoleon and his Marshals."

> Surely it is the most monstrous thing the world ever saw, that eighteen hundred years' profound devotion to a religious teacher should not preclude flagrant and all but universal violation of his most obvious precepts; that Napoleon and his Marshals should be some of the best ripened fruit of our time; that our own people, so unwearied in building up temples of wood and stone to the Prince of Peace, should be at this era mad with boyish exultation at the winning of battles, and in a bad cause too.[52]

In downtown New York, as one moves rapidly by, what do these great men, represented on placards with only a chance of temporarily catching the eye, represent? Fuller's opening sentences are directed to the hypocrisy of passersby taking offense at Napoleon's juxtaposition with Jesus, when the nation of which they are presumably citizens is engaged in war with Mexico. She subsequently uses the fact of this material spectacle of juxtaposition to insist that the greatness of Napoleon is actually manifest in this very reconstitution of the moral, historical, and geographical distance ordinarily thought to separate the two men. The micro-level, temporary, urban spectacle makes him great. She continues:

> Admit, then, that he was not a good man, and never for one moment acted disinterestedly. But do not refuse to do homage to his genius. It is well worth your while to appreciate that, if you wish to understand the work that the spirit of the time did, and is still doing, through him; for his mind is still upon the earth, working there through the tributary minds it fed. We must say, for our own part, we cannot admit the right of minds severely to criticize Napoleon, till they are able to appreciate what he was as well as see what he was not. And we see no mind of sufficient grasp or high placed enough to take this estimate duly, nor do we believe this age will furnish one. Many problems have to be worked out first.[53]

Fuller shifts the significance of Napoleon away from *what* he signifies to *that* he signifies, to the fact that he is still a preoccupation of contemporary intellectual and literary life. The great man becomes a category registering history's alterity; he is a form through which the ongoing effects of history are manifest even as they are unclear to interpretation. Fuller's article thus begs another association with Douglass's *Narrative* because it positions the category of greatness as a useful tool for cultural criticism precisely because this category does represent, act as the form of, cultural and affective investments that exceed the discourse of representativeness—that exceed the capacity of certain modes of representation, such as "narrative," to account for them. That is, she discusses Napoleon the way Douglass discusses himself.

Fuller uses the "great man" as a conceptual apparatus for developing a theory of historical temporality. Those interested in participating in the cultural sphere, she suggests, need to pay attention to a figure like Napoleon on two levels. They should be attempting to make sense of him—to sort through the record of his achievements and failures, and assess his worth as a representative figure. But they should also be attentive to the ongoing, unisolable history of how he is discussed, where, and to what purpose. Indeed, his is less a "history" than a series of present moments added onto one another, a quotidian diary of genius.

Fuller's depiction in the Napoleon piece of the moment the U.S. government began to make war on Mexico was a particularly compelling example of how deeply phenomena apparently so remote in physical and symbolic terms could exert direct influence on the most fundamental, structural levels through which culture was imagined. Genius was able to serve a crucial role as a category in this trend because it could be cast as both a subject and an object—it mapped the changes even as its form was subject to the stress of them. It was able to do this, in part, because Frederick Douglass, cosmopolitan author and American slave, so readily embodied the paradoxical pull between agency and historical circumstance that new representations of genius were attempting to embody.

I find it particularly extraordinary that Fuller and Douglass can be conceived as related in their notions of the ordinary, because scholarship concerned with the antebellum life of middle-class white women has so persistently focused on domesticity as the orienting space of the quotidian. Fuller, on the other hand, emphasizes the public world, exterior spaces, and mobility; hence the heroic, oppositional role she plays in a widely read critical study like Ann Douglas's *The Feminization of American Culture.*[54] Without reconstituting that book's reified opposition between an apolitical literature of private life and a stalwart literature of social criticism, I want to draw attention to this aspect of the preceding analysis, as my next chapter examines the critical rhetoric around a very public female genius, Jenny Lind. For although Fuller was an exceptional intellectual figure in many ways, her success needs to be viewed within the wider context that genius played as a category mediating women's appearance, in body and text, in the public sphere, particularly in public performance venues. In her most well-known book, *Woman in the Nineteenth Century,* Fuller specifically singled out actresses and singers as the foremost examples of female genius, and Fuller herself was often portrayed by people around her as a performer, more effective with language in conversation than in writing.[55] Indeed, in September 1845, Fuller integrated Lind into an article on George Sand's novel *Consuelo,* then "in process of translation in 'The Harbinger,' a periodical published at Brook Farm, Mass.," where a group of men and women associated with Transcendentalism had established an experimental social community based on the writings of Charles Fourier; Fuller speculated that Sand (whom Fuller admired greatly) had based her heroine on Lind, who, on the basis of news from abroad, Fuller termed one of "the priesthood of Muses, who have conferred the higher benefit of refining, raising, and exhilarating the popular mind."[56] Identifying Lind with Sand, and (implicitly) herself with both women, Fuller crossed the conventional boundaries of media and genre, and positioned the notion of genius as a conflation of body and text, a force of immediate personal presence that certain writers and writings shared with certain performing artists.

Although Fuller died earlier in the very year that Lind arrived in the United States for the first time, her description of the singer, along with her association of Lind with a rogue literary figure like Sand, accurately predicts one underexamined strain of the significance of the Swedish singer's legendary, Barnum-sponsored tour: the influence Lind and other female performers would exert on notions of literary genius for both male and female writers in the coming decades. What is particularly striking is that, despite the Lind legend's tendency to trumpet the singer as hyperfeminine (as in her famous nickname, the "Swedish Nightingale"), Fuller's linkage of Lind and Sand associates the former with an intellectual exceptionality given embodied form as unruly gender performance. This insightful prereading of Lind sets the stage for understanding a major strain in the critical response to her performances, in which Lind became an icon not simply of traditional femininity but of certain American audiences' ability to understand themselves as daring and broadly receptive. To achieve this self-understanding, critics increasingly portrayed genius as the attribute of artists, performers, and writers capable of entering and transforming their audiences psychologically.

CHAPTER 2

Cosmopolitan Whiteness: Writing Jenny Lind

Each front page of the *New-York Tribune* from the 1840s and 1850s is a small-scale topography of the antebellum cultural field as it appeared from the nation's emergent intellectual hub. As one of the most successful of the penny dailies that had been springing up in U.S. cities since the 1830s, the *Tribune* was part of the same market expansion that generated this boom in cultural production. Peter Buckley writes that the widespread emergence of the penny press "broadened and refined the boundaries of the 'public' so that wholly new areas of urban life—from night court at the Tombs to costumes at elite balls—became open to continuous surveillance and narration."[1] But the front page of the *Tribune,* more than those of its chief local rivals, the *Herald* and the *Sun,* placed culture on equal footing with other items of local, national, and international concern. Thus did the *Tribune* structurally insist on culture's integration with the stories that narrated to readers their sense of the "everyday."

The range of audiences addressed by the paper, however, can seem broad to the point of incoherence. Strewn among the articles each day are advertisements for stage entertainments taking place in the city—theatrical performances that readers presumably might elect to attend later that day or week. Next to Margaret Fuller's reviews of Balzac and George Sand, for example, sit notices of performances by blackface minstrel companies; some of the more established, such as Christie's Singers and the Ethiopian Opera, advertised virtually every day. When Fuller left New York in 1846 to report on the revolutionary movement in Italy, the paper's founder and editor, Horace Greeley, demonstrated his continuing commitment to literature as an integral part of his readers' everyday lives by bringing in George Ripley—another former Transcendentalist and the founder of the Brook Farm social experiment at West Roxbury, Massachusetts—as her successor. Ripley's pieces on literature appeared alongside continuing announcements of minstrel productions, melodramas, and opera. Sometimes, prominent space was occupied by notices of upcoming visits by Italian divas, such as the famed Madame Alboni.

Yet few cultural events can have generated more inches of newsprint than Jenny Lind's arrival in New York, for the first performances of her U.S. tour, in September 1850. The *Tribune* and its competitors were responding to Lind's celebrity, promoted by P. T. Barnum and materialized in the massive crowds that followed her around Manhattan—a matter itself newsworthy for its disruption of the city's daily routines. But Greeley devoted more resources and space to the singer, committing the paper to an extended examination of Lind as an aesthetic figure. Once again treating post-Transcendentalist Boston as a form of intellectual farm club, he invited John Sullivan Dwight, known in the relatively small circle of readers of the *Dial* as an eminent music critic, to cover Lind's arrival and first performances. Although the idea that music was a field for serious criticism was far from widespread in 1850, Greeley published a series of articles by Dwight, long texts combining accounts of the singer's daily activities, including rehearsals, with assessments of the actual concerts focusing both on Lind's performance and on the character and behavior of her audiences.[2]

Dwight constructed Lind's visit as an event of serious historical significance. In the piece published the day after her first performance, he wrote, "Jenny Lind's first concert is over and all doubts are at an end. She is the greatest singer we have ever heard, and her success is all that was anticipated from her genius and her fame."[3] A bit farther on, he described Lind as "the divine songstress, with that perfect bearing, that aid of all dignity and sweetness, blending a child-like simplicity and half-trembling womanly modesty with the beautiful confidence of Genius and serene wisdom of Art."

That the range of topics appearing on the *Tribune*'s front page today seems either a jumble or an anticipation of our own time reflects the many things Greeley and his staff were asking culture generally, and genius specifically, to *do* within the world as

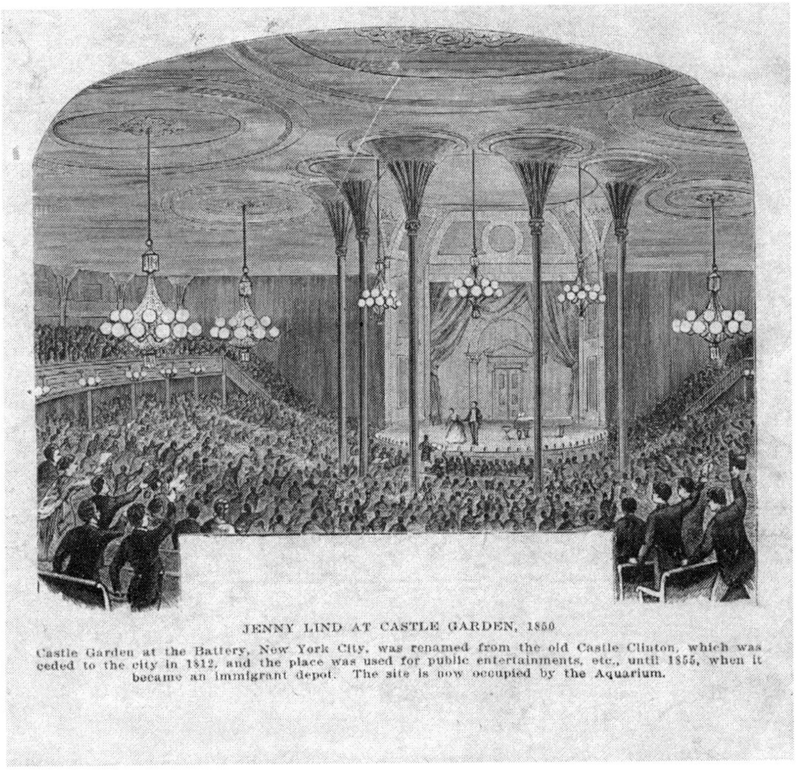

Figure 1. Magazine illustration of Jenny Lind in one of her five performances at Castle Garden in September 1850. From Journal of American History, *1917. Courtesy of Picture Collection, The Branch Libraries, The New York Public Library, Astor, Lenox and Tilden Foundations.*

the paper constructed it. With Dwight, Ripley, Margaret Fuller, and others, the paper embedded a mass-addressed appeal to the redemptive value of aesthetic and intellectual culture within its representation (and embodiment) of a varied but unified everyday present. In his highly influential study of cultural hierarchy in the nineteenth-century United States, *Highbrow-Lowbrow,* Lawrence Levine has cited the extraordinarily enthusiastic American response to Lind, along with Shakespeare's pre–Civil War popularity with audiences of diverse economic standing, as exemplifying the weakness of applying "arbitrary and imprecise cultural categories" such as "high" and "popular" to antebellum culture, the performing arts in particular. According to Levine, the anachronistic application of such categories has "helped obscure the dynamic complexity of American culture in the nineteenth century."[4] What Levine does not point out is that the rich texture of this complexity requires acknowledging that the concept of culture at this time existed less in articulated theory than in the material connection, on a single sheet of paper like the *Tribune*'s front page, of the three "general categories" through which Raymond Williams has defined culture: "the 'ideal,' in which culture is a state or process of human perfection"; "the 'documentary,' in which culture is the body of intellectual work in which, in a detailed way, human thought and experience are variously recorded"; "the 'social,' . . . in which culture is a description of a particular way of life, which expresses certain meanings and values not only in art and learning but also in institutions and ordinary behaviour."[5]

As I have been suggesting, genius, unlike culture, is *not* an anachronistic concept. When Dwight and other critics repeatedly described Jenny Lind as a genius, they were using a term with significance on local, national, and international scales.[6] They were, in fact, juggling the relationship of these scales as they chose to emphasize different aspects of the tour's significance and different aspects of Lind herself. With her Nordic appearance, Lind easily stood out against the background of blackface minstrelsy and Italian opera. But this context had a deeper impact on the shape of her genius, as rendered in writing by Dwight and other critics convinced of her broad significance as an aesthetic figure. Bucking any inclination to consider an "aesthetic turn" in criticism a move away from historical, cultural, and political context, the acclaim for Lind wears its situation in the social tensions of the midcentury United States quite prominently. As Buckley puts it in his account of antebellum New York, "The divisions of class and ethnicity in the 'mercantile period' [1820–1860] extended beyond the workplace or formal politics, to the street, to cultural spaces and options, and to representations of the city itself" (27).[7]

No event illustrated the inseparability of culture and politics more explosively than did the conflagration outside the Astor Place Opera House on May 10, 1848, when police attacked a crowd of largely working-class men gathered to express their alienation from the mercantile classes by harassing a performance of *Macbeth* starring the Englishman William Macready.[8] At least twenty-two civilians were killed. For many better-off New Yorkers, as Buckley writes, the violence signaled that "the need to reconstruct a middle ground for urban culture was clear and pressing" (43).[9]

In the critical response to Jenny Lind, one version of this "middle ground" expressed an increasingly common way of thinking about the arts, their increasing proliferation and variety, and their relationship to the more broadly conceived "society." In this view, genius emerges not against but in a privileged position alongside other cultural forms, all of which are granted legitimation. Criticism espousing this view worked not so much to prescribe aesthetic principles as to encourage a new, more variegated way of understanding cultural production and consumption, as well as cultural discrimination, as a redemptive part of everyday bourgeois life.

The criticism I examine in this chapter strives to specify the nature of such redemptiveness by wrestling with the question of whether genius, as Lind gives form to it, is primarily individual or collective. Although Dwight, especially, was committed to the former, he and other critics nonetheless portray Lind as a genius so as to promote the notion of cultural practice as valuable for *civic* reasons. This cultural politics reflects the republicanism that Meredith McGill's scholarship has shown to have oriented the social and legal status of literature in the United States well into the mid-nineteenth century.[10] What changes in this criticism, and what begins to bring a contemporary understanding of culture into focus, is that the civic sphere is no longer so directly tied to the nation. The collectivity imagined is national, but its strength depends on an overall perspective that is cosmopolitan and actively seeking the infusion of genius from non-American sources. I will argue, however, that these critics redraw the boundaries of legitimate cultural practice along lines implicitly defined by race, by a classed and gendered historical configuration of whiteness.

It becomes clear that Lind embodied a specifically blurry relationship of race and nation that made her particularly adaptable to these critics' view of genius. Moreover, one reason for her appeal to certain critics involved their perception of the shape of more popular cultural forms, particularly blackface minstrelsy. Even as Dwight praised Lind, he was working through his recognition of blackness as a cultural force; in particular, he was becoming aware of the complexity of minstrelsy, which Eric Lott has argued can be "read as a new infusion of 'blackness' and black cultural practices into American life" in the 1840s and 1850s.[11] Dwight's cosmopolitanism emerged almost simultaneously with an insistent effort on his part to value cultural manifestations of blackness by identifying them with the circumscribed realm of national culture. Examples of such culture symbolized the nation, but did not contribute to the process of individual and collective improvement that underwrote the civic ideal of Dwight's cosmopolitanism.

Ultimately, the Lind criticism with which this chapter is concerned attempts to differentiate the roles that culture and nation play in understanding, if not reconciling, tensions between individualist and collective forms of identity at a particular moment of the antebellum era. The standard point these critics construct is not a critique of nationalism but an effort to portray nationalism and internationalism as complementary. Culture and nation become in this view constitutively different entities, joined only obliquely; indeed, their difference ascribes greater historicity to nation, and thus to art aimed chiefly at symbolizing the nation.

A final introductory note: the ideal of genius put forth by Dwight through his discussion of Lind appears at first glance like a proto-Arnoldian or proto-Jamesian "sacralization" (to borrow Levine's useful term) of culture. And, indeed, Dwight's professional biography as a critic follows the outlines of Levine's story of the "emergence of cultural hierarchy," later in the nineteenth century, around the categories of "high" and "low" culture. Less than two years after his work on Lind for the *Tribune,* Dwight founded *Dwight's Journal of Music,* widely considered the most influential American publication on music of the nineteenth century. For the duration of its existence from 1852 to 1881, "Dwight used [the journal] . . . to articulate tirelessly," as Levine puts it, "the conception of a sacralized art," in particular advocating the founding of metropolitan orchestras devoted to "the great unquestioned masterworks."[12] From the standpoint of more than a century's hindsight (a view most concisely reflected in Levine's work), the writing on Lind was a signal part of an overall project that took perhaps three decades to complete—to describe culture as a realm of free-floating subjective purity defined against not only capitalism but politics. Yet the writing on Lind is specific to the situation of the middle class of the North in the mid-nineteenth century—to this class's sense of everyday life and of culture's role in it. Recovering this specificity with a more historically localized view provides a glimpse of this project as it progressed, and alerts us to the possibility that it may remain unfinished, may in fact be constitutively incomplete.

"She Sings Herself"

Dwight's articles about Lind for the *Tribune* are remarkable for their degree of emphasis on understanding of the singer as essentially singular and hence essentially outside the symbolic economy of representativeness. Thus we encounter sentences in his work like this one, from his account of a rehearsal before the first concert of the tour in New York's Castle Garden amphitheater:

> She sings herself. She does not, like many skillful vocalists, merely recite her musical studies, and dazzle you with splendid feats unnaturally acquired; her singing, through all her versatile range of parts and styles, is her own proper and spontaneous activity—integral and whole.[13]

Or this, from Dwight's review of the first concert:

> A moment more, and JENNY LIND, clad in a white dress that well became the frank sincerity of her face, came forward through the orchestra. . . . [T]he divine songstress, with that perfect bearing, that aid of all dignity and sweetness, blending a child-like simplicity and half-trembling womanly modesty with the beautiful confidence of Genius and serene wisdom of Art, addressed herself to song, as the orchestral symphony prepared the way for the voice in *Casta Diva*. A better test piece could not have been selected for her debut. Every soprano lady has sung it to us; but nearly every one has seemed only trying to make something of it, while JENNY LIND *was* the very music for the time being. We would say no less than that; for the wisest and honestest part of criticism on such a first hearing of a thing so perfect, was to give itself purely up to it, without question, and attempt no analysis of what too truly fills one to have yet begun to be an object of thought.[14]

Dwight presents Lind as, essentially, embodied tautology: "She sings herself"; "JENNY LIND *was* the very music for the time being." This thesis shapes his other observations, such as Lind's "child-like simplicity and half-trembling womanly modesty." Many antebellum critics described Lind in terms of childish innocence and feminine virtue, but in Dwight's writing such qualities are ultimately designed less to integrate her into the ideology of domesticity than to clear the path for a complete identification between Lind and her expressivity in song, in the "serene wisdom of Art." The telos of Dwight's writing dissolves, for the time of performance at least, the referentiality of Lind's "Art." He touts this quality of genius by foregrounding his own susceptibility to it, with his assertion of "the wisest and honestest part of criticism" as the postponement of criticism's exigencies, which include making art "an object of thought."

This rhetoric asserts that genius is most itself, most "integral and whole," when it represents nothing outside of itself; at best, what it represents is "Art," but the unique effect of genius in action is to suspend even this degree of referentiality. Yet this assertion obviously does not invalidate the act of writing criticism for Dwight, and he shares a number of the preoccupations of writers from other New York newspapers covering the Lind performances. Dwight, like others, was impressed by, in addition to Lind's femininity, the range of material she presented: arias, Swedish folk music, and a special song commissioned in honor of the tour. Lind's talent for working within various frames of signification appears to have fortified Dwight's view of the singer as ultimately signifying her self.

In addition, Lind's Scandinavian background was a prominent focus for critics. Dwight, like many others, specifically referred to this as her Northern origin and character. The lack of specificity of the epithet "Northern" was especially effective for maintaining rather than resolving the complicated questions of Lind's representativeness; such a resolution was not encouraged by Whig-affiliated cultural politics. "Northern" displaced the frame of reference around her from the contemporary, politically entrenched category of nation onto a signifier at once vaguely racial, regional, and international. More, the term resonated harmoniously with the contemporary vernacular of domestic politics, increasingly organized around sectionalist tensions between "the North" and "the South."[15] Its frequent appearance also reflected Lind's correlation with the growing tendency of Anglo-American thinkers, in sciences as well as arts, to consider the ideals of U.S. republicanism a racial inheritance from the "Teutonic" people of Northern Europe. This view was invigorated by the rise and recent fall of European revolutionary movements of the 1840s, with a number of intellectuals claiming that racial differences within Europe had saved Northern Europe, Britain, and the United States from the violence occurring in nations where republicanism had not taken hold.[16]

That "Northern" could suggest several different associations relieved Lind from the burden of direct historical reference. The vagueness of the category "North" for topography and political geography meant that it could signify in a usefully unstable manner, suggesting a connection to the U.S. North that was easily disavowable. In shuttling between general and specific modes of reference, it followed the logic of the epistemological paradox with which Richard Dyer has described whiteness: "Whites must be seen to be white, yet whiteness as race resides in invisible properties and whiteness as power is maintained by being unseen. To be seen as white is to have one's corporeality registered, yet true whiteness resides in the non-corporeal."[17]

A sense of this particular aspect of whiteness emerges by comparing Dwight's work for the *Tribune* with that of the equally enthusiastic reporter who covered Lind's first concert for the *Herald*. Where the *Tribune* generally aligned itself with Whig politics, and played a central role in the formation of the Republican party, the *Herald* advocated the positions of the Democratic Party, including sympathy for the slaveholding South.[18] Such differences of ideology resonate in each newspaper's Lind coverage. A significant portion of Dwight's review of the first concert describes her within the parameters of "Style" by differentiating her from Italian divas of the "South":[19]

> True, you would not say of her, in the conventional Italian sense of the word, what is often said in first acknowledgment of a good singer: "She has *style*"—meaning the one style which is assumed as the standard. If we are to limit style to that sense, Mdlle. Lind has more than style; she has genius—Northern genius, to be sure, which is precisely what she should have to make her greatness genuine. . . .
>
> It is, perhaps, too late to await the advent of a Queen of Song from the warm South. The South has had its turn; it has fulfilled its mission; the other end of the balance now comes up. The Northern muse must sing her lesson to the world. Her fresher, chaster, more intellectual, and (as they only *seem* to some) her colder strains come in due season to recover our souls from the delicious languor of a music which has been so wholly of the feelings, that, for want of some intellectual tonic, and some spiritual temper, feeling has generated into mere sensibility, and a very cheap kind of superficial, skin-deep excitability that usurps the name of passion.[20]

The aesthetic framing of this contrast reflects Dwight's intense interest in music as a serious aesthetic arena. But the geographical rhetoric demonstrates his certainty that race shapes the measure of aesthetic excellence, favoring the "intellectual" North over the "mere sensibility" of the South. In an odd twist of rhetorical logic, Dwight argues that "Northern genius" is "precisely what Lind should have to make her greatness genuine," but directly precludes the possibility of a "Southern" singer achieving the parallel effect by genuinely embodying Southernness. What seems to justify this contradiction is the identification of Northernness with the nonreferential category of "Style," thus preventing the evaluation of her art through its material effects, its "skin-deep excitability."

Lind's independence from referentiality, her ability to "sing herself," is, then, a racial quality shared by Dwight and his readers (at least as he imagines them) in the domestic version of her international North—the Northern states of the United States. We can begin to see the earlier description of Lind's genius—"she sings herself"—as contributing to a rhetoric of *self-possession* linking U.S. republicanism and whiteness. As Matthew Frye Jacobson has shown in his discussion of the 1790 naturalization law's use of the phrase "free white persons," the ideals of American republicanism "seemed to call for a polity that was disciplined, virtuous, self-sacrificing, productive, far-seeing, and wise—traits that were all racially inscribed in eighteenth-century Euro-American thought." Thus, in an overdetermined paradox, slavery marked people of African descent as unfit for the demands of republican self-rule.[21] The independence of genius from reference, formulated by Dwight through Jenny Lind, can be seen as a reformulation of republican notions of political independence. Lind emancipates herself and her audience, her embodied singing voice guaranteeing them shared entry to the exalted, disembodied realm of "Art"; she even, as we saw, liberates critics from the necessity of mastering her art as a critical object.

By midcentury, however, any identification between national civic virtue and whiteness had to contend with the national conflict over chattel slavery, a conflict increasingly present on a national level in mass-distributed culture and increasingly articulated in sectional terms. Dwight's way of contending with the national crisis was to omit reference to it, to place it beyond the parameters of his aesthetic and cultural concerns. The *Herald* greeted Lind with almost as much enthusiasm as the *Tribune,* which might suggest that the journalistic arbiters of antebellum culture saw her as an essentially apolitical phenomenon. The *Herald* also emphasized Lind's "Northernness," but placed it in a different context:[22]

> As a sign of the progress of civilization among northern nations, [last night's concert's] importance cannot be exaggerated. As a *cantatrice,* she is as much superior to all her northern predecessors as Napoleon was to his contemporaries, or as Eli Whitney, the inventor of cotton, was to the first 'gemman ob color' who used it. She has changed all men's ideas of music, as much so as Bacon's inductive system revolutionized philosophy. It is a new era in art, as much as Raphael's birth. It is chiefly interesting, too, as coming from a new and unexpected quarter—the North; and it shows, among other signs, that the wand of civilization has fallen from the hands of the southern nations, and passed to the hardy northern races.

The *Herald*'s writer, whose identity I have not been able to ascertain, also casts Lind as a "sign" of the "North," identifying her more boldly than Dwight with modernity itself by giving her a space among a range of military, technological, scientific, and artistic achievements that represent the "progress of civilization."[23] As in Dwight's writing, these qualities are contrasted with those that characterize "southern nations." But the crucial difference here is the coterminous presence of the *American* South, in the reference to the cotton gin and to a slave, a "'gemman ob color'" refracted through the dialect voice of blackface. Slavery, in this view, is compatible with modernity, and does not pose an obstacle to modernization; rather, it advances the "progress of civilization among northern nations" by providing opportunities even for nonslaveowners, like Connecticut's Eli Whitney, to develop technologies so innovative as to earn titles such as "inventor of cotton."

But the contrast in cultural politics evident here is not reducible to an opposition between nationalism and cosmopolitanism. Indeed, critics who embraced Lind as a scion of cosmopolitanism positioned their internationalist view of culture alongside various views of the United States, and of nation as a category. One such position was that of Nathaniel Parker Willis, arguably the most relentlessly cosmopolitan of antebellum literary editors, and a hugely enthusiastic supporter of Lind.[24] In 1845, Willis wrote, controversially, in the *North American Review,* "Mere nationality is no more nor less than so much provincialism. The demand for nationality bounded historically and geographically by the independent existence and territory of a particular race or fraction of a race . . . is a sublimer sort of clownishness and ill-manners. Genius is cosmopolitan."[25] When Lind arrived in the United States, however, Willis reinscribed her within the nation's symbolic economy by linking her to excellence in cultural consumption. In an article published just before Lind's tour in his *Home Journal,* and later included in a volume he compiled, *Memoranda of Jenny Lind,* Willis wrote, "Let America be the *country of fresh impressability,* where there is no crust of corruption, for genius or greatness from another land to break through, but where all who come are sure to be received kindly, judged fairly and promptly, and rewarded liberally according to desert."[26] He continued, "In no country (we thank Heaven that we can truthfully say,) has Jenny Lind, in all her gifts and qualities, been, ever before, so completely recognized, and so thoroughly *at home.*" Foreshadowing some of the themes we will examine in the following chapter, Willis saw no contradiction between economic and cultural vitality, a viewpoint that seemed to portend commercially bustling New York's future as the cultural capital of the world. In another 1850 article for the *Home Journal,* Willis announced "The Jenny Lind Epoch of Artistic Migration," in an article claiming that New York, through its newfound wealth, had surpassed Paris as "the world's golden centre": "The truth is that the world is not a globe, as is erroneously represented, but an amphitheatre whose civilized radii have an irresistable declivity toward one centre—*the point where money is spent most freely for pleasure.*"[27]

Despite its modicum of nationalism, Willis's writing, with its attention to money and pleasure, places him outside the principles of republican civic virtue. But Lind's presence spurred another antebellum New York critic, Parke Godwin, to write an extraordinary text that seized on the singer's arrival as a way of recontextualizing U.S. national identity within world history. *Vala: A Mythological Tale,* composed loosely on the model of the Icelandic saga, tells the story of its eponymous heroine's voyage away from desperation and misery to the social utopia of "New Earth."[28] On the one hand, Godwin embraced Lind by making her the equivalent of American "founding father" figures; on the other hand, this embrace relied crucially on defining nation as a category limited by historicity and social relations, in a manner that art was not.

Because the arc of Godwin's career has some close analogies with Dwight's, *Vala* helps fill out the politics embedded in the *Tribune*'s construction of Lind's genius. Each critic pledged his allegiance to Lind in prominent print venues during the first months of the tour, Godwin in the *New York Evening Post.* Each viewed the notion of genius through the lens of English and German Romanticism. Indeed, in 1846, Godwin edited the first complete English translation of Goethe's *Autobiography*; on the book's title page, the work of translation was attributed to "the editor and some friends," one of whom was Dwight.[29] Godwin and Dwight also shared an interest in utopian social theory, primarily that of Charles Fourier. Along with *Tribune* editor Greeley and New England intellectuals such as George Ripley and Henry James Sr., they were among a group of culturally privileged antebellum northeastern white men who saw the nation as beset by social ills caused by its inability to keep pace with modernity, and believed that the problems required a vast reevaluation of economic and social principles.[30] Members of this circle were generally opposed to slavery on philosophical grounds but not actively committed to abolitionism, which they saw as a largely sentimental struggle that did not address the deep structure of social relations.[31] As antebellum U.S. interest in Fourier faded, especially after the failure of the experimental Fourierist community at Brook Farm (which Godwin advocated and in which Dwight was a participant), both men became more exclusively engaged in journalism and arts criticism: Godwin at the *Evening Post* and later at *Putnam's Monthly*; Dwight in a series of books and, most prominently, in his own *Dwight's Journal of Music,* the inaugural issue of which featured a front-page article on Jenny Lind.

As the century progressed, both men played active roles in the institutional consolidation of criticism around the sacralization of culture; both Dwight and Godwin embarked on this route by moving away from social radicalism and toward sectionalism, in a shift Eric Foner has described as characteristic for a number of Northern intellectuals in the 1850s:

> It is possible that the growing ideological conflict between sections had the effect of undermining a tradition of radical criticism within northern society. Men like Horace Greeley, highly critical of certain aspects of their society in the 1840s, became more and more uncritical when faced with the need to defend the North

> against southern assaults. The choices for America came to be defined as free society versus slave society—the idea of alternatives within free society was increasingly lost sight of.[32]

Dwight and Godwin supplement Foner's point by suggesting that, for a number of these men, culture came to substitute for "radical criticism" as the venue in which social change was imagined.

Generically identified by its author as an "Extravaganza," *Vala* casts Lind's visit as an occasion for cultivating aesthetic taste in the nation's citizenry. But, more so than Dwight's criticism, it identifies true artistic genius with a "North" whose genealogical connection to the United States is fully traceable. Unlike the *Herald*'s version of Lind's "Northernness," however, which made room for the states of the South in its national political geography, Godwin's text wants to reconceive the nation *as* the white U.S. North.[33] Godwin's depiction of Lind's genius is at all points bolstered by his conviction that her "Northernness" also embodies *republican* qualities of which the U.S. North remains the world's foremost exemplar. Thus the text begins by invoking the legend of Scandinavian explorers as the first Europeans to land in North America—on the coast of New England. The usurpation of the Italian Christopher Columbus erases the more southern-oriented origin story of a landing in the Caribbean; it also supplants the greatness of a Southern European in a manner analagous to Dwight's use of Lind to supplant the preeminence of Italian opera singers. Godwin uses this origin story, popular with James Russell Lowell and other influential northeastern literati, to cast Lind's tour as a kind of second coming of the continent's supposed originary whiteness—projecting, in "New Earth," the image of an "America" free of Southern Europeans, African slaves, and indigenous people.

More specifically addressing the moment of its composition, the text portrays Vala as driven out of her homeland by social upheaval, a violent conflict between poverty and wealth redolent of the recent events of 1848 in Europe generally. "New Earth," the allegorical America to which she travels, provides a refuge from the despotism of title and inheritance. Thus Godwin portrays Vala's escape:

> As she approached the shore [to depart], there was heard behind her a roaring and a clamor as of ghouls mingled with hissings and wild sobs. A fearful quaking came over her that seemed bodeful of the crash of worlds. Then a Voice said, "Behind you is the past—

> look!" And she looked and saw a vast black cloud drawn over the east far back, in the dim vistas, deep down in the dread abysses, of its many foldings, dubious phantoms and spectres wandered and vanished. Foul Faiths and Bloody Rites, and Lies, and Oppressions, and the agonies of Battle, all monstrous and oppressive Things, flapping their heavy wings, like vultures in a vain struggle against the storm, were swallowed up by that tremendous darkness. (40–41)

When she reaches New Earth, she "receive[s] into her being, with the perfume of the balmy atmosphere, a sense of indescribable peace and joy"; soon after, she finds herself greeted by "multiplying groups of happy and free people." Vala is journeying not only out of her homeland, but out of the past, with its premodern, unchangingly rigid forms of social structure—all "monstrous" manifestations of the undead past, the "darkness" that sucks all things backward toward itself. Here as elsewhere, the text exemplifies the contemporary ideal that Alexander Saxton calls "Republican innovation": the sense among the men from whom the ideology of the Republican *Party* was soon to be formed that they stood on the vanguard of global modernity.

It is important to remember that only a few years earlier, Godwin, like Dwight and Greeley, had been caught up in many of the intellectual currents that drove the European revolutionary movements of the 1840s.[34] Traces of internationalism remain in the text's revisionary account of the nation, most of all in the assertive national nonspecificity of the name "New Earth," which displaces the history of colonialism implicit in nonfictional place names like "New England" and "New Amsterdam." Thus the text is careful not to commit itself to the nation as its symbolic telos. Lind, it suggests, exemplifies genius whose appreciation requires a receptive framework of a scale broader than that of nation. But after Vala arrives in New Earth, the contemporary national crisis is also carefully maintained within the text's frame of reference. Upon the Lind-figure's landing on New Earth's shore, separate choruses of children, women, and men dance and sing to her in succession, whereupon all join together to intone:

> Discord-queller,
> Woe-dispeller,
> Song-queen of the mystic North;
> Saga-singer,

Rapture-bringer,
Pure in heart and rich in worth . . .

From wild New England's stormy coasts,
To California's golden gates.
Thy children spread in restless hosts,
Through circling brotherhoods of States,
Across thy vast unlorded plains,
Freedom for aye shall build her home.
The Arts shall rear their fairest fanes,
Religion raise her noblest domes.
(43–44)

The proto-camp excess of this passage (and of the text as a whole) ought not obscure the specifics of this version of national geography, which names New England and California—admitted as a free state under the terms of the Compromise of 1850 only days after the real Jenny Lind landed in New York Harbor—but includes no southern representatives among its "brotherhoods of States." At the same time, Godwin's flamboyant literary performance enacts the heat of not only his aestheticism but his imagination of the national community along lines more sensual, gender-mixed, and salon-like than is typically associated with antebellum nationalism; perhaps this qualifies as his version of Willis's "country of fresh impressability." For instance, Godwin describes in New Earth "the forms of noble women, of heroic men—ministered to by innumerable spirits, who laughed from rose buds and danced in the rainbows [and] sat in lofty circles conversing in tones more inspiring than music or delicious wine" (44–45). The intoxication this conversation offers is mirrored in the note of transcendence with which the story of Vala herself ends. Like an angel, she flies "beyond the reach of mortal eyes," and "across the heavens were written in mystic fire characters" a scene represented with great flourish in one of the book's final illustrations: "Harmony/E Pluribus Unum/Glory/Forever/To/Art" (46–47).

It is highly significant, I think, that this page of Godwin's book refers to the nation only to subordinate it to the more transcendent realm of "Art." The text is not critical of nationalism; indeed, it sees retelling the nation's story as a necessary part of readying the contemporary nation for Art's arrival. But in Vala's hierarchy of transcendence, art precedes nation in overall importance. Indeed,

Figure 2. "Glory Forever to Art": the final page of Parke Godwin's Vala: A Mythological Tale *(1851), an allegory of Lind's U.S. tour, from a woodcut by Thomas Pritchard Rossiter. Courtesy of General Research Division, The New York Public Library, Astor, Lenox and Tilden Foundations.*

Godwin suggests that not just the quasi-divine creation of art, but participation in culture as a whole, is a human activity of innate value, for which desirable or necessary social forms such as nation serve largely as vehicles.

With their attention to the eager throngs who gather before the "Song-queen of the mystic North," the later pages of *Vala* also address the matter of everyday cultural practice, the realm Michel de Certeau describes as "modes of operation or schemata of action."[35] Its scenes of the people of New Earth greeting Vala are fantasies of enlightened mass publics, of citizens for whom mass gatherings mean not the chaos and violence associated with the Astor Place Opera House, but added opportunities for cultivation and stimulation. Thus Godwin remains attached to a version of republicanism, for "Art" is portrayed not as the cultivating instrument of refined individuality, but as the initiator of a civic realm, however fantastic. This aspect of the text has analogies, as will become clear, in Dwight's writing for the *Tribune.* Indeed, the behavior of Lind's audiences was a concern of many of the journalists covering the New York concerts. These audiences served as examples of the enlightened collectivity whose configuration these critics saw as the practical power of genius.

First, however, we must understand more of the role whiteness played in the cosmopolitan culturalism of critics like Godwin, Dwight, and Willis. To do this, let us look briefly at how Dwight's commitment to the redemptive social value of cultural participation positioned *blackness.* This is important not simply because of the two terms' dependence on one another—indeed, what is interesting about Dwight's writing is its effort to reposition blackness not so much as the opposite of whiteness but as a trailing cultural formation, cut off from genius, and burdened with the historicity of national politics. But formulating his viewpoint required confronting the specific, highly vitiated form that dominated the cultural consumption of blackness by Northern whites—minstrelsy.

Lind and Blackness

In the previous chapter, I argued for the constitutive presence of the idea of black culture, most fully embodied in the notion of Frederick Douglass as genius, in the work of antebellum intellectuals like Ralph Waldo Emerson and Margaret Fuller. With different emphases, Emerson and Fuller both described Douglass's significance as directly proportional to the distance he was able to establish from the United States and from abolitionism (or, in Fuller's case, certain strains of abolitionism). Douglass, we saw, was himself struggling to reconcile contemporary antislavery politics with a not wholly compatible self-identity as an intellectual. We also saw the central role that Fuller accorded to music in her understanding of black culture, particularly in her foregrounding of the "sorrow songs" passage of Douglass's *Narrative.* Indeed, before she left Boston for New York, Fuller had served as editor of the Transcendentalist organ the *Dial,* where John Sullivan Dwight published many of his earliest essays on music. Although Dwight did not address black music directly in his writing on Lind, he mentioned it regularly, often in highly positive terms, in the writing he produced and edited for the *Journal of Music* in the years immediately following the end of Lind's tour.[36] If we take these pieces as articulated from the same overall understanding of the antebellum cultural field as that through which his writing on Lind's genius was composed, we discover more about the cosmopolitan whiteness of this singer's figure—as well as the supportive role played by class and gender in that whiteness.

Dwight's *Journal of Music* repeatedly discusses black music when it tackles the issue of the relationship between nation and genius. This topic was a running controversy for Dwight in the 1850s. In an 1853 column, Dwight described "musical genius" as "distinguished not by narrow nationality, but by . . . glorious universality." As part of what seems to have been an ongoing debate that this editorial sparked with readers, in an 1854 essay titled "Complaint on Behalf of Native Composers" Dwight responded angrily to the tendency among foreign critics to describe "songs of the American stamp" as "'negro melodies, or namby-pamby sentimental ditties, sung and manufactured by the numerous singing 'families' that traverse the States."[37] He insisted, "We did say, and we do say, that the highest genius is not national."[38] This rhetoric reflects an assumption implicit in his Lind pieces and familiar from our readings of Emerson and Fuller: the relegation of culture generated within slavery to a subordinate position—its spirit perhaps emblematic of an innate national commitment to "freedom" but its words and music always limited aesthetically by its connection to historical and political struggle. By making it the duty of every culturally right-minded person to consign black and popular cultural forms to the ephemeral, Dwight's rhetoric identified the uppermost principles of aesthetic practice and taste with whiteness.

Yet this link between blackness and nation is a tricky one, for its criticism of nation as a framework for cultural practice derives centrally from a sense that such a framework dilutes the genuineness of art at a level of deeper significance. Part of what drives Dwight's hostility to the notion of an "American stamp" on music is that the "negro melodies" labeled such by foreign commentators are inauthentic according to conventional standards of artistry. One article from the *Journal* notes that "We at the North hear these songs only as burlesqued by our Negro Minstrels, with faces blackened with charcoal."[39] Meanwhile, the celebrations of slave spirituals appearing in the *Journal of Music* in the 1850s convey his drift toward relegating "blackness" to a form of hypostatized authenticity even today maintained in the classifications "folk" and "roots" culture. Such a viewpoint resembles the position struck by Theodore Parker's comments on slave narrative in his 1849 essay "The American Scholar":

> Yet, there is one portion of our permanent literature, if literature it may be called, which is wholly indigenous and original. The lives of the early martyrs and confessors are purely Christian, so are the legends of saints and other pious men; there was nothing of this in the Hebrew or heathen literature, cause and occasion were alike wanting for it. So we have one series of literary productions that could be written by none but Americans, and only here; I mean the Lives of Fugitive Slaves. But as these are not the work of the men of superior culture they hardly help to pay the scholar's debt. Yet all the original romance of Americans is in them, not in the white man's novel.[40]

Described in this fashion, black culture could be representatively American, but it could not be effectively *genius*. This view positions blackness, and black lives, as embodying organic national identity. Parker places slavery at the center of that identity, while simultaneously subordinating nationally representative art to the significance of work produced by "men of superior culture." Moreover, this view limits blackness's cultural presence to the realm of described experience, distinguishing it (as well as the degraded "white man's novel") from the provinces of literature produced by the imagination of the "superior men."

In the 1850s, *Dwight's Journal* took up an analogous position in articulating its broad definition of genius. This view was stated most concisely in an article, "National Music," that the journal reprinted in 1853 from the Philadelphia *Evening Bulletin*. The anonymous author condemned what he saw as a tendency to over-identify the value of American cultural production with its representation of "native" subject matter. The specific occasion for the piece was the offer by Ole Bull, the celebrated Norwegian violinist, of one thousand dollars in prize money to the author of an American opera written on an "American" topic, a stipulation this critic found highly objectionable: "The idea of national genius, as entertained by many, is a fallacy; for genius is an attribute shared by the whole race, though in different degrees; and neither climate, geographical lines nor naturalization papers can so modify it as to give it a distinct character in each land, or in each nation of the earth."[41]

Nation is here subordinated to genius on the basis of the latter's status as "an attribute shared by the whole race"; the writer would seem at first to mean something like the generalization embodied in the phrase the "human race." She or he develops the point, however, by citing a contrast between genius and a specific antebellum way of living racial embodiment, American slavery. Citing the example of Hiram Powers's famous sculpture *The Greek Slave,* the author asks, "Is Power[s] not an American artist because his *chef d'oeuvre* is a Greek and not an American slave?" The blackness of an American slave guarantees the obvious, implied answer, "Of course not," and obviates any need to press the question beyond the boundaries of its rhetorical cast. The remainder of the piece confirms that blackness was the specific haunting this perspective on cultural nationalism:

> [W]hen [American artists] try to make their statues American, they necessarily violate the standards of beauty, and produce men and women of rather ungraceful outline. When they try to make their music American, what can they do, unless they reject the models of the old world and fall back upon Yankee Doodle, the Star Spangled Banner, or the negro melodies?[42]

It is unclear whether this critic shared Dwight's opinion that what most white Northerners referred to as "negro melodies" were in actuality counterfeits. Nonetheless, his or her writing performs a striking juxtaposition, making "negro melodies" a constituent of the same cluster as a nationalist standard and the national anthem itself.

This formulation values cultural embodiments of blackness in music, literature, and elsewhere. Rather than constructing an oppositional model of cultural value by means of the racial binarism distinguishing white-identified and black-identified forms of cultural production, this view constructs a graded hierarchy, with genius of the sort embodied by Lind at the top. The place black cultural production occupies on this grid is necessarily limited by certain innate qualities that do not constrain its national resonance: in particular, an emphasis on collectivity at the expense of individuality, and an emphasis on practices understood as "imitative" (Dwight used the term "manufacture[d]") in contrast to the originality of genius. Purposely absent in this formulation is any assertion that there cannot be good black music, or a good rendition of the national anthem: these forms are simply different and circumscribed by limits of social and historical circumstance.

But the ability to recognize this hierarchy is written as one of the entitlements of cosmopolitan whiteness: even if blackness is authentically rendered, it still carries the burden of what Parker called black "lives," the experience of slavery, which precludes its victims from the conditions and insight necessary to appreciate genius. Indeed, a particularly notable mechanism within the Parkerian form of cultural politics inscribes within itself a critique of ideology, a claim to insight that exceeds the promises of nationalism. This subordination of nation portrays (as we shall soon see) the establishment of a redemptive engagement with culture as a matter of individual affect and discrimination; in doing so, the fuller context of its derivation—the construction of the individual specifically and simultaneously against nation and blackness—is rendered invisible.

Genius is a category of fundamental importance to this position not only because of its usefulness for removing cultural evaluation from a national framework, but also because it describes the alternative to these more "native" cultural forms in terms that displace racial hierarchy onto a hierarchy of cultural value. Thus the cosmopolitan view I am describing and the everyday participation in culture it advocates for the educated Northern bourgeoisie deserve consideration as a nationally invested form of *whiteness*. Whiteness underwrites the exercise of cosmopolitan aesthetic taste and the capacity to identify genius.

As we look at more of the ways Lind was described as a genius, it is important not only to keep this context in view, but also to be aware that such criticism was modeling not so much unvariable principles of aesthetic value but the essential vitality of a practice of discrimination. Alongside the loosening of the national framework evident in the critical response to Lind is a focus on the nature of audience response, both individual and collective.

"The Spectacle of a Whole People As It Were, Worshiping at the Shrine of Art"

If *greatness* refers to the external manifestations and range of effects of an internal property called *genius,* then we might assume that the aesthetically oriented Lind critics saw genius as an intervention in greatness. But the criticism these men produced is, from the vantage point of the early twenty-first century, surprisingly free of disdain for the scale of Lind's fame, or for her association with the era's most capitalized figure in what Horkheimer and Adorno called the "culture industry."[43] Indeed, in a manner quite unfamiliar to readers accustomed to later conventions of arts journalism, a striking degree of their writing concerns material beyond the moment of her performance. Even the coverage of the performances blends the perspective of aesthetic judgment with that of a cultural commentator, as even a critic as committed as Dwight to making music a field for serious criticism attends to the greater cultural scene of the performances, honing in particularly on the behavior and demographics of the audiences.

This attention suggests that Dwight, Willis, and Godwin did not conceive the magnitude of Lind's mass celebrity as necessarily opposed to the extent of her aesthetic achievement. The emphasis that the rhetoric of genius placed on Lind's self-possession that we have seen was not, I think, individualist in a generic sense. Overall, this criticism carries traces of a continuing republicanism that refuses to draw individual and collectivity into the sort of opposition that Lawrence Levine describes as a staple of later nineteenth-century music criticism. As a pedagogical practice, the earlier criticism's attention to "ways of doing" (to reiterate de Certeau's phrase) balances civic-republican and aesthetic-individual concerns. It proposes guidelines for both group and individual response. The Lind critics propose blueprints for a middle-class version of what Christopher

Newfield describes, in his study of Emerson, as the "orderly crowd," feared deeply when constituted by the urban working class.[44] I want to look closely at these guidelines now. We have already seen some of the attention accorded to group response in Godwin's bizarre prose-poem *Vala,* which cast Lind's U.S. tour as a new origin-moment for the nation, a slate-cleaning evisceration of the cultural and political burdens on national progress incurred, in the view of an increasing number of intellectuals from the Northern states, by the presence of the South, slavery, and (to differing degrees) blackness itself. The end of Godwin's text, with its sequence of choruses greeting Lind's arrival on the shore of New Earth, may be less fanciful mythology than a piece of civic choreography mapping an idealized yet potentially practical way of participating in the mass scale of this cultural event.

Indeed, the emphasis on gender in *Vala*'s climax—groups of men and women first responding separately, then together—complements the connection that many writers covering the New York performances made between civic order and gender heterogeneity in describing the audiences. Even the Democrat-identified *New York Herald* participated in this:

> [I]t was not the aristocracy who were there; it was the middle classes—the mechanics and storekeepers, with their wives and daughters and sisters, presenting an array of dazzling beauty, in which the upper ten were lost as a drop of water in the ocean. . . . From the ceiling to the stage it was one dense mass of human beings. . . . Yet was there *no confusion* [my emphasis]; for every seat was not only numbered, but the color of the paper on which the number was printed was the same as the color of the ticket.
>
> . . . It is very probably *[sic]* that many ladies were kept away for the first night for fear of being crushed; but when they find that their apprehensions were groundless, they will doubtless take the Castle by storm tomorrow night.[45]

The passage glowingly records the mixture of men and women, merchants and artisans, becoming "one dense mass." It also notes with admiration the system of management—color-coded tickets and seats—that literally ensures the order of a mass whose constituent individuals are spared the burden of "confusion," presumably leaving them in a state more attuned to the aesthetic purity of Lind's performance.

Dwight's analogous descriptions more specifically thematize the mass audience response as a model of civic behavior. In his work, the health of a culturally formed civic sphere is measured in terms of its middle-class identity. Dwight equates this health with heterogeneity of gender. Attributing such properties to a "mass" was to reappropriate mass entertainment from its association with the working class. As Lott, Saxton, and David Roediger have noted, minstrel performances were long considered the domain of the white urban working class, a theatergoing public that was constitutively male homosocial. To persuade middle-class readers that a mass public performance could be an orderly affair meant persuading them that this was not a working-class event, which meant persuading bourgeois individuals of both genders that women could safely attend.

According to Mary Ryan, "The first [antebellum] public den of male sociability to be sexually integrated was the theater," a transformation that began around the time of Lind's arrival in New York.[46] Dwight's writing on Lind shows that his notion of her as genius was designed to advance this process. Indeed, in his criticism, Lind as genius becomes a model of a middle-class woman safely insulated from social danger by her cultural sophistication.[47] More broadly, Dwight and other critics emphasize practical methods with which to make the reception of female genius a heterosocial marker of cultural modernity, in which the mass is no longer a mob but an agent of internal cultivation constituted in public space across gender lines.[48]

Dwight addressed these concerns most fully in his review of the third Castle Garden concert. He notes in the second paragraph that "none of the usual disagreeable features of such an event were experienced," an apparent reference to the risk of physical injury many middle-class New Yorkers associated with large-scale performances, particularly after the Astor Place events. He continues:

> At seven o'clock, when we took up the line of march for Castle Garden, both sides of Broadway were thronged, and the main avenue of the Battery was filled with a steady stream of persons pressing into the Castle gate. As on the first night, a double line of policemen had been formed, which effectually prevented all disorder. . . . We should, at a rough guess, estimate the number of the auditory at *seven thousand*. A much large *[sic]* proportion than

> on former nights, were ladies. . . . It is worthy of note, that the first and second concerts, immense as they were, were composed almost entirely of the intelligent and appreciative middle-class.[49]

This passage does not describe a panicked or phobic response to the crowded event; instead, it tells the story of a middle-class mass, with a discernible note of triumph. It embraces terms such as "thronged," and the notion of a "steady stream . . . pressing" the gates to the theater. The tone is not fearful, nor is it designed as an assurance to individual middle-class readers that they will be physically and mentally safe despite the scale of the event. Rather, this is an account of the successful harnessing of that scale, success that Dwight writes as dependent upon the "intelligen[ce]" and "appreciat[ion]" particular to the middle class.

By the review of the fifth concert, Dwight was prepared to more fully integrate this account of the audience's civic excellence with his assertions of Lind's genius:

> The Nightingale may sing in halls of much more musical dimensions, to audiences select and closely gathered within the more immediate circle of her potency: audiences not too large to keep still, and halls where each accompanying instrument may have some good chance, as well as her miraculous voice, of a good hearing. But to Castle Garden is reserved *this sublime spectacle of a whole people as it were, worshiping at the shrine of Art,* and receiving the voice of Art as that of "deep calling unto deep." Jenny Lind is evidently most her self and most inspired when she sings most for *all* [my emphases]. . . .
>
> The triumph has been two-fold: first, the highest refinement of Art, not only achieved but personified before us; and secondly, to complete and justify the beauty thereof, the widest possible and heartiest reception of it.[50]

Dwight here forcefully asserts the specific importance of massive scale to the success of an international artist in the United States. Indeed, he seizes a key category of modern aesthetic discourse, the sublime, and attaches it not to the specific quality of Lind's singing but to the mass "spectacle" of audience reception that in turn inspires Lind to be "most her self." For Lind to be "her self" is to attain the heights of aesthetic genius. As in *Vala,* the quality of genius emerges with the woman's capacity to unite a mass of people, illustrating within the bounded, concrete space of the performance hall the ideological operations she performed within the discursive spaces of nation, art, and genius. Lind's singing results in a "sublime spectacle" consisting in, as Dwight oddly phrases it, "a whole people as it were." The qualification at the end of this phrase prevents the passage's reference point from too directly becoming nation or nationalism. Like the people of New Earth, Lind's audiences may be illustrations of an "E Pluribus Unum" whose ultimate guarantee is art more than nation.

For Dwight, Lind's sublimity arises out of her binding effect on the large-scale live audience, her ability not simply to allay anxieties about mobs or mass culture but to actually make the mass into a "sublime spectacle." Her perfection consists in her ability not only to embody "the highest refinement of Art" but to inspire its "widest possible and heartiest reception." Gender diversity, specifically, gauges the breadth of this model of republican cultural sophistication. This diversity, however, is constructed through an implicit distinction from not only male homosociality but its specific connotations of class (working class) and race (trafficking in culture derived from black slaves in distorted form). In other words, these detailed descriptions of the experience of consuming a cultural event on this scale inscribe their own admission ticket of sorts: specifically, the middle-class cosmopolitan whiteness I have been describing.

Dwight's description of Lind's genius, then, is constructed through a series of cues to *Tribune* readers that signal the safety and propriety of attending a mass event, and that construct attendance at the event as an expression of white middle-class identity. But criticism of the sort exemplified in Dwight's articles also assures readers that Lind's art will provide an experience of individuation, will embody genius in the sense Kant meant when he located aesthetic judgment at the core of human subjectivity, in his third *Critique*. This vein of the criticism constructs the notion of genius as perfected self-expression ("she sings herself"), as the pedagogical model of an experience that cultural consumption makes attainable for audience members in the course of their everyday lives. Moreover, it does so by emphasizing its disregard for gender difference. The paradoxical quality of this perspective—discussing gender difference in order to assure readers that it doesn't matter—plays an important ideological role in suppressing the racial entitlement that underwrites participation in this cosmopolitan, republican realm of arts appreciation.

Dwight, in particular, portrays Lind's singing as cultivating *depth* not only in the generalized field of aesthetic achievement but in the individual members of her audience: what the review of the fifth concert called "deep calling into deep." That is, *genius* names her ability to make *them* more fully individuals, more fully themselves. Again, the difference from later nineteenth-century highbrow notions of aesthetic reception is noteworthy. Specific aspects of Lind's style are less important than the fact of the audience's attunement to the figure of genius she embodies, and the consequent effects on audience members as individuals.

Thus, even as the criticism emphasizes Lind's originality and individuality, touting those qualities as ideals for readers and audience members, it also enthusiastically portrays the apprehension of these ideals as a collective process taking place in public. What is also notable is how the simultaneous idealization of collective and individual experience registers *as* paradox, as tension. Indeed, what may be *least* republican about this criticism is its essentially erotic investment in such tensions. That is, republicanism is finally not the only force through which this work portrays the limits of individualism; genius also makes *sexuality* available for ultimately redemptive, class- and race-affirmative play between loss of self and self-expression.

A convergence of racial, classed, and sexual factors made up a coherent model of genius with which to describe Jenny Lind in the setting of mid-nineteenth-century New York. But the point of critics' describing this convergence as a coherent notion of genius is not strictly symbolic. It is equally important to see the construction of genius in Lind as, in a sense, routinizing the sublimity of such phenomena—making them a self-transformative event that middle-class Americans might realistically expect in their everyday lives as the result of an ordinary commercial transaction (the purchase of a ticket, in this case a color-coded one). In his essay on Lind, Henry T. Tuckerman elaborates on the temporal structure of these events, and integrates them more fully into the course of the quotidian. He describes the experience of Lind's presence in terms similar to Dwight's, but gives it a still more practical bent by depicting it as a two-step process:

> The peculiar charm of Jenny Lind, as an artist, is her unconsciousness. We are disposed to regard this as one of the most reliable

> tests of superior gifts. It at least proves the absorption of self in what is dearer—a condition essential to all true greatness. The most acute observers of this beautiful vocalist fail to detect the slightest reference either to her audience or herself while engaged in a part. For the time being her very existence seems identified with the character she represents. It is the afterthought, not the impression of the moment, that brings us to the artist. Infected by the complete realization of the scene, we think of it alone; and only when it has passed away do we become aware that the genius of another has, as it were, incarnated a story or a sentiment before us, through will, sympathy, and talent. The process is quite as unthought of as that by which a masterpiece of painting or sculpture has been executed, when we stand before it rapt in that harmonious spell that permits no analysis and suggests no task-work, any more than the landscape of the summer, or the effulgence of a star. We feel only the presence of the beautiful, the advent of a new creation, the irresistable appeal to the highest instincts of the soul.
>
> Carlyle says "the unconscious is the alone complete"—an aphorism which Jenny Lind robs of all mystery; for her superiority consists in the wholeness and unity of her effects, and this is produced by a kind of self-surrender, such as we rarely see except in two of the most genuine phases of humanity—genius and childhood.[51]

We encounter many familiar terms and tropes from Dwight in these lines, from the portrayal of Lind as a performer who dissolves her self and audience into unity through the art of her physical presence, to the specific emphasis on her capacity to suspend even critics' ability to think rationally during a performance. Tuckerman also emphasizes this form of genius as *genuineness,* a particularly urgent point to note when his emphasis on "the character she represents" might quite conceivably be understood as a celebration of her skills in *artifice.* More specifically, Tuckerman gives Lind's genius a structure that closely approximates the sublime of the Longinian tradition, in which an experience of subjective breakdown or "blockage" (as Neil Hertz has called it) is followed by a process of self-recollection.[52] The explosive affective experience of the performance is the kernel of a contemplative exploration of the self, which the individual audience member performs later. Thus, Lind's "unconsciousness" easily becomes the enactment of an individual audience member's realization of his or her *unconscious*. She or he realizes, in the second step of the encounter with genius, the "afterthought" that the mind is not always present to itself, and that affects register with it in ways varied, complex, and comprehensible only with time and reflection. Genius thus becomes a projective figure through which the participant in the realm of "Art" experiences a form of ecstatic self-loss that ultimately cultivates psychological depth and accommodates itself to the rhythms and spaces of bourgeois leisure. Genius sends the audience members home to reflect on their rich, unprocessed affective experience in private space, where they transform such experience into an interiorized, discursive appreciation of its value.

Genius's overwhelming effect, in this model, is to render the presence of individual interiority out of an experience in a mass public setting. One experiences genius in its pure, sublime state in public, then takes it home, where it can be fully and individually realized in all its depth. This extended temporal structure of genius-reception makes this process a portable part of a new middle-class urban life of cultural consumption. The portable efficacy of presence was perhaps intensified in the case of female performers, as a way of both enabling and containing the erotic charge of the audience members' experience of the presence of performance.

The possibility of encounters with the presence of female genius figures—highly mediated by the factors we have been discussing—opens up space for diversifying our understanding of gender and sexuality as lived in the antebellum United States. In particular, the celebrity of figures like Lind, Madame Alboni, or Fanny Ellsler, and the premium that the notion of genius put on a self-transformative experience of their presence, demands a reconsideration of the monolithic tendency to understand antebellum cultural producers through the "cult of domesticity" and to understand antebellum middle-class erotic intimacy as domestic through and through.[53] Dwight's, Godwin's, and Willis's writings on Lind as a genius complicate the definitiveness of this domestic frame on a number of levels. First, they portray authoritative advocacy for viewing the performing arts as opening space for cross-gender relations—between audience members as well as between audience and performer—taking place within the framework not of marriage and parenthood, but of culture. The cultural politics of this view suggested that men and women strengthened the nation not (solely) by conceiving and raising children together, but by attending cultural events together, experiencing the effects simultaneously, and through individual reflection transforming this common experience into the cultivation of good taste.

Lind certainly does fit any number of the ideals most commonly associated with the antebellum "cult of True Womanhood," as scholars like Bluford Adams have emphasized; she is repeatedly portrayed as pure, sincere, charitable (she was continually praised for her philanthropic efforts in every city she visited on the tour, and the many contemporary biographies of her emphasized her work with the poor and orphans), benevolent, and, in *Vala*'s climax, directly associated with angels and heaven. But the criticism we have been looking at does not envision her primary benefit for middle-class U.S. audiences to be service as a moral exemplar. She is positioned rather as offering possibilities for self-cultivation of a kind that, like her genius, resists referentiality and representativeness. Moreover, her ability to achieve this effect depends on her violation of certain precepts we have come to understand as considered natural for the Northern, white middle-class of the antebellum period.

I want here briefly to discuss the role of sexuality in the critical acclaim for Lind—in part to suggest the importance of what we have been seeing for a broad history of rhetorics of "cultural value" in the nineteenth-century United States, and hence this chapter's importance for those that follow. In some sense, the criticism we have been looking at raises expectations for *genius* along lines that anticipate the full-blown emergence later in the century of the self-defining discourses of psychology and sexuality. Moreover, it positions cultural production, or art, as a mode of self-expression, and emphasizes the importance of not fully knowable aspects of the self in producing self-expression. This may seem no different from, say, the model of the Romantic poet put forth by Coleridge and Wordsworth: the basis of "true" poetry in the "spontaneous overflow of powerful feelings."[54] But what we are seeing is an ongoing process of imagining such ideals through particular historical conditions of mediation, conditions shaped by political circumstances such as slavery and sectionalism, and producing different, shifting ways of thinking about literature, music, and the other arts considered constituents of the domain of aesthetics. What the Lind model of genius seems to have in common with the later emergence of psychology and sexology is a secularized, professionalized emphasis on the viability—indeed, the practicality—of self-transformation during the course of everyday life. In other words, the criticism we have been looking at seems marked by traces of a *therapeutic* way of thinking about life, and about (among other things) the role individuality and collectivity play in it.

In preparing to examine the role sexuality plays in this rhetoric, we need to look more closely at the way Dwight and other cultural critics bolster the substitution of white racial genuineness for national genuineness with a rhetoric describing cultural consumption as a *psychological event* experienced by individuals in their everyday lives. We have already seen evidence of this; in one representative depiction of the dynamic between audience and performer taking place at a Lind concert, Dwight noted that "JENNY LIND *was* the very music for the time being" and described the incapacitation of his own critical facility by her presence. Dwight thus modeled an encounter with genius as an event that ruptures self-awareness and self-possession, a rupture reconstructed into communicable meaning, along with the self, later—in his case, in the act of writing criticism. But he was careful to identify his own experience of the concert with that of other concert-goers rather than, say, to insist on his absolute difference from them as an *expert.*

Genius in this model is not only an "integral and whole" figure; it becomes a site of projection that integrates psychological self-affirmation into the course of everyday life. Genius achieves that integration specifically by allowing the individual cultural consumer to depart from the collective aspect of that life and then return to it directly. As a genius figure, in Dwight's portrayal, Lind enacts the dissolution of all surroundings and mediation, ultimately making her performance representative of nothing beyond her self. However, the criticism portrays this as a process that opens Lind's efficacy to her audiences. In the following passage from Willis's *Memoranda,* the attention audience members pay her is described as longing, which in turn is portrayed not as lack but as a realization of individuating desire:

> There was attention of a peculiar kind—the ladies all studying her intensely, like a puzzle they could not make out, but of which they were dying to absorb the secret for their own use, and the gentlemen leaning toward her with troubled and thoughtful absorption,

> lips open, and heart and eyes bent on her with abandoned entireness. . . . Her eyes, if we remember rightly, have dark lashes, but of that we are not sure, nor of what it is, in them, that calls up, in the heart of the beholder, a far-down and hitherto scarce suspected want, the voice of which speaks from his better nature.[55]

This description fleshes out Dwight's picture of Lind in performance as "deep call[ing] unto deep." Indeed, the detailed descriptions of the audience members' bodies, particularly those of the males, matches the attention accorded to Lind's "dark lashes." The specificity with which the passage describes bodily postures, however, is a frame for portraying the psychological drama that Lind's singing draws audience members to participate in. Across gender, they are imbued with the expectation that their mental engagement will lead to the realization of some "secret" or generally unknown part of the self. This recalls Dwight's discussion of Lind's "intellect," which distinguished her from Italian divas and ultimately supplied the racially cast narrative of triumph that made it possible to imagine Lind's presence in the country as "an era in our History of art."[56] Lind's singing replaces the sensual intensity ascribed to female Italian singers with a more "integral and whole" presence (in another of Dwight's phrases), in which the corporeal and the intellectual are intertwined. Erotics can't be strictly associated with body; aesthetics can't be strictly associated with intellect. The audience response is so powerful, so *sublime,* because it makes such a distinction unimportant. But the transcendence of the distinction takes place specifically by means of the exclusion of the Southernness from which this Northern whiteness distinguishes itself.

In Lind's case, whiteness moderated, but did not fully elide, the sexuality that critics tended to associate with Italian divas. In a summary essay for the *Tribune* written after Lind's first five concerts, Dwight reiterated the widely iterated difference between Lind and the Italian women. He asserted that "Every Italian Opera is inspired mainly by one passion, that of sexual love, and hence the sweet sadness which it has led many persons to associate with the very thought of music." On the other hand, he writes of Lind, "The passion in her (without which there could be no genius) lies deep. It is not on the surface." Dwight's opposition between Lind and the Italians is not exactly one of virtuous sexual purity versus polluted promiscuity. Genius necessarily implies passion, which necessarily implies erotic energy. (Indeed, it is interesting to note the concerns expressed in many U.S. papers later in the tour when it became known that Lind was planning to marry her accompanist.[57] Although it would be possible to view this reaction as a concern with maintaining the singer's purity, I think such an impulse itself qualifies for consideration as an attempt to regulate and maintain erotic access to the singer's iconicity.) For Dwight, Italian opera isn't immoral because of its sexuality; it simply ends up registering as "sweet sadness," which Dwight suggests is a resonant if ultimately superficial emotion. As a genius, Lind transforms what could be languorous, draining affect into fulfilling, inward, "deep" experience. Indeed, in this essay, Dwight repeats a phrase (already cited in a review we have seen), writing that Lind's voice "seems to come out of the inmost depth of a soul in harmony with nature—'deep calleth unto deep.'"[58]

In *The Anatomy of National Fantasy,* her study of the "national symbolic" in Nathaniel Hawthorne's work, Lauren Berlant writes, "It would not be too strong to say that the political deployment of the feminine icon has a pornographic structure."[59] Berlant's point is not simply to argue that symbolically invested female figures are "objectified" by a patriarchal gaze; rather, she depicts this "pornographic structure" as one form in which erotic feelings are tapped by ideologies like nationalism. The Lind criticism's interest in drawing a clearer distinction between culture and nation sought to tap eroticism as a resource in making itself more popular with more middle-class Americans.

For the most part, we have seen eroticism as one resource among others, such as whiteness, republicanism, and middle-class identity. But because this notion of an analogous relationship between sexuality and cultural participation is vitally important to our discussion of the category genius in subsequent decades, I want to conclude by looking at a text from the initial response to Lind that is more explicitly eroticized.

Publishing in the *United States Democratic Review,* the anonymous poet wrote in "Impromptu on Hearing Jenny Lind":

> Methought some bird had left its native sky,
> To breathe its melody in mortal ear;
> So wildly sweet, those strains now swell, now die—

So exquisitely soft, so bold and clear.
I sit, and drink the pure delicious sound,
Alone—tho' hundreds throng the crowded hall;
With rapturous joy, my throbbing pulses bound—
I dae not break the soul's bewitching thrall.
For, oh! to waken from a dream like this—
To feel the world's debasing touch once more!—
'Tis hushed! that voice that woke my soul to bliss;
Sweet Jenny Lind, my dream of heaven is o'er.[60]

The imagery of sublime transcendence here derives not from mass spectacle but from privatized erotic fantasy. What are the particular dimensions of these erotics? The basic structure, it would seem, is a heterosexual dyad, uninterrupted by the mediation of public space. Yet the context for the heterosexual intimacy described is quite different from the form of marriage and parenting; it takes place in two spaces quite cut off from the family: the downtown public performance space and the man's head. The isolation and the melancholia suggest a shame-suffused autoerotic stimulation and release, a sense bolstered by the poem's ever more private and self-focused telos. Indeed, the process of interiorization we saw in the Lind criticism as a response to her genius occurs here, again, but in a way we may understand as more fully sexualized because more fully privatized. Again, this greater sense of privatization arises from the greater tension of the speaker's relationship to public space. Unlike what we have seen, his portrayal does oppose art and the public: the speaker throbs *despite* the "throng" in the "crowded hall." This opposition makes the concert experience more structurally parallel to a sex act, particularly sex as identified with melancholy and the risk of waste, in lyrics this poem seems to imagine as its forerunners, such as Shakespeare's sonnets and Keats's odes.

The poem seems to anticipate an increasing interiorization of aesthetics, a process that may make us recontextualize what we have been observing as the early stages of the move toward the more fully individualized notions that framed what Levine calls the "sacralization" of culture in the late nineteenth century. This poem also enacts the further mystification of the whiteness of cultural value that characterized the postbellum decades. But the poem's reliance on older antecedents may be a helpful reminder that the eroticism it both displays and enacts are (more than are the works I examine in chapters 4 and 5 of this book) opaque to the discourse of sexuality per se.[61] The poem suggests that the erotic energy it portrays Lind generating in its speaker is more a mode of self-access than predetermined by the sexuality that already forms the core of the participants' selves. The poem begins to map cultural participation as a form of *sublimation.* But in doing so it leaves open the central distinction Freud would make several decades later, between desire and identification. And to this extent the poem suggests that the enthusiasm some male critics felt for Lind had to do not only with heterosexual erotic attraction, but with a form of self-recognition across gender. Here the critical response to Lind resembles a contemporary tradition of writing on female actresses, including Rachel Felix, who would play an important role as an antecedent for Henry James's novel *The Tragic Muse,* which we examine in chapter 5. Yet Lind, too, may have played a role in the construction of female genius in the performing arts as a specifically *queer* figure, one whose vision of collectivity may have also included the creation of real and imagined communities of queer men.

Coda

Making genius the focal point of mass audience reception was one way influential antebellum cultural arbiters sought to harness the "market revolution"—with its newly proliferative, diverse technologies of production and distribution—to the growing investment in the social value of cultural consumption. This impulse shaped one vein of the critical response to Jenny Lind's tour, but this was not the way her warm welcome in the United States looked to everyone at the time; the satirist writing an account of the tour in *Holden's Dollar Magazine* used Lind's tour as an occasion to render a different vision of the American economic infrastructure. The article parodies Lindmania by, among other things, depicting an American selling a slave in order to purchase a ticket to attend the singer's concert.[62] With this conceit, the writer alluded to one of the more legendary public spectacles with which Barnum promoted the diva; several days before her first concert in New York, he held an auction for tickets. Bidding climbed steadily, ending when John Genin, the proprietor of a hat shop and an associate of Barnum's, offered $225—a sum high enough to cause a public sensation but nevertheless not nearly enough money to procure a "prime field hand" in a Southern slave auction.[63]

But the parody is less concerned with accurately portraying exchange values than with the auction itself as a proscenium upon which acts of exchange in the United States take on cultural meanings. The perception that a slave and access to the presence of a genius were of equal exchange value speaks to the multiple cultural variables informing mid-nineteenth-century Anglo-America's view of the issue. Genin's publicity stunt echoed Barnum's well-established acumen at staging capitalist relations, emphasizing the theatrical aspects of market value—its dependence on performance, on promise and credit—and embracing the public's eagerness to see capitalist modes of social relation turned into mass spectacles of fascination.[64] The "Yankee" point of view articulated here was, on one level, the work of an "enterprising fellow" who had studied the "philosophy of advertising." But as with many of Barnum's own schemes, the strength of the sensation drew from the contrasting scale between act and effect, between the negligible labor of raising one's hand at an auction, or wearing a hat, or having a brilliant idea, and becoming a dominant marketer. This fantasy of agency is also decidedly a fantasy of ease, of labor so alienated that it barely feels or looks like labor at all. It mirrors the description of Lind's genius as her ability to "sing herself"; unconventionally, it suggests that value accrues in an inverse relationship to work.

The *Holden's* critique reasserts the presence of the labor underlying these fantasies, the labor of the slave body. Yet, like Genin's ploy, and like Barnum's presentation of Lind, its motive energy arises from the scandalous juxtaposition of commerce and human beings, or of commerce with the pinnacle of human faculties, genius. The critique placed the Swedish Nightingale's aesthetic excellence and feminine beauty beside Barnum's entrepreneurial tactics. It surrounded qualities considered unique and priceless with mass publicity fascinated by sums, prices, and fees.[65] Barnum's gambit was a flagrant challenge to the central opposition between the faculty of genius and economic interestedness in modern aesthetics.

Yet Barnum's insertion of genius into the context of commercial exchange was not a simple assertion of the capitalist cliché that "everything has a price." Like many of his most famous schemes, it had a purpose that exceeded an isolated profit motive, garnering Barnum more symbolic capital for his reputation as an "artist" of modern capitalism. Moreover, his representational strategies had a surprising contemporary analogy in depictions of slave auctions in abolitionist literature and visual culture. The crux of such texts was, again, the shock of incompatible realms brought together in the form of a human commodity. The auction, with its stage-like platform, audience, and ritualized movements, was a particularly direct manifestation of capitalism as theater. But, instead of challenging the boundary between the two, the theatricality of the auction was seen as intensifying the scandalous encounter between money and persons.

In this sense, Barnum and abolitionism made public *scenes,* seeking to rivet large audiences by staging relations it expected them to find *ob*scene. Their potency derived from a willingness to represent capitalism exceeding its proper bounds. They shared the notion that economic exchange has symbolic properties exceeding the fact of exchange. This stance anticipates several later revisions of Marx's theory of value and the commodity form—writings by Walter Benjamin, Pierre Bourdieu, Jean-Christophe Agnew, and Bill Brown, to name a few—that share what Brown has recently called "a concern with returning the question of value to the aesthetics of the everyday."[66] In *Outline of a Theory of Practice,* Bourdieu characterizes modern capitalist discourse as purposefully "misrecogni[zing]" acts of exchange as significant solely as the "objective truth of economic activity." The fact of exchange relegates its context—its setting, the interpersonal relationships, feelings, gestures, and movements involved—to the "irrationality of feeling or passion" (177). Counterintuitively, Bourdieu urges an end to such "economism" by:

> extend[ing] economic calculation to *all* the goods, material and symbolic, without distinction, that present themselves as *rare* and worthy of being sought after in a particular social formation—which may be "fair words" or smiles, handshakes or shrugs, compliments or attention, challenges or insults, honour or honours, powers or pleasures, gossip or scientific information, distinction or distinctions, etc. (178)

Recontextualizing economic relations within the broad field of social practice, Bourdieu fundamentally refuses the opposition between economic and cultural activities that underwrites the sensational representational strategies of Barnum, the *Holden's* satirist, and the abolitionist movement.

By the logic of Bourdieu's critique of "economism," all of these strategies rely on a script portraying black slaves as the drama's objects, subject to the whims of white traders or a white citizenry. The mechanics of the market erase black agency, recontaining slaves by consigning them to the status of passive victims of commerce. Thus this mode of critique does the same thing it condemns capitalism for doing, repeatedly inscribing the readiness with which black minds and bodies collapse on the stage of the market. This is a more specifically economic version of the problem that Frederick Douglass complained of in his second autobiographical book, *My Bondage and My Freedom* (1855): the abolitionist representational strategy that reiteratively cast him, during antislavery rallies, in the role of a "thing."[67]

The next chapter examines the ways that notions of genius shaped a decidedly different response to similar pressures, in the career of one of Douglass's black abolitionist colleagues, William Wells Brown, a writer, activist, and professional "man of culture."

CHAPTER 3

Stages of Genius: The Traveling Productions of William Wells Brown

"The experience of above twenty years' travelling had prepared me to undergo what most persons must, in visiting a strange country."

WILLIAM WELLS BROWN

In *American Civilization,* C. L. R. James employs the useful term "abolitionist intellectual" to describe the men and women active in antebellum antislavery politics who regularly performed labor of cultural, mental, literary, visual, and performative dimensions beyond the boundaries suggested by more traditional classifications accorded them, such as "reformer" or simply "abolitionist." Regrettably, James's unfinished book offers no sustained consideration of the ways racial ideology shaped the experience and performance of this labor differently for black and for white abolitionist intellectuals. However, he draws near this sort of analysis when he describes fugitive slaves' work for the cause as taking the form of "self-expressive presence . . . embodying in their persons the nationally traumatic experience of bondage and freedom [without which] antislavery would have been a sentiment only."[1] For the black abolitionist, this self-expressive presence carried associations, questions, and limitations not in play when antebellum music critics used similar rhetoric to identify Jenny Lind as a genius. Unlike the bottomless depths of internal insight that Lind's cosmopolitan whiteness offered a culturally engaged, WASP-identified middle class, cultural and intellectual labor performed by any figure marked by blackness bore the burden of representing both the antislavery cause and the "race" itself. As Emerson made especially evident in his 1844 journal entry on Frederick Douglass and Toussaint L'Ouverture, the discourses of race and culture in the mid-nineteenth-century United States placed black intellectuals and cultural producers in a paradoxical position: to be celebrated as geniuses, they needed to demonstrate their significance beyond the confines of contemporary racial politics, but to do so was also to represent something essential about the category "black" (see chapter 1). This paradox led to Douglass's break with William Lloyd Garrison and the poignant account of his ongoing experience of racialist constraint as an abolitionist intellectual that appears in his second autobiography, *My Bondage and My Freedom* (1855).

Douglass's writing depicts not only the paradoxes of nineteenth-century racial ideology, but the more specific contradictions that burdened the work of the racialized intellectual according to the fundamental terms and syntax of early- and mid-nineteenth-century notions of culture, within which the transcendent value of genius was considered to depend upon distance from the materiality of commerce and politics. The present chapter examines similar issues in antebellum writing by Douglass's longtime associate William Wells Brown, also a fugitive slave who had become an abolitionist and, with the publication of his *Narrative of William W. Brown* in 1847, an intellectual and cultural laborer. Epistemological instability in the conventional oppositions between culture and commerce, and between culture and politics, fuels Brown's great interest in discussing genius and genius figures in his early writings—an interest most apparent in the two books in which he described his sojourn in Britain between 1849 and 1854: *Three Years in Europe; or, Places I Have Seen and People I Have Met* (1852) and its expanded version, *The American Fugitive: Sketches of People and Places Abroad* (1854). Although Brown modeled these texts on the conventions of travel writing established by white authors, most notably Nathaniel Parker Willis, he resisted the tendency of his contemporaries to employ the category of genius as a signpost drawing attention away from the workings of economic systems of value. Indeed, as Brown built upon the reputation he had established in abolitionism and produced himself as a man of culture trafficking ideas among the great minds of Britain, he produced a distinct view of genius. This view depicted genius as significant insofar as its appearance demonstrates, in readily visible tableaux, the paradoxes and contradictions that haunt the conventional presumption that artistic and intellectual practices serve as a *preserve* from materiality. As a black abolitionist intellectual, Brown is of course well attuned to the role racial ideology and slavery play in making this supposedly universal preserve a domain of whiteness. But he produces a particularly interesting critique of the paradoxes that economic logics bring to the situation of black men and women doing intellectual and cultural work.

The racial cast of one of these paradoxes is evident in a letter from one white abolitionist leader, Edmund Quincy, to another, Caroline Weston, contrasting the ways that the intellects of Brown and Douglass made them "valuable" for the antislavery movement:

> He [Brown] is an extraordinary fellow. I do not know that his intellectual power is equal to that of Douglass, but he is of a much higher cast of character. There seems to be no meanness, no littleness, no envy or suspiciousness about him. His mind seems to be singularly healthy & he never seems [to] (& he says he never does) think uncomfortably about his being a black man. He understands everything about the Cause . . . & has no twaddle about him. He is the most valuable man we have got since Douglass—& in many respects he is more valuable than he.[2]

Although it is highly unlikely that Brown ever saw this letter, his intimacy with Quincy must have made this attitude perceptible. Quincy does not simply compare the effectiveness of the two men; he fantasizes about exchanging Douglass for Brown. Quincy's use of evaluatory rhetoric places the two fugitive slave intellectuals within the relations of exchange that, for Marx, were the basis of the commodity form and the abstraction of human labor.[3]

My point is not that the leaders of the Massachussetts Anti-Slavery Society treated their black colleagues in what amounts to the way slaveholders had treated them. It is rather to illustrate a concern I believe to be one of the most powerful and unique undercurrents of Brown's work—the pervasive use of economic language and metaphors in social realms ordinarily conceived as refuges from commerce. It is noteworthy that Quincy's negative assessment of Douglass is essentially a pathological interpretation of his "intellectual power," i.e., of the *genius* that Margaret Fuller discussed in her review of the 1845 *Narrative* in the *New York Tribune*. Notions of genius as a mental disease or as a sign of dissipation were not yet as common as they would become later in the century, but they were in wide circulation. Quincy seems to be playing off of this association, which allows him to laud Brown's "singularly healthy" mind as a way of expressing discomfort with Douglass's inhabitation of blackness.

Quincy's attempt to differentiate Brown from Douglass assumes but does not address the fact that each man made his livelihood working as what historian Larry Gara has called the "professional fugitive slave."[4] The mild insouciance of the phrase reflects the difficulties that lives of ex-slave intellectuals like Brown pose for isolating the relationship between labor and remuneration, which could range from royalties from book sales to the symbolic capital Frederick Douglass was referring to when he joked to a correspondent that "It is an advantage to be a nigger" in Britain.[5] Douglass's remark both acknowledged and critiqued what to many may have come to seem the essence of the professional fugitive slave's profession: performing oneself. Like that of Douglass and other ex-slave activists, a considerable amount of Brown's work was in some sense to *be* what he *was,* to act as an exhibit who brought audiences into the most immediate presence of slavery they would ever experience.

Brown's model of genius drew on modes of performance and veneration of personal mobility that defined the market cultures in which he moved, first as a slave and then as a cosmopolitan abolitionist intellectual. Life as a slave and a fugitive had taken him to an astounding range of places, in which he had performed numerous types of labor. Born in 1814 on a Kentucky plantation, Brown was taken to the Missouri Territory as a two-year-old, along with his family, by his owner John Young. When Brown was thirteen, Young attempted to stave off financial difficulties by selling Brown's mother, sister, and two brothers, and contracting Brown's labor out to other white men. Over the course of his life as a slave, Brown had three owners, who both worked him themselves and sold his labor to at least seven other men. His light skin (his father was "a white man, a relative of my master, and connected with some of the first families of Kentucky") seems to have inclined his owners and lessors to use him as a service worker rather than at heavy physical labor.[6] For six months, as a young teenager, he worked as a hand for a tavern keeper. After Brown made an unsuccessful attempt to flee to the North, Young contracted him to work on a pleasure steamboat and in a St. Louis hotel. His owner's next contract took him to the printing office of the *St. Louis Times*. Subsequently, he was hired by a slave dealer, James Walker, who plied his trade on passenger steamboats sailing between St. Louis and the massive slave markets of New Orleans.

In 1833, Brown's sister and mother were again sold and taken to Natchez and New Orleans, respectively. Brown wrote in his *Narrative of William W. Brown* that their formerly nearby presence had prevented him from persisting in his attempts to flee bondage; in 1834, he did so successfully. His flight from the slave South took him to Ohio, Canada, Michigan, and Buffalo, New York; he also apparently visited Haiti, Cuba, and other nations in the Caribbean. During the early years of his life as a fugitive, he earned money as a steamboat worker, barber, and even proprietor of a "wildcat" bank. This last endeavor seems a particularly ripe illustration of how insight into economic matters informed Brown's work.

Throughout this time, he also contributed his knowledge of navigation to groups assisting runaway slaves. In 1843, Brown began his long labor of public speaking and writing against slavery. He eventually moved to Boston, where he quickly gained favor with William Lloyd Garrison and his associates. In 1847, with the financial support of the Massachussetts Anti-Slavery Society, Brown published the *Narrative of William W. Brown, a Fugitive Slave, Written by Himself.* Two years later, Brown sailed across the Atlantic to attend the World Peace Convention in Paris, then settled in Britain, the location that served as a base for his writing and activism for the next five years. He lectured, constructed a panorama exhibit about slavery, toured with it, and published *A Description of William Wells Brown's Original Panoramic Views* in 1850. He published the two volumes of his travel memoirs. In 1853 he wrote and published *Clotel; or, The President's Daughter,* now widely considered the first published novel by an African-American author. In 1854, he published a history tract, *St. Domingo: Its Revolution and Its Patriots.*[7] During that year, the same British abolitionist who had purchased Frederick Douglass's manumission papers secured Brown's for three hundred dollars. Brown returned to the United States in the fall.

As this thumbnail biographical sketch of his early career demonstrates, Brown's exceptional mobility was matched by an exceptional adaptability to many different modes of work. As a result, Brown has sometimes been portrayed as a genius of the sort most frequently represented by Benjamin Franklin, the figure whose authority and adaptability to circumstance stems from his or her inventiveness in manipulating social relations as they are structured by market capitalism. In Brown's case, this quality can lead critics to circumscribe the significance of his writing; for instance, Benjamin Brawley opens his sketch of Brown, in *Early American Negro Writers* (1935), "In his day William Wells Brown attempted more things than any other writer connected with the Negro race, and he won success; but his importance is now almost wholly historical."[8] Nevertheless, Brown himself advertises his fit with this form of iconicity in these lines from the "Memoir of the Author" that prefaces *Clotel* and seems to have been written (by British abolitionist Edward Farmer) under Brown's close supervision:[9]

> Most of the fugitive slaves, and in fact nearly all of the coloured men who have visited Great Britain from the United States, have come upon begging missions, either for some society or for themselves. Mr. Brown has been almost the only exception. With that independence of feeling, which those who are acquainted with him know to be one of his chief characteristics, he determined to maintain himself and family by his own exertions—by his literary labours, and the honourable profession of public lecturer.[10]

This passage indicates the primary role "literary labours" was playing in both his livelihood and his public self-fashioning. But more crucially, it illustrates Brown's keen awareness of how his relationship to money, despite its supposed irrelevance to literature, deeply affected perceptions of his value as a writer. This awareness was likely fortified by contact with the manner in which William Lloyd Garrison expressed his admiration in a letter from around the time Brown left the United States for Britain, wherein he noted that Brown did not "go out to be a pecuniary burden or to make himself an unwelcome guest to any one; but he hopes that, by the sale of his Narrative, (the stereotype plates of which he takes with him,) he shall be able to meet such expenses as may arise."[11]

The readings that follow trace the ways that Brown's first-person antebellum writing stages the operation of different regimes of value production while narrating the stages of his development as an intellectual. As Brown fashions his life into one identifiable with the category of literary genius, this development depended upon his continuous attention to the relation between culture and commerce, a focus maintained as he went from work in the slave market to idle flaneurie in modern London. Femininity plays an especially important role in the maintenance of this focus, as the refined female slave type called the "fancy girl" serves Brown as an origin figure for the model of refinement and mobility he strove to attain as a cosmopolitan man of genius. Although Brown's most famous book, *Clotel,* shows the importance of the fancy girl to his literary imagination, his autobiographical writing reveals her broader significance to him as a figure of identification. In particular, she is incorporated into his understanding of the continuity in the ways racial ideology frames both his labor as a slave and his labor as a "professional fugitive" and abolitionist intellectual.

Fancy and Fantasy: Brown's Narrative

The fancy girl was a type of slave that Brown was particularly committed to representing in the late 1840s and early 1850s: she surfaces both at a key moment in the *Narrative* and as the eponymous heroine of *Clotel* six years later. Several factors made the fancy girl a particularly useful figure of identification for Brown as a "literary laborer." Her work did not go directly into producing capital; her sexual labor generated pleasure for slaveholders rather than solely the reproduction of the slave system (although the possibility always existed that any offspring a slaveholder produced with such a woman would be sold back into more common forms of slavery). As a number of scholars have made clear, a significant part of a fancy girl's value to a slaveholder stemmed from the cultural capital she provided. Her purchase indicated the degree of the buyer's wealth, but she was also very often prized for a degree of education and cultivation off limits to other slaves.[12] Her association with superstructure over base, with culture, refinement, pleasure, and leisure rather than as alienated labor, puts her in a position homologous with the ideals ascribed to literary genius within market capitalism.[13]

In his recent introduction to the Modern Library edition of *Clotel,* Hilton Als describes this knowledge as identificatory, portraying Brown as "a writer who sees in [Clotel's] nearly white skin and nobility of purpose not only his sister, but himself. *Clotel* is a kind of autoerotic writing."[14] Several factors suggest Brown's self-projection onto the fancy girl more broadly. Her exceptional value resembles, structurally, that of aesthetic objects; the insistence that she/they are outside the economy—*in*valuable—is precisely what makes them so commercially valuable. Anticipating Brown's slightly later period of cosmopolitan exile in Britain, let us look at his *Narrative* as connecting its portrayal of labor, leisure, whiteness, and femininity with a broad sense of the aesthetic meanings of "fancy." This nexus ultimately provides a more focused view of how the notion of genius, as a figure outside the valorization of labor, proved a practical frame in Brown's subsequent writing and authorial self-fashioning. Ultimately Brown employs genius's conceptual alienation from labor as a way of reframing ideas about what labor looks like—and about how race and gender figure in its embodiment.

As the *Narrative* relates, much of Brown's work as a slave took place within the leisure industry, in hotels and onboard passenger ships. His notion of work took shape, that is, in a realm in which no tangible commodity was being produced other than pleasure. To an extent, this influenced Brown's experience of the work: "My employment on board was to wait on gentlemen, and the captain being a good man, the situation was a pleasant one to me" (385). In such a situation, his body's appearance and comportment were fundamental elements of his work; his relative whiteness may well have played a role in his attractiveness to his "employers." Under these conditions, Brown's person—being himself—thus made up a substantial portion of his work even before he became a "professional fugitive."

His work in hotels and ships was also a realm defined by the constant transience of its consumers and, on the ships, its laborers. Thus Brown had access, however mediated, to a far wider world than the typical person held in Southern slavery; he had a richer, more palpable sense than most of the world beyond the local. This may have helped Brown to formulate a critique of slavery addressing its systematicity as part of ordinary life; his account of his work becomes the *Narrative*'s means of demonstrating the inextricability of slavery and the slave trade from other forms of commerce in the South. Several weeks into his work on a ship called the *Enterprise,* Brown writes, "on our downward passage, the boat took on board, at Hannibal, a drove of slaves, bound for the New Orleans market." The "drove" is made up of "fifty or sixty . . . men and women from eighteen to forty years of age." What for Brown is a spectacle of considerable note merely blends in with all things quotidian for both the leisured and laboring people around him: "A drove of slaves on a southern steamboat, bound for the cotton or sugar regions, is an occurrence so common, that no one, not even the passengers, appear to notice it, though they clank their chains at every step" (385).

Brown portrays the chains' silence to the white passengers as an ideological function of both capitalism and racial formation, as the result of the routinized submergence of slavery and certain forms of blackness in the everyday world of commodity consumption. But this submergence is countered by the surplus fascination brought about by a slave whose body is couched as different from the "drove" in terms of race, gender, and class. The fancy girl, a light-skinned, well-coiffed woman, emerges against the mass of slaves as a rare, exceptional human commodity—a fetish in both the economic and the sexual senses.[15]

> There was, however, one in this gang that attracted the attention of the passengers and crew. It was a beautiful girl, apparently about twenty years of age, perfectly white, with straight light hair and blue eyes. But it was not the whiteness of her skin that created such sensation among those who gazed upon her—it was her almost unparalleled beauty. She had been on the boat but a short time, before the attention of all the passengers, including the ladies, had been called to her, and the common topic of conversation was about the beautiful slave-girl. She was not in chains. The man who claimed this article of human merchandize *[sic]* was a Mr. Walker,—a well known slave-trader, residing in St. Louis. There was a general anxiety among the passengers and crew to learn the history of the girl. Her master kept her close by his side, and it would have been considered impudent for any of the passengers to have spoken to her, and the crew were not allowed to have any conversation with them. When we reached St. Louis, the slaves were removed to a boat bound for New Orleans, and the history of the beautiful slave-girl remained a mystery. (*Narrative,* 386–87)

The "beautiful slave-girl" appears here as physically separate from the other slaves, both in the unchained position presenting her as in some measure the trader's companion, and in her physical features: white, near-blonde, blue-eyed. Brown's narration is thus at some level ideologically complicit with both Walker and the white passengers on the boat, setting her apart from the "drove" on the basis of a femininity formed through notions of whiteness and class distinction.[16] But the narration also suggests that the woman's value as a sex worker stems not simply from her whiteness and beauty, but from the knowledge or knowingness—the epistemological dynamic surrounding sexuality and identity that Eve Sedgwick (in another context) labels "We Know What That Means"[17]—that she produces for the people who gaze at her. This passage does everything it can to insist upon the fancy girl's exceptionality, but in such a way as persistently to emphasize the paradox that everyone is *familiar* with her as a type of slave laborer even if not with her particular "mystery." She embodies what Brown would portray with special emphasis in *Clotel,* the open secret of slavery as a market in interracial sex patronized by propertied white men.

In this way, despite what we might be tempted to see as her total bodily "objectification" or "commodification," the fancy girl emerges as a kind of *knowledge* or *cultural* worker. She produces knowledge and fantasy (a word whose etymology is much like that of *fancy*) for audiences. This knowledge is routinely disavowed, so that the institution of slavery survives as an element of the quotidian, and so it can again produce the same sensation of revelation. But at a fundamental level, Brown portrays the fancy girl as occupying a position similar to that of the artist or intellectual. More, she does little visible labor in this role other than to be herself; indeed, her value depends on her maintaining her individuality to the similar extent that the value of the slaves in the "drove" depends on their remaining unindividuated, pure, purchasable labor power.

This scene on the boat is a crucial one, too, because it dramatizes Brown's initiation into market capitalism as a form of theater, his recognition of value as the product of manipulations of the visible.[18] This insight would extend into his career as a "professional fugitive," when he performed the mental and physical labor of re-creating himself as a cosmopolitan intellectual. But here it sets up his description of his year spent in the exceptional position of a slave working *in* the domestic slave trade, as a "hand" or assistant to a slave trader. His labor during this time put him in a liminal social position, partly inside and partly outside slavery, anticipating the role he would occupy as an abolitionist and intellectual. It is also likely that this experience was crucial for the perceptiveness with which both the *Narrative* and *Clotel* portray the symbolic forms of capital that slavery in general and the fancy girl in particular traded in. In the description of the "beautiful slave-girl," for instance, both Walker and the ship's passengers are engaged in a fantasy of power, status, and wealth—an assertion of social authority through conspicuous consumption, through the purchase of luxury commodities. The "beautiful slave-girl" offers a way of coordinating class, gender, sexuality, and race so that they all fortify such an assertion. Indeed, in *Soul by Soul,* his study of the everyday culture of the huge slave market in antebellum New Orleans, historian Walter Johnson has suggested that to purchase a fancy girl was to a large measure a performance staged by white men in a homosocial setting before a group of colleagues they considered an audience.[19]

Thus, even though the scandalousness of the fancy girl was connected to the role of her body in her work, she was also sensational because much of what her labor produced was so *abstract*—or conversely, because she didn't produce any *thing,* any commodity. This aspect of her work allows us to draw a connection between her nomenclature and the category "fancy" in aesthetic theory. If we take Coleridge as an exemplary theorist of central importance to nineteenth-century Anglo-American letters, we find in *Biographia Literaria* that "fancy," as a faculty, names a mental quality that arranges already extant materials yet produces nothing new[20]—much like the fancy girl, both in her production of an open secret as a commodity and in her sexual labor, which is meant to produce ephemeral pleasure more than new labor power for the slave economy.[21]

The "beautiful slave-girl" appears as a kind of wasted whiteness, valued for the sexual titillation provided by its physical beauty, rather than for the moral purity it symbolizes. She violates the customary equation of whiteness and free labor, and her invisible blackness ultimately maintains this equation. Visibly, however, she looks quite a bit like Jenny Lind, her role generated by the same fascination with blonde, blue-eyed femininity that energized the sensational success of the singer's U.S. tour three years after the publication of Brown's *Narrative.* However, her sexual labor identifies her more closely with the Italian opera singers condemned by critics as excessively emotional and embodied. Yet all of these feminine figures are models of embodied whiteness, whiteness that because of some particularity of race or nation can be *named.* This suggests that we may see them on a continuum of salable whiteness, with the beautiful fancy girl or "white slave" from the *Narrative* on one pole and Jenny Lind on the other. As a commodity, this whiteness provides pleasure, aesthetic refinement, and emotional intimacy for white men outside the domestic sphere, where feminine whiteness is supposed to inhere in moral purity rather than in physical characteristics.[22]

The marketability of whiteness in these culturally and (more or less) sexually invested forms of femininity is what Brown goes on to describe, in the *Narrative,* as resulting in his own hiring by James Walker, the slave dealer. Brown's identification with the fancy girl takes place through their parallel feminization; this parallel is bolstered when he reveals, soon after he describes her spectacular appearance on the boat, his own objectification by the slave trader's gaze, and the subsequent purchase of his labor. Just a few pages after the girl disappears into "mystery," we learn that, while virtually everyone on the boat had been admiring her, Walker had been looking admiringly at Brown. Brown describes Walker as assessing him for his refinement and authority: "Seeing me in the capacity of a steward on the boat, and thinking that I would make a good hand to take care of slaves, he determined to have me for that purpose; and finding that my master would not sell me, he hired me for the term of one year" (389). While Brown, the rest of the ship's crew, and the ship's passengers had been transfixed by the beautiful slave woman, Walker had been visually processing the environs as well and evaluating those on board for their suitability as possible laborers. Since Brown, like the woman, is light-skinned and, as a waiter, quite possibly gives off the impression of gentility, he is coming under much the same process of evaluation as the fancy girl. The episode thus implies that Brown's own whiteness and femininity is on display both in his body and in the atypically gendered and raced nature of his labor, which is what makes him particularly visible. The parallel between Brown's selection by Walker and the eventual fate of the woman upon her sale is fortified by the fact that laboring in this position of "hand" will involve an exceptional measure of intimacy between Brown and Walker, including far more access for Brown to Walker's person. It is strongly suggested here that, because of its feminizing effects, whiteness underwrites the value of a slave as an *intimate.*[23]

Thus Brown enters the strange, liminal situation of slave labor producing value in the slave market. To be chosen as a "hand" by

Walker was to be granted the edifying, emotionally challenging privilege of seeing slavery operate as an economic network on both micro and macro scales. William Edward Farrison, Brown's only modern-day biographer, called this year of his enslaved life "an opportunity to do what might have been called advanced field work in the 'peculiar institution.'"[24] Walker carried on his business as a slave trader by moving droves of slaves like the one we have seen Brown describe, taking them on commercial steamboats to stand at auction in cities on the Mississippi between New Orleans and St. Louis. This work exposed Brown to a vastly larger scale of geography than the typical slave would ever see, except perhaps if sold from a border state to the Deep South. It also brought him a behind-the-scenes view of the theater of value that slave capitalism, like capitalism generally, becomes in the market setting.[25] Although used by historians to fill out accounts of the antebellum slave market, Brown's depiction of this work is not highly detailed; indeed, it is marked by silences that (like the unheard noise of the drove's chains) resonate with a sense of traumatization, as when he writes a single-sentence paragraph describing the boats' lower hold where the chained group of slaves was kept at night: "It was impossible to keep this part of the boat clean" (390).

Within these silences, too, likely lies another definitive experience in Brown's intellectual biography, his understanding of the ties between physical and intellectual labor, and his view of the workings of market capitalism as dependent on manipulable symbols and forms of symbolic capital. Walter Johnson argues compellingly that the antebellum slave market was a space relatively rich with situations for slaves to exercise agency. It was a locus of information sharing in which knowledge could be transferred, including tactical intelligence about what behavior would be likely to encourage or discourage certain buyers. As Johnson puts it, "By knowing what slaveholders were looking for, slaves could turn their own commodification against their enslavement."[26] Because New Orleans served as a capital of the domestic slave trade, the market there was also a focal point for the circulation of information about specific individuals, temporarily bridging thousands of miles of distance between relatives and friends. Thus the slave market produced an alternative economy in which slaves acted as agents: an economy of information. The primary movers among these agents were people in positions like Brown's, whose role was in a sense not only to procure but also to capitalize this information by delivering it to the contexts in which it held significance, or by transforming it into new possibilities for action.

But maintaining this economy would have been entirely dependent on carrying out one's labor in the above-ground slave market, on continuing to maintain the market's quotidian routines, and on continuing to contribute to increasing the value of both individual slaves and the slave economy as a whole. Brown describes how this market's dependence on appearance pervades all its levels of commodity production, not solely the sales of fancy girls. The most harrowing task Brown describes performing for Walker is "prepar[ing] the old slaves for market," a process involving plucking the beards and blackening the faces of older male slaves, before the staging of another drama of value:

> Before the slaves were exhibited for sale, they were dressed and driven into the yard. Some were set to dancing, some to jumping, some to singing, and some to playing cards. This was done to make them appear cheerful and happy. My business was to see that they were placed in those situations before the arrival of the purchasers, and I have often set them to dancing when their cheeks were wet with tears. (391–92)

Here again Brown displays himself in the position of producing ephemeral value (the fake skin color attempting to satisfy racial ideology's assumptions about dark-skinned [and younger] male slaves as stronger because of a more "pure" Africanness) and pleasure—or its simulation, again meant to increase the bids that buyers, seeing apparently docile chattel, would be willing to make.[27]

Brown is straightforward in his description of this process and his impression of its brutality. The tableau and face-painting anticipates a central aspect of his future life as an intellectual, as he would portray it in his travel memoirs. Brown's time in the slave market forms the basis for understanding him and perhaps other "professional fugitives" as men and women whose critique of slavery was also a critique of the "knowledge-producing projects" of modernity, with their consignment of varieties of social experience to representation in discrete realms—aesthetics, economics, and so on.[28] For we have been witnessing Brown, in his *Narrative,* constructing a view of how ideologies of race, gender, and class determine the ramifications of such distinctions, ramifications that involve the value ascribed to certain kinds of laboring bodies and minds. Indeed, his concerns and situation suggest that he might usefully be considered a cultural materialist of the sort generally tied to the antebellum United States, if at all, by the genealogical line Benjamin → Baudelaire → Poe. Putting Brown alongside these central figures in the Euro-American history of criticism calls attention to the incompleteness of canonical accounts of modernity: namely, the extent to which they ignore or misconstrue the centrality of slavery and racial ideology in undergirding such key terms as "shock" and in enabling what Meaghan Morris calls the "boudoir talk" of commodities in critics' celebration of nineteenth-century urban figures like the flaneur.

Moreover, the reference point is useful as we witness Brown coming to consider genius, particularly in his rambles around London, as a kind of commodity: available for consumption within the routines of everyday life. For this is the position of the prostitute in Baudelaire's and Benjamin's depictions of modernity and urban space. In *Charles Baudelaire,* Benjamin described the prostitute, like the poet, the flaneur, and the dandy, as one of the "heroes of modern life." Indeed, all three authors hone in on sex workers as embodying a problem they want to generalize: the collapse, in modern capitalism, of distinctions between the agency of labor and the commodity object. Baudelaire, a historical contemporary of Brown's and Willis's, is noted for having written in his journals that "there is, indeed, no exalted pleasure which cannot be related to prostitution."[29] Baudelaire, in other words, views modern capitalism as threatening the survival of the distinction between sex and aesthetics. Indeed, in a much cited essay by Catherine Gallagher, and elsewhere, the prostitute has been described as a figure for understanding the profession of authorship in modern capitalism.[30]

Yet economically cast configurations of femininity inform Brown's self-conception and performance as an intellectual in ways that exceed the metaphorical use to which they are put in Baudelaire, Benjamin, and many recent scholars of their work. Of crucial importance here is the *Narrative*'s portrayal of Brown as the *object* of the assessing white male gaze. Brown's movement into a liminal position in the slave economy is inextricable from the memory of his own bodily commodification. In describing his encounters with figures of both national greatness and cosmopolitan genius, Brown also stages this experience of commodification as a central aspect of what modernity defines as genius. Written in the vein of travel narratives by the dandyish antebellum American literary celebrity Nathaniel Willis, his depiction of his life in London during his years abroad closely associates mobility with modernity, and his view of genius becomes largely based in assessing cultural figures' ability to accommodate the kinds of mobility that modernity makes necessary and available, even within everyday life.

"Free" Markets: Brown's Cosmopolitan Years

Elisa Tamarkin has suggested that genius might be seen as a useful category through which to understand the activities of antebellum black intellectuals from the United States living in Britain, a category that "shapes a style of intellectualism that lets black abolitionists operate on an open terrain of cultural concern, one where investments in British customs do not always circle back to slavery, and where race counts among a variety of interests that are as undiscriminating as the British themselves"; Britishness here stands for a voracious, promiscuous cultural appetite skipping "wantonly" between topics of interest and concern without any concentrated, overriding purpose.[31] Genius, in this sense, is markedly different from the sense of the term propounded in key tracts of Anglo-European Romanticism like Coleridge's *Biographia Literaria,* which opposed "fancy" to the "imagination" required of true genius. In the more fully circum-Atlantic context that frames Tamarkin's analysis, genius values whimsy and consumption; it seems the product of a much wider range of available commodities and experiences than characterized aesthetic theory in the eras of Coleridge or his influential predecessor, Immanuel Kant. Indeed, this later notion of genius overhauls the fundamental distinction in Kant's definition of the category, which Jacques Derrida glosses as the assertion that "free art is more human than remunerated work. . . . The free man, the artist in this sense, is not *homo oeconomicus.*"[32]

An especially important reference point for Brown's revised conception of genius seems to have been Nathaniel Willis, the hugely successful author, editor, and publisher who played a central role in fashioning the ideal of cosmopolitan genius and taste that surrounded Jenny Lind upon her arrival in the United States. Brown alluded to Willis in the titles of his travel memoirs, and Willis was also cited as a reference point in reviews of the books, citations that Brown subsequently recycled into prefatory materials for later books. Brown's tactical use of Willis's symbolic capital is a testament to the latter's centrality as both a writer and an institutional force in antebellum literature, a phenomenon only beginning to be recognized by scholars of American literary and cultural studies.[33] Politically, Willis was an odd figure for Brown to juxtapose with himself—avowedly apolitical, occasionally an apologist for the slave-owning South, literary doyen of what Brown called "the pro-slavery, Negro-hating city of New York."[34] Indeed, many readers know Willis mainly as the man who hired Harriet Jacobs after her escape from slavery and in many respects treated her poorly. Willis periodically expressed his admiration for white Southern gentility, and it seems clear that his treatment of Jacobs played some role in her conclusion that life in the North was essentially a second slavery.[35]

Yet despite the obvious differences between the two men's status vis-à-vis American citizenship—one born in Southern slavery, the other in a New England family whose patriarch published one of the nation's first religious newspapers—Brown found in Willis's work a readymade structure for his own personal narrative of travel in Europe. Both authors devoted a considerable amount of their books to visiting historic sites, attending theater, looking at art, and paying calls on men and women prized by their nations as geniuses. For Willis, this work was instrumental for a broader project of internationalizing the taste of the American middle class; he repeatedly argued that criteria of genius did *not* include specifically nationalist qualities. Willis's writing usually brought forth such notions in a truncated form, the "sketch" or what he sometimes called the "Hurry-graph." Casting himself as a narrator in frenetic motion, he rendered encounters with men and women of genius as an element of the everyday life of modernity. Indeed, genius, for Willis, was a category closely resembling modern celebrity, a form of personhood whose public power grew the more it was mediated by capitalism and its technologies of publicity. As is most clear in his one novel, *Paul Fane* (1857), Willis was also interested in genius imagined, as Kant and Coleridge imagined it, as an interior faculty. But Willis did not oppose this interest to his appreciation of the significance of genius as a public effect, constituted in relation to a mass audience. Like Andy Warhol, over a century later, Willis seems to have been fascinated not just by genius but by the way figures of genius looked to a mass public. His representations of Lind and Emerson, among many others, employ a mass audience as a screen through which the lineaments of genius appear.

It may seem surprising that Willis would have stood out as a point of reference or identification for an antislavery activist. But for someone who had experienced slave labor, particularly of the sort Brown describes in the *Narrative,* the most striking aspect of Willis's career may have been its relentless advertisement of his alienation from the valorization of labor widely current among the northeastern white working class and bourgeoisie.[36] In an excellent essay on Willis's persistent celebration of idleness in his paradoxically voluminous work, Sandra Tomc argues that he both resisted the antebellum ethical premium on productive labor and successfully professionalized his stance, marketing it in his writings and in the journals he edited.[37] Willis was a tremendous commercial success, as author, editor, and publisher. Yet he tried hard to dissociate his achievements from the masculine work ethic associated with capitalist achievement and free labor ideology. In effect, Willis wrote copiously about what little work he did.

Robert Reid-Pharr connects the central role that sex scandal plays in Brown's *Clotel* with a "powerful tradition of female discursive practice," yet we might also connect it to a tradition of writing by men who disidentified from normatively masculine notions of both labor and sexuality, a tradition perhaps most commonly associated with Wilde (and models such as Byron and Baudelaire). To do this would mean bolstering our sense of the diverse genealogies of queer male writing in the United States, supplying models that extend beyond yet further specify the crucial roles played by writers such as Whitman and Melville. But because of the role that iconic female figures play in the connection between Brown and Willis, this pairing also opens up new perspectives on the relationship between embodied and mental labor in modern capitalist economies of pleasure.[38]

A relentless champion of leisure, consumption, and aesthetics who, like Oscar Wilde, did much of his writing for women's magazines, Willis staged his public persona as a queer masculinity, produced in the public glare of admiration, denigration, and self-promotion. He met phobic responses from rival publications, where he was called "Namby-Pamby Willis" and "an impersonal passive verb—a pronoun of the feminine gender."[39] He outraged many British readers by poking fun at members of the aristocracy in some of his earlier travel writings. This flippant attitude pervades the brief articles in which he recounts his encounters with male figures of genius highly invested with nationalist symbolic capital. He brings out details of these encounters that render these men real bodies in real space and that consequently interrupt their symbolic status as representative men. In an essay on Webster, he wrote of the advantage of having seen the national leader when he was *ill,* a condition that allows Willis to envision Webster as a man who would have been a great poet (17). In another piece, Willis complains about Emerson's battle with the material conditions of a lecture hall. At the beginning of the essay, Willis becomes preoccupied with the difficulty of getting a clear look at Emerson, though he is soon struck by the latter's voice, which he describes as "inspired and foreign to his visible and natural body" (171). In making such remarks, Willis insists, he is "gossiping only—not trying to estimate or criticise." This distinction is in essence what differentiates him from Emerson, whom he calls "too great a man to be triflingly or easily appreciated . . . He is a suggestive, direction-giving, soul-fathoming mind, and we are glad there are not more such. A few Emersons would make the every-day work of one's mind intolerable" (173). Willis thus depicts Emerson's body as unfit for the quality of genius that he and other critics found so radiant and transformative of space in Jenny Lind: the immediate availability of self-presence.[40]

Although Willis could in no way be described as sympathetic to antebellum activism for women's rights, his nonnormative masculinity informed his nevertheless somewhat condescending view of women as more highly attuned than men to refined culture. Indeed, Willis regularly derided American men for their apparently inborn desire to keep women confined to domestic duties.[41] The nature of this enthusiasm, I suggest, is similar to Brown's fascination with the "beautiful slave-girl," a fascination centrally attuned to her power to elicit fascination—a focus that recalls the sizable attention that Willis's and other reports of Lind's performances paid to the "rapt" attention the singer garnered in her audiences.[42] That is, both men's writings display a preoccupation with both spectacular femininity and its bodily charged psychic effects on audiences—i.e., its faculty to incite fantasy.

Moreover, Brown, Willis, the "beautiful slave-girl," and Brown's fictional character Clotel, across conventional patterns of gender and racial affiliation, experienced intense public scrutiny of their sexual behavior. Brown, like Frederick Douglass, was the victim of rumors that his trip to Britain was motivated by a desire to have sex with white women there. During his early career, he was largely estranged from his wife (who died while he was in Britain), and was frequently pressed by associates to reconcile with her in order to quiet rumors of miscegenation that some felt would damage the public reputation of the antislavery cause.[43] Although not subject to the specifically racialist cast of the talk surrounding Brown, Willis's sexual behavior was the target of much rumor throughout his life. He was both indicted for his excessive femininity and insinuated to have carried on numerous adulterous affairs with women other than his wife. In the most explosive of these allegations, in the spring of 1850, he was accused by the Shakepearean actor Edwin Forrest (also a key player in the then-recent Astor Place riot) of having "seduced" Forrest's estranged wife, a charge that brought extraordinary levels of attention to the details of Forrest's divorce case as it was playing out. The scandal's proportions grew in June when Forrest assaulted Willis with a whip in Washington Square. But Willis's authorial identity was such that his career largely capitalized on these events, much as it had for years with the rumors concerning his sexuality. Anticipating later nineteenth-century Anglo-American celebrity genius figures such as Wilde and Adah Isaacs Menken, Willis was unwilling to retreat from the spotlight or to attempt to straighten out conflicting knowledges and knowingness about his sexuality. In other words, he employed scandal as a cultural medium through which to produce a commodity of his sexuality's epistemological status, along the lines I portrayed as appropriate for understanding Brown's portrayal of the fancy girl in his *Narrative.*

Recent work by Sandra Tomc and Meredith McGill effectively depicts Willis as an author for whom the antebellum "market revolution," and the attendant expansion of cultural production in the United States, was a generative, performative context rather than a threat to the unalienated labor of writing. That Willis did not romanticize labor, I suggest, may have made him a figure of particular noteworthiness for a professional fugitive slave. Citing Brown and Douglass specifically, David Roediger has delineated efforts by black abolitionists to prevent the extension of the slavery metaphor to wage workers and to "portray southern slavery as *sui generis.*"[44]

Willis's alienation from the principle of "free labor," then, would have made his apparently apolitical stance an appealing, and politically invested, node of affiliation for Brown. Moreover, both writers were deeply fascinated by the cultural capital the antebellum era attached to femininity, a fascination that for both was connected with the association between bourgeois femininity, culture, and *not* working. According to Roediger, fugitive intellectuals had far fewer objections to women's rights' activists' use of the slavery metaphor than they did to the "free labor" appropriation of it: "The inability of white women and of slaves to possess and control their individual labor, wages, property, and bodies" made such a link far more plausible.[45]

The labor of the travel memoir genre, as Brown adapted it from Willis, *is* leisure. At times, Brown insisted that he had spent a significant amount of his time abroad working diligently for the antislavery cause. In the biography of Brown that she published the year after his return to the United States, his daughter Josephine asserted that "few persons could have accomplished more labor than did this fugitive slave during his five years' absence from America" (94–95). However, *Sketches of People and Places Abroad* shows little concern for legitimating the juxtaposition of his specifically abolitionist activities and his observations about British character, everyday life, landscape, cityscape, literature, and art. Indeed, the English antislavery leader George Thompson wrote privately of his regret that Brown's accounts of his travel in Europe discussed so little material directly relevant to the cause.[46] Reviews of *Sketches* that Brown and his daughter chose to excerpt in subsequent publications portray the book as written very independently of abolition while also emphasizing Brown's origins; the *Glasgow Examiner* review quoted in Josephine's biography announced, "This is a thrilling book, independent of adventitious circumstances, which will enhance its popularity."[47] Indeed, the memoirs' publication, especially in two volumes following closely one after the other, attests to work having become, for Brown, a comprehensive category rather than grounded in an opposition to the activities of the "man of culture."

That individual women do not figure prominently among the genius figures that Brown recounts having seen or met is almost certainly the result of diverse anxieties about the white Anglo-American reading public's attitude toward black male sexuality. More than anywhere else in his writing, with the possible exception of the first version of *Clotel,* Brown in these books distances himself from understandings of masculinity that resist positing the male body as a material entity. He not only declares and enacts his appreciation of leisure; he describes his body as subject to the modern technologies of leisure and modernity. Indeed, the "Memoir of the Author" of *Clotel* does this in a manner that attempts to strike a balance between his image as abolitionist and his image as cosmopolitan intellectual. This piece estimates that "since [Brown's] arrival [four years earlier] he has travelled above twenty thousand miles through Great Britain, addressed one hundred and thirty public meetings, lectured in twenty-three mechanics and literary institutions, and given his services to many of the benevolent and religious societies on the occasion of their anniversary meetings" (107–8). The image of motion here is striking, given the small size of Britain; to map Brown's tour would be to end up with a confusing collection of criss-crossing lines, a picture of chaos that belies the supposedly singular nature of his mission—to promote the abolitionist cause in the interest of human progress. Brown represents his travel as a kind of hyperactive mobility in such a way that it cannot shape anything resembling the geographically conceived journeys of selfhood operative at this time, such as "going North," "going West," "going to Canada," or "going to England." Instead he seems, rather like Margaret Fuller walking in downtown Manhattan, to conceive of motion as deeply tied to *work.* At the same time, Brown displays the intensity of his labor by means of what, from a large-scale topographic view, is its directionlessness. Much like Willis and his "Hurry-graphs," the textual impression of Brown's time in Britain, even his work for abolitionism, has the quality of spatial disorientation and "shock" that Baudelaire and Benjamin associated with modern urban space.

In a significant way, though, Brown is more aligned with these European theorists of modernity than is Willis, because racism and its attendant effects on cultural capital leave the fugitive far less personally connected to the people and places he sees, a situation that introduces the alienation effect associated with the protoethnographical mode characterizing Benjamin's *Arcades Project* and aspects of Baudelaire's journals. Like Willis, Brown depicts his encounters with genius as arising arbitrarily within the course of everyday life in urban spaces. (Indeed, Willis claimed that he equated visits to living international geniuses with visits to tourist sites.)[48] Yet, far more than Willis, Brown attains access to genius not through entitlements based on race, class, or cultural capital, but through the technologies of modernity, particularly transportation technologies. In the modernity Brown portrays, modes of travel such as the steamship, the railroad, the omnibus, and the underwater tunnel provide a wide range of people access to mobility, creating a world of dense crowds to which the cultural trope of genius is forced to respond, and that some figures typically identified with the trope are depicted as unlikely to survive.[49] Modern genius walks in the same streets and rides the same buses as a mass public (but also has still largely privileged access to forms of travel such as crossing the Atlantic). Brown uses this notion of a distinctively modern type of genius to mark the United States as abject, as premodern. He repeatedly heaps abuse upon the railroads of the United States. In contrast, he writes of the magnificence of British rail travel, with its speed that reaches "a rate unknown to those accustomed to travel only on American railways," and of British steamers, which he describes in nearly sublime terms:

> The boat appeared to be conscious that we were going on a holy mission, and seemed to be proud of her load. There is nothing in this wide world so like a thing of life as a steamer, from the breathing of her steam and smoke, the energy of her motion, and the beauty of her shape; while the ease with which she is managed by the command of a single voice makes her appear as obedient as the horse is to the rein. (54–55)

British steamships thus reclaim the technology from its degraded use in the degraded culture of Mississippi River slave commerce of which Brown gave a firsthand account in his *Narrative*. Elsewhere, Brown explicitly contrasts the full access he is given to a Scottish train's amenities with the "pro-slavery, negro-hating spirit of America" (265).

These modern global and local forms of mobility provide virtually anyone access to figures invested with cultural and political stature; these forms do not discriminate, at least outside the United States, on the basis of bodily particularities.[50] For instance, one of the first sketches appearing in Brown's travel writings narrates the apparently random coincidence of his arrival in Dublin with a visit by the British Royal Family. Brown stands along the piers amid crowds of people watching as a fleet of steamships enters the harbor; the crowd goes through a chain of moments of recognition and misrecognition of various princes, until "as if by some magic power, we beheld a lady, rather small in stature, with auburn hair, attired in a plain dress, wearing a sky-blue bonnet, standing on the larboard paddle-box, by the side of a tall, good-looking man, with a mustache" (47). The technology of intercontinental travel here provides an opportunity for localized public contact with a figure who embodies national (and in this case colonial) authority. Significantly, the affirmative exclamations of the crowd claiming recognition are what make this a moment of contact rather than any direct interaction. Brown implies that the person may not have been the queen at all, but that this is an issue of negligible importance.

Although he depicts a flaneurial existence in London similar to Baudelaire's in Paris, in representing his experience of this modern, urban quotidian, Brown is careful not to elide the presence of slavery and racism as a palpable part of the international West he is discovering.[51] He notes the apparition of "colored men arm-in-arm with whites" in the streets of Edinburgh, where he also takes note of the integration of civic institutions such as universities and hospitals (265–66). And just as his wanderings bring him close encounters with Carlyle, Horace Greeley, and the Queen, so he describes encountering a down-and-out fugitive slave from the American South on the street; he almost passes the man by, but turns back to speak with him. The fugitive is from Maryland, Brown learns. He originally escaped slavery to New York, "but not feeling himself secure there . . . made his way to Liverpool; and not being able to get employment there, he had come up to London. Here he had met with no better success, and having been employed in the growing of tobacco, and being unaccustomed to any other work, he could not get labor in England. I told him he had better try to get to the West Indies; but he informed me that he had not a single penny, and that he had had nothing to eat that day" (119). This incident takes place as Brown is experiencing his own period of destitution, but he hands over half of his one remaining shilling nevertheless. The episode's inclusion in *Sketches* complicates the more utopian claims other U.S. fugitives, as well as Brown himself, at times made about the life of a black exile in England. It also renders the deeply cosmopolitan framework within which Brown represented and experienced slavery, depicting the Northern and Southern United States, two highly international British cities, and the Caribbean as key positions in a fugitive slave's geographical sense of the world.

The chance encounter with Thomas Carlyle that Brown narrates several chapters later in *Sketches* brings together Brown's interests in genius figures, race, slavery, sexuality, cosmopolitanism, and urban modernity. Given Carlyle's national significance and theoretical interest in genius (his *Heroes and Hero-Worship* was widely read in the United States as well as Britain, and was an ambivalent pre-text for Emerson's work in *Representative Men*), along with Carlyle's vitriolic racism, the episode is, in a sense, hilarious. Rather than breaking out of his flaneurial mode to address these issues, Brown describes Carlyle as a shell of a man, left behind by modern urbanity; he notes of Carlyle's outfit, "his dress did not indicate a man of high rank; and had we been in America I would have taken him for an Ohio farmer." Brown portrays Carlyle's symbolic stature in much the way Willis depicted Emerson: awkwardly confronted with his own embodiment when forced into the presence of a crowd. Brown, on the other hand, found the crowd a generative site from which to describe his glimpse of the royals. Brown encounters Carlyle on an omnibus, while returning home with a white woman friend from a visit to the World Exhibition at the Crystal Palace. The passage subtly and potently subjects the body of the author of "Discourse on the Nigger Question" to the discomfort of a coach made crowded by an event that was, for Walter Benjamin, a manifestation of modernity's displacement of any fixed standard of value: "World exhibitions glorify the exchange value of the commodity. They create a framework in which use value recedes into the background. They open a phantasmagoria which a person enters in order to be distracted."[52]

Brown's narrative of this encounter is nonchalant, an approach that lends a good deal of bite to the fact that, in merely having boarded the bus, he subjects Carlyle to the presence of not only a black man, but a black man enjoying leisure in the company of a white woman. Indeed, this incident is the single moment in *Sketches* in which Brown discusses interacting with white women outside the context of antislavery work. It is Brown's companion who first picks Carlyle out of the faceless crowd on the bus; Brown doesn't notice him until she attempts to signal with gestures that "we were in the presence of some distinguished person." Brown looks around the crowded bus without seeing "any one who by his appearance showed signs of superiority over his fellow-passengers." Directly, he notices the man who resembles an "Ohio farmer" except for a scholarly stoop to the shoulders and a "forbidding and disdainful frown, that seemed to tell one that he thought himself better than those about him" (199–200). Only after a few stops during which several passengers exit does Brown get close enough to his friend for her to whisper "that the gentleman I had been eyeing so closely was no less a person than Thomas Carlyle." In the setting of an urban conveyance, amid a crowd of passengers that includes at least one person of color, Carlyle's body overcomes his symbolic value as a national literary genius. His bad temper and physical dessication come into view.

Ultimately, the encounter with Carlyle dramatizes the challenge everyday modernity presents as the stage upon which modern genius must perform. A routine aspect of that modernity, as Brown portrays it, is inclusion not only in a mass but in a mixed-race mass, a site of spatial and personal intimacies among people of differing racial identities. The incident is a compact drama in which a U.S.-born fugitive slave, returning from probably the most modern form of leisure in the world, views a British man—widely regarded throughout Euro-America as a genius—as abjected by modernity. The sketch becomes a kind of parodic Oedipal drama in which Brown seizes authority from the writer who, on the basis of *Heroes and Hero-Worship,* was considered the leading thinker on the concept of genius in the Anglo-American world. Brown directly states that although he had had a "high opinion of [Carlyle's] literary abilities" from books like *Hero-Worship* and *Past and Present,* his distaste for the man after "his laborious article in favor of the reestablishment of the lash and slavery" (referring to "The Nigger Question," though Brown suppresses the title) made it difficult to stay on the same public conveyance with him. It is as though Carlyle himself is dragging the bus's movement down, the "laborious"-ness of his writing cramping the efficiency of the carriage. Indeed, the sketch plays off the same anxiety about modern mobility that Emerson evidenced in his journal comment that "the great man walks, never runs, to lecture." (Emerson, however, left the question of the genius on mass transit unaddressed.)

The Carlyle encounter also serves as a preface for Brown's depiction of "the greatest genius I met in Europe," a man whose skill navigating space in the modern city is as great as is Carlyle's difficulty. This man is Joseph Jenkins, whom Brown describes as African, directly descended from royalty, and "neither black nor white." Despite the extended attention Brown accords Jenkins in his travel memoirs, I have been able to find no evidence that the man actually existed; instead, he appears to be based in some measure on the African-American Shakespearean actor Ira Aldridge; to some degree on the first president of Liberia, Joseph Jenkins Roberts; and to some degree in Brown's fancy—that is, his fantasy of a genius who integrates experiences of blackness and slavery into modernity. The description of Jenkins as "neither black nor white" is a bit of a cipher, but it groups Jenkins with both Brown himself and the fancy girl of the *Narrative* as figures whose racial liminality marks their exceptional relations to other realms: class, domesticity, nation.

Brown begins the chapter on his "greatest genius" by emphasizing this genius's fit with the everyday texture of life in modern London:

> No one accustomed to pass through Cheapside could fail to have noticed a good-looking man, neither black nor white, engaged in distributing bills to the thousands who throng that part of the city of London. While strolling through Cheapside, one morning, I saw, for the fiftieth time, Joseph Jenkins, the subject of this chapter, handing out his bills to all who would take them as he thrust them into their hands. I confess that I was not a little amused, and stood for some moments watching and admiring his energy in distributing his papers. A few days after, I saw the same individual in Chelsea, sweeping a crossing; here, too, he was equally as energetic as when I met him in the city. Some days later, while going through Kensington, I heard rather a sweet, musical voice singing a familiar psalm, and on looking round was not a little surprised to find that it was the Cheapside bill-distributor and Chelsea crossing-sweeper. He was now singing hymns, and selling religious tracts. I am fond of patronizing genius, and therefore took one of his tracts and paid him for a dozen. (268–69)

Jenkins next appears *literally* on stage, playing the lead in a production of *Othello*: "During the following week, I saw, while going up the city road, that Shakspeare's *[sic]* tragedy of Othello was to be performed at the Eagle Saloon, and that the character of the Moor was to be taken by *'Selim, an African Prince'*" (269; Brown's italics). Brown makes the impulsive decision to attend that night, the sort of excursion he describes as routine practice: "It was the same interest that had induced me to go to the Italian opera to see Madames Sontag and Grisi in Norma, and to visit Drury Lane to see Macready take leave of the stage."

Here Brown emphasizes what Elisa Tamarkin describes as the indiscriminate cultural consumption and exercise of discrimination that a number of American fugitive slaves living in London represented in their writing. But Brown's account of Jenkins's apparition before him as he sits in the audience at the Eagle differentiates the latter from a series of men associated with that very community. If Brown has all along been describing Jenkins as unhindered by the disorienting multiplicities of modernity, in implicit contrast to Carlyle, he here takes his portrayal of genius a step further, contrasting it with certain embodiments of blackness:

> Who could this "prince" be, thought I. He was too black for Douglass, not black enough for Ward, not tall enough for Garnet, too calm for Delany, figure, though fine, not genteel enough for Remond. However, I was soon satisfied as to who the *star* was. Reader, would you think it? It was no less a person than Mr. Jenkins, the bill-distributor from Cheapside, and crossing-sweeper from Chelsea! For my own part, I was overwhelmed with amazement, and it was some time before I could realize the fact. (270)

This account is remarkable for its articulation of a black male form of charismatic greatness, physicalized in an Emersonian manner that stands out starkly against more conventional descriptions of black bodies during this era. But given the context within *Sketches,* so close upon the description of Carlyle, it is a remarkably double-edged passage that also recalls the structure of Quincy's letter comparing Brown and Douglass. On the one hand, it elevates Jenkins into the highest tier of modern black American genius, as represented by some of the most eminent names among its cultural elite: Frederick Douglass, Samuel Ward, Henry Highland Garnet, Martin Delany, and Charles Redmond; in this vein, the passage anticipates the book Brown published in 1863, *The Black Man: His Antecedents, His Genius, and His Achievements.* Yet in another sense these lines work to reduce the stature of these specific, actual men by describing them as defined by their bodies in a way that Jenkins is not. Whereas each of Brown's colleagues bears some remarkable bodily trait, Jenkins is a chameleon figure, able to cross among forms of labor—manual, service, cultural—without any difficulty. Playing Othello (and having been described as the descendant of African royalty) lends Jenkins a (non-American) status that the other men lack.[53] They are not abject in the manner of the book's representation of Carlyle, but they seem static in comparison with Jenkins's less fixable characteristics, which underlie his overall fluidity. Indeed, the stiffness of the group echoes softly but consonantly with the statuesque figures described as embodying genius in Emerson's "Uses of Great Men."[54] In contrast, Jenkins always appears as if emerging from the darkness of backstage—with the sudden, startling appearance of his face or figure in an unfamiliar place. Jenkins is a better genius than Carlyle or Queen Victoria because he is able to maintain his visibility across the fragmentary, ephemeral social relations of modern urban life. He is a better genius than Douglass, Delany, et al. specifically because he can be anywhere.

Ultimately, being "African" and "neither black nor white" means less that Jenkins transcends race than that because he is spared the burden of an outdated form of representative masculinity, his body collapses work and culture into one continuum of value production. In this way more than any other, I think, Jenkins illustrates the manner in which a specific concept of genius shaped Brown's transformative concept of his own career as a fugitive intellectual. Jenkins's appearance marks the transition in the nexus of ideas about the body, spectacle, and labor that has taken place for Brown since he described his encounter with the fancy girl in his *Narrative*. The probably fictional genius figure is not portrayed as subject to sexual commodification in the same manner as that enslaved woman, but the emphasis on his ability to produce value in various contexts, across various "regimes," portrays him as exceptionally acclimated to the various ways that modernity commodifies his labor. Jenkins is always working—labor makes him visible in each particular instance of Brown's depiction—and he is exceptional not because of what he does beyond work, but because his way of embodying work disarticulates the differentiation between subject/producer and object/thing–produced upon which alienation is based.

The fact that Brown makes his "greatest genius" an African deserves further comment. There is, of course, an element of black nationalism at play here. Indeed, ascribing Jenkins African origins and naming him (in part) after the president of Liberia anticipates Brown's later work, *The Black Man,* in which he articulates a more explicitly Afrocentric view of history. But the emphasis on the impossibility of imagining an American fugitive in this role is the most salient aspect of the passage. This current in Brown's model of genius reflects a broader nineteenth-century trend, identifying the value of aesthetic culture as distinct from the framework of nation. Indeed, the ideas in Brown's writings that we have been examining anticipate the destabilization of gendered models of authorship and cultural labor whose queerness becomes increasingly visible late in the century.

CODA: CLOTEL AND JEFFERSON

Throughout the 1990s, Thomas Jefferson's sexual relationship with a slave, Sally Hemmings, continued to be disputed even as DNA evidence established its factuality with an overwhelming statistical probability. Although there is no equivalent lab test of college and university course content, it seems reasonable to assume that public interest in the Jefferson-Hemmings relationship has deeply influenced the way Brown's novel, *Clotel,* has been taught in recent years, notwithstanding Ann Ducille's incisive 2000 essay "Where in the World Is William Wells Brown?" which registers surprise that the novel has not become still more central to English department curricula in the light of late twentieth-century sexual and racial politics.[55] What risks getting lost in such arguments is how *absent* Jefferson is from the novel: mentioned just four times and excised from the two revisions Brown later published (in the United States rather than Britain). Jefferson's absence only affirms the relevance of teaching and discussing Brown's novel in tandem with the facts of the Hemmings-Jefferson relationship. In fact, absence is the most salient aspect of Jefferson's presence in the novel—the founding father's absentee fatherhood. Critics have yet to do justice to the radically experimental form of the first version of *Clotel*; instead, they have largely consigned aspects such as its abrupt shifts in perspective to Brown's inexpertise and implied a kind of primitivism by emphasizing the text's status as the first novel by an African American. But the text's display of dispassion toward Jefferson is brilliant. By not centering the novel in the revelation of Jefferson's intimate relation(s) with black women, Brown implies that this is no news at all—that his nation knows such relationships occur all the time, and that any claim to be scandalized is merely a strategic assertion of an ignorance attributable to white privilege. Indeed, Brown's narration speaks in this double-edged manner regularly, the first paragraph tossing off references made to black-white sexual relationships by, for instance, Henry Clay and John Randolph.

Like other midcentury representations of historical and political greatness, Brown's treatment of Jefferson operates by reembodying what was formerly a far more abstract, generalizable, "representative" figure. Indeed, Brown essentially reminds his readers that Jefferson had not only a symbolic phallus but a material penis. In this way, Brown's Jefferson occupies a crucial position in a historically deep, ongoing genealogy of Jefferson's standing as a national figure, an iconicity in which the constituent elements *are* complication, hesitation, self-contradiction, and other Hamlet-like traits.[56] As Jay Fliegelman has shown, Jefferson's anxieties about public speaking shaped the writing of the Declaration of Independence, and he was later beset with widespread charges that he had plagiarized the document—a claim that has also been made, with varying degrees of condemnation, regarding *Clotel.* To police for plagiarism is to subject a text to notions of authorial originality largely based in Romantic and post-Romantic literary conventions idealizing an organic relationship between a text and its author's mind. But as Paul Giles's recent work on Jefferson has shown, such a model, which also underwrites the "representative man" structure of national-historical genius, hardly fits Jefferson's intellectual or biographical profile. Attempts to clear Jefferson's hypocritical behavior and writing about slavery, among other issues, "seek . . . simply to erase contradictions by [the] assumption that Jefferson should have been operating within the kind of organic logic, the rhetoric of integrity and integral wholeness, that was intellectually much more characteristic of the mid-nineteenth century than the late eighteenth."[57] Without collapsing the vastly more important differences between the contexts in which the two men became intellectuals, it is noteworthy how ripely this resistance to "the rhetoric of integrity and integral wholeness" applies to a text like *Clotel* and to a career like Brown's.

I have been arguing that the fancy girl was a figure of identification for Brown, a projection of his own situation as a literary and intellectual figure in the Anglo-American public sphere. But one can simultaneously argue that Thomas Jefferson himself was a figure of identification in this way, a possibility for which Henry Louis Gates Jr.'s recent essay on Phillis Wheatley provides a potential framework.[58] Jefferson's contradictions, in juxtaposition with his literal and symbolic authorship of American independence, illustrate the bind of representativeness that men like Douglass and Brown found themselves in, and which continues to shape the careers of many writers and intellectuals of color.[59] Moreover, that Jefferson's sexual history should be subject to probing, widespread surveillance brings him closer to the historical experience of many African-American men and women—and, although I am admittedly overgeneralizing, sympathetic discussions of the affair between Monica Lewinsky and President William Jefferson Clinton by commentators from Toni Morrison to Chris Rock may serve as illuminating analogies here. As I have noted, black abolitionists frequently found themselves under scrutiny for their behavior around white women, as well as for their treatment of their wives. I have suggested that this situation may have made Nathaniel Willis a figure of special interest to Brown, and it would seem equally suggestive—though I lack the space to develop the thesis here—to place Jefferson, Willis, and Brown together in a tradition of American figures of cosmopolitanism and vexed, excessively sexual masculinity.

That Brown should be looking to both the mysterious fancy girl and a figure of problematically sexualized national masculinity like Jefferson makes sense within the broad cultural history of genius in the United States as it was changing around midcentury. Such dynamics reflect the centrality of gender and sexuality in the discourse of genius as the century proceeded. This shift is the context of the following two chapters, which examine a world where, for the educated Anglo-American bourgeoisie, *culture* has become coherent as something more deeply formative than a process of self-cultivation. The psychic dramas allegorized in Brown's and Willis's writing about genius become more minutely detailed representations of interiority in the postbellum writings of Louisa May Alcott and Henry James.

CHAPTER 4

Genius Burns: The Queer Performativity of Louisa May Alcott

As Ralph Ellison wrote in 1964 in *Shadow and Act,* the North-South conflagration was "a war which left even the abolitionists weary of those problems associated with the Negro."[1] Consequently, representations of race as an issue of politics, of social relations of power, all but disappeared from writing produced in the most influential institutions of the postbellum literary sphere. For most white Americans, the defining voice of literary blackness became Joel Chandler Harris's Uncle Remus, spinning tales of an antebellum South that bolstered the dominant political ethos of regional reconciliationism. Even the sector of this white audience that had supported abolitionism and, to varying degress, Congressional Reconstruction, looked at recent history with what Saidiya Hartman has called an "amnesiac" view of slavery. By celebrating emancipation, military victory, and reunion as components of a triumphant chapter in the story of American democracy, this Northern reform-oriented demographic, chiefly associated with the Republican party, abandoned African Americans in the context of ongoing political and economic struggles. Thus, according to Hartman, emancipation became to a large extent a nonevent in the history and everyday life of African Americans.[2]

But these developments in the postbellum cultural field ought not to obscure what a genealogy of the notion of genius can extract as a buried counternarrative. Elements of antebellum cultural commentary looked ahead to the more important role that gender and sexuality would play in postbellum concepts of genius. William Wells Brown's antebellum engagement with the category struck an antislavery stance that included a critical perspective on whiteness, femininity, and the construction of regimes of value; in Brown's work, unconventionally gendered bodies and minds increasingly came to serve as the sign and identifying proof of genius. The next two chapters examine writing that manifests these qualities, performatively, as *queer.*[3] The texts in question attempt to contain gendered qualities that would otherwise be seen as highly contradictory, and they eroticize—often without regard to normatively gendered patterns of eroticism—the work of cultural production, literary and otherwise. In the figure of the genius, writers as apparently different as Louisa May Alcott and Henry James construct an iconic subject whose liminality seems to challenge the standards of normativity even as it helps to perpetuate the normative's sense of cultural self-worth.

Although Alcott and James were each born into families at the center of the nineteenth-century New England intelligentsia, their very different professional trajectories reflected the cultural politics and economics of the postbellum period, as Richard Brodhead has emphasized.[4] More important than establishing any direct or indirect relationship between these two people, however, is the possibility of grasping genius as part of a queer "structure of feeling" during this era, in which both modern culture and modern sexual identity were becoming recognizable. Alcott's and James's texts dramatize ways in which the discourses of both genius and sexuality merged from and contributed to the diagnostic, pathological, epistemologically suspicious understandings of selfhood, models of identity that Michel Foucault has associated with this period.

In the years just after the end of the war, Alcott's treatment of genius responds to her consignment to a particular corner of the literary field by the elite circles in which James was beginning to thrive, and which would soon produce conditions permitting him to imagine himself a novelist of masterpieces on a par with the internationally reknowned works of Balzac and Turgenev. For Alcott, genius was a persistent if ungraspable preoccupation; the assurance in *Little Women* that Alcott stand-in Jo March "did not think herself a genius by any means" (265) only sets the stage for later Alcott efforts such as the unfinished novel *Diana and Persis,* a narrative rumination on balancing domestic responsibilities with artistic talent and passions, and perhaps for the apparently never-developed idea for a book titled simply *Genius.*[5] While continually representing genius as a subject position she herself cannot occupy, from which she cannot speak, Alcott repeatedly portrays the figure of genius as oddly productive for those intimate with it but apparently excluded from its mantle.

The queer dimensions of this energy are evident in a spirited exchange between Jo and Laurie in *Little Women.* While Jo is verbally sparring with the lovesick boy in a game loosely resembling "Truth or Dare," she is asked by him what her greatest desire is. Jo replies sassily and sharply, "Genius. Do you think you can give it to me?"[6] Jo is flirting here, but she is also explicitly substituting "genius" for the boy-sister named Laurie, who is as contradictorily gendered as Jo herself, though a more conventional object of desire. The term "genius" performatively defers Laurie's request that she orient her desires through his easily attainable person and perpetuates the erotic energy of their relationship. It both affirms and disorients their intimacy.

Although this is a brief moment, it should be recalled that Jo's brazenness in this exchange, and throughout the novel, emerges from a period during which a small circle of grown men were increasingly assuming control of the process Lawrence Levine has called the "sacralization" of the work produced in certain provinces of culture in late-nineteenth-century America.[7] Over the course of the 1860s, Alcott found herself excised from the list of contributors to publications representing themselves as the nation's venues of aesthetic innovation, such as the *Atlantic Monthly.* Founded by James Russell Lowell and the publishing firm of Ticknor and Fields in 1857, the *Atlantic* published four stories by Alcott between 1859 and 1863, but rejected both "M. L." and "My Contraband" because of their antislavery themes. As Alcott put it in a February 1860 journal entry, "Mr. _____ [presumed by the journals' editors to be Lowell] won't have 'M. L.' because it is antislavery, and the dear South must not be offended."[8] Lowell's decisions reflected a broad trend among editors of the influential journals one critic has usefully dubbed the "*Atlantic* group," as over the course of the 1860s they ceased to solicit work from Alcott and other female authors such as Harriet Stowe, Rebecca Harding Davis, and Gail Hamilton, many of whom had written abolitionist fiction and some of whom, such as Davis, continued to address the politics of labor. After her novel *Moods* failed to capture a significant audience, Alcott turned largely to writing children's fiction and to sensational tales published pseudonymously in venues such as *Frank Leslie's Illustrated*

Newspaper (presumably the model for the *Spread Eagle* of *Little Women*).[9]

This encroaching confinement of Alcott's career must have resonated with a long-standing tendency, evident throughout her journals and letters, to marginalize herself in paroxysms of reverence for "great authors." As a girl, she refers to Emerson as the "god of my idolatry," calling him "Master" after the fashion of Mignon in Goethe's *Wilhelm Meister's Apprenticeship.* After having a story accepted for publication, she writes with reference to Charlotte Brontë, "Wonder if I shall ever be famous enough for people to care to read my story and struggles. I can't be a C. B., but I may do a little something yet."[10] She describes Margaret Fuller, a former intellectual colleague of her father's and frequent visitor at the Alcott family home in Concord, with a similar elocution; indeed, while writing some reminiscences of Emerson upon his death she compares herself unfavorably to two genius figures, with extraordinary rhetorical economy: "They [Alcott's memoirs of Emerson] may be interesting some day, for though I am no M. Fuller I have loved my Master all my life."[11]

Disavowals of this sort exemplify the remarkable degree to which shame structures her representations of both herself and genius.[12] But at the same time as this rhetoric suggests the littleness of the author of *Little Women* next to "gods" such as Emerson and "C. B.," its repeated invocation, and its dissemination into Alcott's fiction, suggests that these acts of self-belittlement were also important acts of self-presentation for Alcott, stagings of her relationship to the institution of literature, literary history, and the act of literary writing.[13] Perhaps the most memorable example of this theater in which Alcott and genius costar occurs in the chapter of *Little Women* titled "Literary Lessons," that portrays Jo's writing process:

> Every few weeks she would shut herself up in her room, put on her scribbling suit, and "fall into a vortex," as she expressed it, writing away at her novel with all her heart and soul, for till that was finished she could find no peace. Her "scribbling suit" consisted of a black pinafore on which she could wipe her pen at will, and a cap of the same material, adorned with a cheerful red bow, into which she bundled her hair when the decks were cleared for action. This cap was a beacon to the inquiring eyes of the family, who, during these periods, kept their distance, merely

> popping in their heads semi-occasionally, to ask, with interest, "Does genius burn, Jo?" (265)

The theatricality of this scene is straightforward, the garret acting as a kind of proscenium, the scribbling suit and pinafore as a costume, and the red bow as a form of stage illumination. But Alcott absolves herself of the charge of excessive self-indulgence, or fascination with her own body, by immediately disavowing any lasting, proprietary relationship with genius; directly after this passage, she writes, "Jo did not think herself a genius by any means." Instead, the scene positions Jo as playing both the role of writer (wearing her author's costume) and, when genius chooses to possess her, the role of victim, object of the "vortex" of genius's power. Indeed, even though the family's question, "Does genius burn?" emphasizes Alcott's association of literary generativity with intimate relations, it also portrays Jo as the object of a scrutinous and even suspicious gaze, the family using the rhetoric of genius not only to encourage but to judge her.[14] These factors contribute to a multifaceted eroticism, as Jo works furiously at opening herself to the vortex, the intensity of her potential objectification paradoxically becoming the agent of the scene's theatricality as metonymically represented by the red bow.

Mentions of genius in Alcott's public and private writing persistently follow this structure, flirting with potential self-negation and converting it into highly theatrical scenes, often scenes illuminated by images of flames, blood, or redness. In this sense, her references to genius, even when self-deprecatory, regularly display the insouciant energy and self-assertion of Jo's riposte to Laurie. Alcott deploys her belittling relationship to genius, then, in much the way Eve Sedgwick uses shame to structure her notion of "queer performativity," which she calls "the name of a strategy for the production of meaning and being, in relation to the affect shame and to the later and related fact of stigma."[15] Shame, Sedgwick writes, is "the affect which mantles the threshold between introversion and extroversion, between absorption and theatricality." It signifies as both public and private, both breaks off and constitutes interpersonal relations: "Shame floods into being as a moment, a disruptive moment, in a circuit of identity-constituting identificatory communication. Blazons of shame, the 'fallen face' with eyes down and head averted—and, to a lesser extent, the blush—are semaphores of trouble and at the same time of a desire to reconstitute the interpersonal bridge" (36).

Begging off any intention of "defin[ing] the relation between queerness and same-sex desire," Sedgwick suggests that "Queer . . . might usefully be thought of as referring in the first place to . . . those whose sense of identity is for some reason tuned most durably to the note of shame" (62, 63). Alcott's writing displays this durability again and again as it takes up and disavows the notion of genius. In this high-stakes flirtation, she recurrently associates authorship with various connotations of burning: destruction, embarrassment, eroticism. Jo's genius can burn, but it can also burn her. Getting burned might hurt, as is suggested in the many scenes of manuscript burning in her writing. Her manuscript is sent up in flames when Amy angrily tosses it in the hearth. Later, Jo herself burns one of her own manuscripts after it is condemned as immoral by Professor Bhaer. The novel *A Modern Mephistopheles* (187) opens with a writer planning to immolate himself with his manuscript in his pockets after it has been subject to vicious criticism. Yet it is a signature characteristic of Alcott's writing that as much as each of these scenes reflects a moment of shame, their recurrence connotes her attraction to the eroticism of the form expressed in the Sapphic fragment "You burn me." And this structure is, indeed, most combustible when tied to forms of intimacy between persons of the same sex.

This approach deploys the mischievous wit most often associated with camp, but it is also deadly serious.[16] For Alcott manifests not only her personal frustration vis-à-vis her literary career, but a broader sense in which the notion of culture has become deeply formative for bourgeois interiority and intimacy, marking the borders of selves, the junctures at which their boundaries dissolve. Her work recognizes that culture has become more than a process of self-cultivation, that it has become a matter of self-constitution. Alcott's writing shares with James's a deeply contemporary sense of the urgent personal stakes of the individual's relationship to culture, a relationship most visible in his or her ability to achieve or recognize genius. In Alcott's fiction in particular, this urgency is represented through queer performativity as the potential for culture and genius to victimize people in a manner alternately pleasurable and shaming, alternately self-affirming and self-negating.[17]

Victimhood is a multidimensional, generative model of literary, erotic, and social relations for Alcott. Its foremost self-shaming, self-denigrating qualities concern Alcott's place within and outside the elite literary world of New England. Her sense of objection comes out strongly in her journals and letters, as when she writes, "I shall always be a wretched victim to the respectable traditions of Concord,"[18] or "To have had Mr. Emerson for an intellectual god all one's life is to be invested with a chain armour of propriety."[19] But the hyperbole of such statements is also directly drawn from a rhetoric of genius and victimhood circulating in work by the writers anointed to maintain these "respectable traditions." To demonstrate that Alcott was of her time even as she was in some senses marginalized, I want to look at a parallel model of victimization by culture, a model present in an essay on genius by Alcott's institutional antagonist James Russell Lowell. Lowell's essay helps show how Alcott's performative erotics of shame were tied to a broader historical pattern linking sexuality and culture as discourses of the individual interior.

"THE VICTIM OF HIS SENSATIONS"

In the United States and Britain, imagining oneself as a self victimized by the inadequacy of culture is one of the great legacies of the late nineteenth century. Nancy Armstrong writes, "Perhaps no debt to our Victorian precursors is more enduring than their ability to represent themselves, the agents of an imperial culture, as culturally sapped of instinct and feeling by cultural productions that catered to those below them in rank and education."[20] With its rhetoric of desensitization, fatigue, and dissipation, Armstrong's formulation nicely articulates the transformation of class difference into individual pathology. Yet it should be remembered that this transformation was a response to the increasing undeniability of the "cultured" subject's submergence in *mass* culture—in its forms of distribution, production, and consumption. Jonathan Freedman calls this process the transfer of the "idiom of [Arnoldian] culture . . . into the life-practices and institutions of the middle classes."[21] In the prime of Alcott's career, such principles had major spokespersons in commentators like Thomas Wentworth Higginson, who in his essay "A Plea for Culture" wrote, "What we need is the opportunity of high culture somewhere—that there should be some place in America where a young man may go and study anything that kindles his enthusiasm, and find there instrumentalities to help the flame."[22] Culture, in this drama, informs and cultivates the individual, but also by definition inscribes in its audience a sense of itself as an unrealizable ideal—and hence of resentment, manifest in narratives that specify the agents responsible for preventing its realization: the laboring classes, the "philistine" bourgeoisie, the Church, Spencerian materialism, and so on.[23]

The northeastern bourgeoisie's increasingly broad sense of culture as both antagonist and pedagogue underlies Lowell's 1865 essay on Jean-Jacques Rousseau's genius, "Rousseau and the Sentimentalists," published in the *North American Review.* In this essay, Lowell, one of the most powerful figures in the mid- to late-nineteenth-century aesthetic culture of the United States, addresses this sense by encouraging his audience to take *risks* in reading and to envision genius as a structure of reader-author relations that sanctions such risk taking. Lowell's article makes Rousseau a refracted representative figure of postbellum national reconciliation by noting his origin in the "southern races" and asking tolerance for his difference.[24] More broadly, the essay insists on Rousseau's liminality in moral, political, gendered, racial, and sexual terms, then identifies a willingness to subject oneself to these qualities with the disposition of the cultured bourgeois citizen. Indeed, Lowell specifically connects Rousseau with both Jefferson and Thomas Paine, using the category of genius to construct a mutually reinforcing relationship between good citizenship and the courage to venture into intellectual regions of questionable moral origins.

Lowell's essay affirms Rousseau's reputation as a genius of literary and political innovation despite the scandalousness of the latter's personal life: "[I]t strikes us as a little singular that one whose life was so full of moral inconsistency, whose character is so contemptible in so many ways, in some we might say almost revolting, should yet have exercised so deep and lasting an influence, and on minds so various, should still be the object of minute and earnest discussion—that he should have had such vigor in his intellectual loins as to have been the father of Chateaubriand, Byron, Lamartine, George Sand, and many more in literature, in politics of Jefferson and Thomas Paine" (353).[25] Rousseau's alibi for his behavior, Lowell suggests, is genius, which renders the person whose body it inhabits helpless: "Talent is that which is in a man's power; genius is that in whose power a man is" (356). The unconventional passivity of this type of "man"-hood results from excessive attunement to the senses, to the point that they overpower the will. This quality is what Lowell is referring to when he refers to Rousseau as a "sentimentalist"—an individual who feels too much, who evades the regulation of "taste" and inevitably slides into decadence and dissipation: "the sentimentalist always insists on taking his emotion neat, and, as his sense gradually deadens to the stimulus, increases his dose till he ends in a kind of *moral deliquium.* At first the debaucher, he becomes at last *the victim of his sensations*" (my italics).[26] The genius as sentimentalist is passive in a manner that exceeds any passivity conventionally considered a trait of good women; Lowell describes Rousseau through the language of addiction. He exculpates the Frenchman by diagnosing him, psychologically and physiologically, as a deviant.

Certainly, Lowell is here connecting Rousseau with the authorial legends of a host of other nineteenth-century male literary figures, many associated with Romantic models of genius, men who have been depicted as cultivating their senses, often through the use of opium, to the direct detriment of their bodies—Coleridge, Poe, and De Quincey, for instance. But the earlier mention of Jefferson and Paine suggests that, along with drawing on the myth of this established figure of scandal, Lowell intends to address the relation of this model of genius to the category that defines his readers collectively and individually: American citizenship. That is, he is instructing his readers in how to manage their response to a figure whom they are likely to see as incompatible with the principles of proper self-governance conventionally imagined as necessary for being American. The inclusion of Jefferson and Paine in a list that also includes Byron and Sand is an implicit request that the *Review*'s readers consider that the sensual attunement represented in this model of genius is a property that may nonetheless contribute to both individual and civic freedom.[27] The essay invites its readers to consider reading morally controversial authors as an exercise of such freedom.

This point depends on Rousseau's negative relationship to that freedom. Addled by his senses, the Rousseau that Lowell has described is very much unfit for American citizenship as Jefferson and other "founding father" figures imagined it; the language of victimhood renders him an insufficiently realized individual for participation in representative democracy. Lowell develops his portrait of

Rousseau as genius by emphasizing this impossibility and by lending it specifically embodied dimensions, implying that Rousseau was neither man enough nor Anglo-Saxon enough to exercise the rights and privileges of citizenship. Although Lowell calls Rousseau a victim rather than a slave per se, he nevertheless has recourse to racial discourse as he continues to construct genius as the Frenchman's alibi. "Sentimentalism," Lowell writes, is a property of the "southern races" (races which include the French, apparently), who live in a more fully embodied manner than Anglo-Saxons: "We men of colder blood, in whom self-consciousness takes the form of pride, and who have defied *mauvaise honte* as if our defect were our virtue, find it especially hard to understand that artistic impulse of more southern races to *pose* themselves properly on every occasion, and not even to die without some tribute of deference to the taste of the world they are leaving" (378). Lowell thus asks his readers to extend to Rousseau a kind of liberal tolerance on the basis of a *racial* difference of which the preeminent bodily sign is not dissipation but the "artistic impulse" to "pose." The mention of Rousseau's "impulse . . . to *pose*" is not only racialized, but calls up the association of genius with the expressive self-presence we have seen associated with female performers like Jenny Lind. However, in writing of Rousseau, Lowell has revalued the "southern" valence of embodied presence that Lind's most vocal supporters among antebellum critics used her to offset. Thus Lowell makes genius into a principle of postwar reconciliation.[28]

Although the reference early in the essay to "the vigor in [Rousseau's] intellectual loins" (245) would seem to claim for the Frenchman a kind of sexual potency responsible for his intellectual paternity of Jefferson, Paine, et al., Rousseau's significance, as Lowell paints it, is defined in the *limits* arising from the particularities of his embodiment. Embodiment is the source of his obeisance to his senses; it puts him into proximity with femininity and blackness. Implicit in this portrait lies the suggestion that Rousseau engages in sexual activity that strays from the patterns of racial and cultural convention, a sense the mention of Jefferson may well have reinforced for nineteenth-century U.S. readers. The notion of Rousseau as George Sand's father, in particular, puts the Frenchman in a position of queer progenitor, a parent unable or unwilling to perform the customarily fundamental duty of the parent to assign his or her child a gender.

Indeed, Sand's famous bisexuality is not so far from the more detailed portrait of Rousseau that Lowell proceeds to construct. In the penultimate sentence of his essay, Lowell maps the subjectivity of genius by impersonating it as a cross-sex romance: "If, as some fanciful physiologists have assumed, there be a masculine and feminine lobe of the brain, it would seem that in men of sentimental turn the masculine half fell in love with and made an idol of the other, obeying and admiring all the pretty whims of this *folle du logis*" (266). He maps genius's interiority by portraying it as a heterosexual courtship, a wooing of the feminine lobe by the masculine. Yet this model again quickly slides from a relation of "half love" into one of obeisance, of servitude—or, in not yet emergent psychoanalytic terms, of simultaneous desire and identification, a relationship half love, half idolatry. The recipient of this affective and erotic investment, within the interior of the genius's brain, is the "folle du logis," none other than the madwoman in the attic. Lowell then closes the essay by noting the possible weakness inherent in the necessary presence of femininity within the genius, a threat that Rousseau has been genius enough either to contain or to let emerge precisely in order to elicit the attribution of genius.

Using Rousseau as a figure of genius, Lowell's essay delineates a culturally affirmative queerness by imbuing it with an unconventional figuration of gender and a liminal racial identity. Indeed, part of what makes the scandalousness of Rousseau's androgyny and sexual deviance figurable, rather than unrepresentable, is its association with a liminal form of whiteness believed to originate in southern Europe. Matthew Frye Jacobson has shown that as the nation drifted toward the end of Reconstruction, a nationalism grounding itself in a "heritage" of Anglo-Saxon whiteness reconsolidated across the formerly rival northern and southern sections of the country. But Jacobson also describes the emergence of a new, limited notion of whiteness defined through "fitness for self-government" that encompassed some of the rapidly increasing population of immigrants from southern Europe.[29] Lowell's essay uses the category genius to legitimate this distinctly liminal position, as a quasi-male, quasi-white quasi-citizen. Lowell is clear to mark the difference between Rousseau's whiteness and that of his *North American Review* audience, but this difference is revalued by its basis in the Frenchman's all-encompassing liminality, particularly its gendered queerness.

Ultimately, Lowell's essay is a good citizen's guide to cultural consumption. In an atmosphere encouraging middle-class Americans to consume cultural production of a particularly high quality, the recognition of genius wards off the risk of infection by the toxins and pathologies that circulated through Rousseau's own body and mind. Lowell urges risk taking by implicitly suggesting that genius acts as a prophylactic. Why suggest this? Part of the reason is the readiness with which Rousseau and his queer progeny (Jefferson, Sand, et al.) allegorize reconciliation with the South, with a region of the United States associated with decadence, lethargy, insufficient respect for the value of labor, and sexual deviance.

Yet Lowell's genius performs prophylaxis in a manner that I want to associate with both queer performativity and a newly demarcated form of cultural *labor.* Despite his moral scandalousness, Rousseau, as Lowell depicts him, is a theatrical figure emblazoned with the markings of shame, in a manner analogous to what we have seen running through Alcott's writing. Moreover, he helps us see how Alcott would have envisioned such performances as productive. A "victim of his sensations," Rousseau compensates for his "moral deliquium" by making his passivity a productive display, a process through which Lowell defines genius. Genius, by this logic, is a figure who shames, denigrates, and burns him- or herself so that others, the good citizens of both the nation and Arnoldian culture, don't have to. The idleness attributed to genuises is a "pose" that performs, even as it masks, a particular kind of work, of value production. Lowell constructs genius in the role of emotional laborer, the surrogate to whom the job of *receiving feelings* is consigned. As we will see, both Alcott and Henry James take up this notion in ways that respond to the contemporary institution and profession of literature.

This model of genius appears in Alcott in a form that looks in certain ways like the antebellum trope of the consumptive sentimental heroine, made famous in characters such as Little Eva in *Uncle Tom's Cabin.* Thus Richard Brodhead associates Alcott with this earlier body of writing, and specifically associates *Little Women*'s Beth March with Stowe's Little Eva. But the persistence with which the rhetoric of genius circulates in *Little Women* and in other work by Alcott of the late 1860s suggests how strongly her writing was tied to the modalities of queerness being worked out in the most entitled literary circles of nearby Boston, the circles from which she had recently been rusticated. Both *Little Women* and the long tale "The Freak of a Genius" thematize authorship, and both pair their authorial figures—the ones who do the "real" work of writing—with intimate same-sex companions whose role is to perform the tasks of authorship most alienated from normative conceptions of labor. These latter characters have to *feel,* and to *be,* in certain ways, to create the conditions in which their companions can produce writing most effectively. They are victims of consumption (in the word's many senses) who burn themselves out, leaving their companions behind in a situation of cultural and (hetero-) sexual happiness founded on the mourning of the lost genius figure. In two of James's 1880s novels, this role becomes more professionalized, shaped by discourses of management and therapy. But in texts by both authors, genius figures allow the working out of a cluster of nonnormative relations, emotions, erotics—much like the Rousseau designed by Lowell to provide valuable exercise in the cultivation of a full individual.

Genius Freak

Constructing a lens through which to again look at the role of genius in *Little Women* requires a study of the dynamics of genius in "The Freak of a Genius," a long magazine story that Alcott published across two numbers of *Frank Leslie's Illustrated Newspaper* in 1866, two years before the appearance of her best-known book. Alcott rewrote the tale of frail, seductive genius twelve years later in *A Modern Mephistopheles,* but the earlier version is more illuminating about Alcott's use of genius to scrutinize polarities of gender during the period when men such as Lowell were beginning to institutionalize highbrow literature. Almost everything about the story belies its similarity to *Little Women* except its relational model of genius, which I will eventually discuss with reference to Jo and Beth.

"Freak" concerns the relationship between two men, Kent and St. George, who have entered into what seems to be a productive partnership. Kent is a poet, and St. George wants to be one. St. George is younger, much better looking, and much more charming in public situations, but he is unable to make himself write again after the failure of his first book of poetry. The two make a "bargain" that is almost immediately an open secret in the narrative, although the actual revelation doesn't come until the middle of the story: Kent will write his brilliant poems and St. George will act as their author in public, enjoying the homage of a largely female public that the older man finds embarrassing and stultifying. At the basic level, Alcott seems to be identifying across gender with the figure of Kent. She was famously reticent about embracing the public aspect of the writing life; she also saw herself as much like Kent physically, frumpy and unattractive.[30] St. George becomes in this reading a fantasized prosthetic body with which to battle the rigors of the public sphere, to endure being read in public. The structure here suggests that Alcott, like Lowell, conceptualizes genius as two halves: a feminine half (St. George), and a masculine half (Kent) that relies on the mimetic capabilities of the feminine half. As we will see, St. George's feminized mimetic faculties are given the edge of madness that Lowell described as a necessary component of genius.

Alcott's apparent identification with Kent suggests that her model of authorship finds a generative eroticism in the hermeneutic practices set in motion by the suspect category of genius. For the female public's romance with St. George is mirrored by Kent's erotic attraction to the younger man, whose theatrical grace contrasts with the older poet's blunt awkwardness. The story suggests that Kent's affection is returned, and the attraction between the men is presented in a coy but perfectly clear manner:

> [Kent:] "There was but one blemish in your first [book], the critics said. The poet wrote of love, yet it was evident he had never felt it."
>
> "I'm not so sure of that," murmured the boy [St. George], with a sidelong glance at his companion.[31]

The book referred to was authored by Kent but publicly claimed by St. George, and the "sidelong glance" can refer to both Kent's presumed desire for the young man and St. George's reciprocal desire for the older one.[32] Part of St. George's appeal is that he simply looks the part of a genius, an appearance described in the text in terms of feminine beauty: "large white lids hid [his] eyes, and long lashes rested on his cheeks as smoothly rounded as a girl's" (431). Constructing the outer appearance of genius as white femininity both incites the sexual attraction between the two men and provides it a heterosexual structure. Yet Kent's assumption of a position parallel to that of the girls who swoon over St. George at parties has an implicitly feminizing effect on the older man. These are the charms the "bargain" brings to Kent, who tells St. George near the beginning, "I do not find that I have paid too high a price for affection" (432).

The same-sex desires flourish here amid and through the phantom presence of the cross-sex erotics represented both by the female readers' attraction to St. George and by the effort Kent makes, toward the story's beginning, to provide St. George with a female partner to "understand the passion of which he writes" (431). To create the appearance that his public self has "felt" love, Kent urges St. George, the latter should wed a woman, and Kent takes the young man to a party filled with female admirers. Kent has preselected his neighbors, the sisters Margaret and May, as the most eligible candidates. Margaret, although more intelligent, is more skeptical of St. George's apparent success; echoing a line of thought in Lowell's essay on Rousseau and emergent in other contemporary areas of Euro-American science and aesthetics, she sees the public signs of genius as potential markers of danger; at the party at which St. George meets the women, she remarks on genius's vulnerability to "indolence" and "neglect."[33] At this point we observe a remarkable transformation in St. George: "St. George's eyes fell like a bashful girl's; he colored, and sat silent for a moment; then as Kent moved away he rose, turned the chair and sat down near Margaret with such an altered air that May shrunk back with sudden timidity, for the boy had vanished, and the man appeared" (436). St. George acts to allay Margaret's doubts by moving rapidly across gender roles, a theatrical deployment of the gender duplicity accorded literary genius. His performance apparently quells temporarily Margaret's doubts—doubts inevitably raised, it would seem, by the mention of "genius."

St. George's theatrics here also recall Sedgwick's model of queer performativity. The flush of blood into his face, as Alcott depicts it, signifies both withdrawal and extroversion, both shame and self-assertion, both masculinity and femininity. This moment reflects a broader level of queer performativity in the text's narrative, which analogously works against any simply oppositional model of repression and release. Alcott does not situate her text in such a model; instead, she *frames* the affective and erotic dimensions of it. "The Freak of a Genius" contains no mystery plot culminating in St. George's exposure to the reader as a fraud; we know from the beginning of the story that the men have struck a deal. Instead, the tale maps the patterns of demand and desire for the information it depicts as involved in attributing genius. In this sense, the story dramatizes an epistemology of genius. And this model of epistemology, constructed as a hermeneutic of suspicion, parallels contemporary discourses of information seeking and confession extraction associated by Michel Foucault with the discursive practices of modern sexuality. As St. George first blushes and then responds to Margaret's suspicious questioning, Kent takes up a position as covert spectator of the scene: "Kent stood a little apart, apparently intent on a portfolio of rare engravings, but May fancied he listened as attentively as herself, for she detected an occasional flash of the eye, curl of the lip, or involuntary gesture of the head, which betrayed him though he uttered not a word" (436). His interest in the tussle over the possible secret mirrors the reader's, and implies that the erotic component of this relationship arises as a *result* of the aura of suspicion, not despite it. It is produced directly by the suspicion that genius is empty, a mere screen that shields amoral behavior and disguises a core of shallowness. What "The Freak of a Genius" does, then, as it makes an open secret of St. George's performatively successful but empty genius, is create a drama *around,* rather than *of,* the search for proof. In depicting Kent watching St. George's shame and subsequent dramatic eruption, Alcott's tale transforms the open secret about authorship into a portrayal of the erotic pleasure of observing the extraction of truth—what Foucault calls "pleasure in the truth of pleasure, the pleasure of knowing that truth, of discovering and exposing it, the fascination of seeing it and telling it, of captivating and capturing others by it, of confiding it in secret, of luring it out in the open—the specific pleasure of the true discourse on pleasure."[34]

Alcott's use of "freak" in the tale's title compounds the text's resonance with Foucault's portrayal of a range of pathologized notions of identity extractable from below the surface by trained experts. In particular, it recalls the perhaps most famous line of *History of Sexuality,* in which Foucault declares that, with late-nineteenth-century medical "discoveries" concerned with sexual behavior, "The homosexual was now a species." Indeed, "freak" implies a wide range of associations with pathological understandings of identity. In particular, it connotes excessive attachments to substances, sex, and knowledge. Robert Chapman's *Dictionary of American Slang* lists a late nineteenth-century meaning as "expert, specialist, very good student" and a 1908 meaning as "devotee or enthusiast." In these earlier usages lie the origins of later slang meanings of the term as "addict," in phrases like "speed freak" and "acid freak."[35] But the former in particular also ties together these bodily practices of sensual stimulation and display with a pathology of knowledge, the desire for knowledge of which the story makes a spectacle. *Freak* implies an epistemophilia exceeding the social functionality of a given body of knowledge, and making the "pursuit" of knowledge a process of repeated erotic stimulation. Hence the resonance of a still earlier historical instance of the term: the *Oxford English Dictionary* lists a definition for "freak out" as female orgasm, quoted from John Cleland's *Memoirs of a Woman of Pleasure*—"she had had her freak out, and had pretty plentifully drowned her curiosity in a glut of pleasure" (2: 198).

The story's trajectory submits St. George to this process of obliterative saturation, destroying him while establishing Kent in a position of social sanctity as heterosexual patriarch. For much of the story, we learn again and again that Margaret's suspicions are correct: St. George is indolent and neglectful, or at least lazy and dissipated. He is also party to an erotic attachment, his continuing relationship with Kent, that undermines his interest in heterosexual marriage. St. George does finally marry May, the demure sister, but the marriage leaves both unhappy. St. George spends the bulk of his time engaging in behaviors that have been historically coded as will-shattering, decadent, "addictive," and "queer": frequenting French bohemia, gambling, drinking.[36] His character traits lend credence to the suspicion that he is the eponymous "Freak" of the story. The power of the story's economy of secrecy is most highly dramatized when Margaret deduces the secret of the bargain between the two men and St. George directly drowns himself.

Kent remains unrecognized as an author until after St. George's death and Margaret's revelation. Yet "The Freak of a Genius" is not a simple morality tale in which St. George's deviance is punished and Kent's good will finally given its due. For the posthumous presence of St. George, of St. George-as-performative-genius, remains peculiarly productive of literary activity. Not only does the young nonpoet's penchant for self-destruction construct the story's narrative, but it has a lasting effect on the older man that the text specifically associates with public authorship and its effects on an audience. When Kent finds St. George's body in the Paris Morgue, the story hyperbolizes the tragedy and emphasizes its legacy for the older man:

> Cold and pale as a beautiful statue he lay under the scanty covering allowed the dead in that sad place. A stream of water flowed continually over the rounded limbs, pale face, and drenched hair, and above him hung the plain suit he had worn. Before the grating stood a curious throng, admiring, criticising, pitying "the young man, so charming, so romantic, so pathetic," and at the door, surrounded by sympathizing men and women, leaned Kent, bowed down with a speechless, tearless sorrow, which left its traces on him all his life. (488)

Even in death, St. George's erotic, public efficacy lives on. He remains a spectacle; he remains a public figure in front of a "curious throng." At the Morgue, he is not a corpse but a statue, a monument. Moreover, his supposed lack of substance is marked here not as absence but as the vital power of nakedness (in the sexy image of water flowing over "rounded limbs, pale face, and drenched hair"), contrasted with the "plain suit" hanging nearby. His spectacular force is not to be repressed by the countering force of the narrative's move toward closure; although he has drowned, he will float.

This irrepressible power—and its impression on an audience—is for Alcott the working model of writing, as the final paragraphs of the story make clear. Among the mass gazing at St. George's corpse stands Kent, for whom the spectacle becomes another kind of monument; through his sorrow, he incorporates St. George's "traces" and soon turns them into traces on paper. He embarks on his own successful, openly public writing career. He marries Margaret, settles into a home with her and May, and writes the story of his life:

> Long after, when the young poet was forgotten by all but the faithful three, when Kent was a happy man with children on his knee and a noble wife beside him, when May had put off her widow's weeds and found comfort in Albany's affections, another and an entirely different book appeared, to take the public by storm, give the author a late-won but enduring fame, and stamp his long silence as "THE FREAK OF A GENIUS." (488)

The tale thus maps writing, the establishment of a writing career, and the formation of domestic heterosexuality as results of the process of mourning and incorporating a lost same-sex erotic bond. The freak here is no longer St. George's identity but Kent's act in concealing his authorship, the "bargain"/bond itself, now formally written (the text's capital letters draw attention to their own printed status)—in fact, the story we hold in our hands and activate into literariness as we read. Over the course of the tale, the significance of the word *freak* has evolved, designating first St. George, then the deal Kent strikes with St. George, and finally the act of composing a piece of public writing and the composition itself. It is a freak of genius that it can perform in this polyvalent way. The story's title encompasses the act of reading and consuming St. George, his own consumption by tragedy, and the writing of that story of consumption.

"Like Keats . . ."

Beth March is *Little Women*'s freak. Like St. George, she serves her text's authorial surrogate as an affective surrogate. Both are vulnerable, receptive to others, and embodied spectacles of sensual inflammation, of the suffusion with blood theatrically presented, in characters implicitly bestowed with white skin, in the burning of the blush. Moreover, both are portrayed as igniting their authorial figure's desire by means of this theatrical display, infusing the text with the erotics of queer performativity. Not only is this connection an important thematic link between the texts, but it undoes the logic of repression underlying the frequent descriptions of Alcott's career as having two "halves," sensational writing and sentimental writing.[37] The analogy between the two characters, each in many ways a convention of their genre, points to genius as an important category underlying Alcott's productive, queer erotics of shame. From early in *Little Women,* the shame of Beth's having done the "real" work becomes a bond of shame attaching Jo to her sister (Beth contracts her fatal illness when, in place of a lazy Jo, she visits a poor German family), an inverted version of St. George's shame for not "really" writing his own work. Moreover, as in "The Freak of a Genius," a same-sex relationship is given ostensibly masculine-feminine dynamics and the act of publication is associated with the masculine figure's (Jo's) melancholic, imitative reaction to the feminine figure's (Beth's) death.

In its model of authorship, *Little Women* constructs an ambiguous relationship between activity and passivity similar to that in the relationship between Kent and St. George. Although Kent is in one sense the passive partner (transfixed by the spectacle of St. George's beauty and theatricality), he is also active in his role as the "real" writer. Similarly, Jo March writes after falling into a state of possession, what she (and Alcott in her journals) calls a vortex: "Every few weeks she would shut herself up in her room, put on her scribbling suit, and 'fall into a vortex,' as she expressed it, writing away at her novel with all her heart and soul, for till that was finished she could find no peace" (265). Alcott used similar language to describe the process she went through eight years earlier while writing her first adult novel, *Moods*: "Genius burned so fiercely that for four weeks I wrote all day and planned nearly all night, being quite possessed by my work."[38] The later parts of *Little Women* feature other scenes in which Jo is subject to vortex-like swoons; in one prominent example she attends a party at which she faints on hearing the "world being picked to pieces" in a discussion of philosophy among intellectual "celebrities" whom she admires, leaving her "with a sense of being turned adrift in time and space, like a young balloon out on a holiday" (352).

Little Women is particularly adept in its play with the ideological content of burning as domestic hearth versus burning as genius authorship, a tension mirrored in the word's grammatical doubleness. Burning is used repeatedly in the novel both intransitively (burning as display) and transitively (burning as it effects a change in something or someone). During the preparations for the society party that Meg and Jo attend toward the beginning of the novel, for example, Jo trumps Meg's complaint about not having a silk dress to wear by lamenting, "Yours is as good as new, but I forgot the burn and the tear in mine; whatever shall I do? The burn shows horridly, and I can't take any out" (23). The burn's potential to embarrass the girls at the party associates burning with blushes and the dangers of display. But the scene also reminds us that fires, such as the one that burned the dress when Jo stood too close to it, also burn transitively. The hearth is an active, potentially dangerous, performative agent; it is not simply a reflection of domestic sanctity. Moreover, in Alcott's literary world, a hairdo, a dress, or a schoolhouse can ignite at the blink of an eye, and manuscripts and printed matter seem doomed to the irresistible attractions of fireplaces. Faces continually burn in shame, in love, in anger. Finally, Jo March, sitting in her garret in her ink-stained pinafore, her cap's "cheerful red bow . . . a beacon to the inquiring eyes of her family" (265), faces a perpetual battle to ignite her writing process, to make genius burn.[39]

But no character is more important to this battle than Jo's sister Beth, whom Alcott portrays as someone whose face flames up at the slightest provocation, at the hint of attention, or a deed performed with her interest or pleasure in mind. One of the most compelling representations of the dynamics of burning in *Little Women* comes in the opening scene, as the novel introduces Beth, the shy, blushing March sister. Amid the talk of Christmas, Beth recalls a scene from Christmas past:

> "I used to be so frightened when it was my turn to sit in the big chair with a crown on, and see you all come marching round to give the presents, with a kiss. I liked the things and the kisses, but it was dreadful to have you sit looking at me while I opened the bundles," said Beth, who was toasting her face and the bread for tea, at the same time. (5)

The passage illustrates the pathetic fallacy, for the interior burning of a childhood memory is mirrored by the external burning both of Beth's face and the toast she is charring. This is a moment of shame inspired by memory's internal force as well as by the exterior force of display ("it was dreadful to have you sit looking at me"), a moment of confrontation with the external world. Indeed, the shame itself is similarly double, for it both reflects and performs the intensifying of sisterly bonds. This intensification also calls into question whether Beth's embarrassment is from within: doesn't it come as much from without, from the circle of sisters mirroring the memory? Meanwhile, as with any blush, Beth's face both burns and is burned: the affect registers on the cusp between transitivity and intransitivity and makes Beth both active and passive.[40] In her essay on queer performativity, Sedgwick, we may recall, describes shame as "the affect which mantles the threshold between introversion and extroversion, between absorption and theatricality." Throughout the novel, Beth's role seems to be to embody this powerful union of the apparently opposed forces of display and reticence, passivity and action.

Burning Beth, beginning a long period of physical decline after the unfortunate charity visit to the consumptive child of a German immigrant family, soon refines her role in Jo's life, increasingly becoming an external source of inspiration—or ignition—for Jo's writing. That is, Beth and Jo become a genius pair resembling Alcott and Emerson, Fuller and Emerson, or Kent and St. George. Here, as in "The Freak of a Genius," a same-sex relationship is given ostensibly masculine-feminine dynamics and the act of publication is associated with the masculine figure's (Jo's) melancholic, imitative reaction to the feminine figure's (Beth's) death. And as in "Freak," Alcott's version of the genius pair involves emotional surrogacy—the production of writing by one member as the other is dramatically, spectacularly consumed by her sensitivity.

Beth's drawn-out death from consumption has been read by several critics as the turning point in the novel, the point at which Jo is domesticated as a bourgeois female by the sacrifice of the novel's perfectly mortal heroine, the book's own version of Stowe's Little Eva or Dickens's Little Nell. Brodhead, for example, has commented on the "deep conservatism" of this aspect of the narrative.[41] Viewing Beth's death through the model of the genius pair, however, generates a quite different reading. Like Kent, the older poet who is so deeply impressed by the crowd watching the naked dead body of his protégé, Jo (like Alcott) finds the power of the publicly celebrated figure both seductive and productive, generative of both writing and the embrace of public authorship. Not only does Beth encourage Jo's efforts throughout the novel, with exhortations like "You're a regular Shakespeare, Jo!" but it is finally the force of Beth's illness that leads Jo to send the manuscript of her novel out to be published. Although she has already begun to publish sensation stories anonymously, Jo obsesses and hesitates over her novel because it will be the first of her works to appear under her own name. As various members of the family debate possible changes in the book's narrative, Beth intervenes: "'I should like to see it printed soon,' was all Beth said, and smiled in saying it; but there was an unconscious emphasis on the last word, and a wistful look in the eyes that never lost their childlike candor, which chilled Jo's heart, for a minute, with a foreboding fear, and decided her to make her little venture soon" (270). In a sense, Beth is the one writing here; her dying is enabling the book to take material shape, to become printed.[42] After this scene, Jo does send the book off. The "foreboding fear," the "chill" in Jo's heart, and most of all the mourning that Beth's consumption already allows produce the first published work in which Jo identifies herself as the author.[43]

Upon publication of Jo's novel, the scale and wild unpredictability of the reviews throw the young novelist into "a state of bewilderment, from which it took some time to recover." One reviewer calls it "one of the best American novels written in years," while another denounces it as "a dangerous book" (271). But Jo deprecates the trauma of the experience, claiming "Not being a genius, like Keats, it won't kill me" (272). Jo is alluding here to the legend, popular on both sides of the Atlantic, that Keats's terminal illness had been brought on by harsh reviews of his poem "Endymion."[44] Yet I think Alcott is writing with some irony here, the most obvious aspect of which is that someone *is* killed very soon—Beth. Both Beth and Keats die of that provocatively named disease, consumption, and both succumb soon after an act of literary publishing; in this hybridization of the tragic sentimental heroine and the tragic Romantic genius, Alcott finds a model of authorship in which "consumption" becomes production, becomes the position of authorship.

Alcott may have learned about Keats in discussions among Brook Farm inhabitants, whose attention to the poet is reflected in several numbers of the community's publication, the *Harbinger.* Moreover, 1848 saw the publication to numerous and largely favorable reviews of R. M. Milnes's *Life, Letters, and Literary Remains of John Keats . . . Complete in One Volume.*[45] Keats's friend Joseph Severn, who attended the poet at his deathbed, wrote in a front-page essay in the April 1863 *Atlantic Monthly,* "It is a singular pleasure to the few personal friends of Keats in England (who may still have to defend him against the old and worn-out slanders) that in America he has always had a solid fame, independent of the old English prejudices."[46] Yet it seems likely that much of Alcott's knowledge of Keats, and perhaps that of many American readers, came through James Russell Lowell's writings. And Lowell, even while writing about Keats's verse, participated in the tendency to read Keats's *person;* in fact, Lowell baldly states in his long essay "Keats," "There are few poets whose works contain slighter hints of their personal history than those of Keats; yet there are, perhaps, even fewer whose real lives, or rather the conditions upon which they lived, are more clearly traceable in what they have written."[47] Writing about Keats's person, though, inevitably meant writing about his illness, which led Lowell and a host of other critics to write about his body. What Lowell called Keats's fine "sensibility," another writer described as his "feminine delicacy"; both reflected the impression that "[h]is spirit seemed too ethereal for earth . . .

his sense of beauty was a disease."[48] In "Keats," Lowell provides an extended discussion of the poet's physicality and its role in his lasting reputation:

> We are not without experience of natures so purely intellectual that their bodies had no more concern in their mental doings and sufferings than a house has with the good or ill fortunes of its occupant. But poets are not built upon this plan, and especially poets like Keats, in whom the moral seems to have so perfectly interfused the physical man, that you might almost say he could feel sorrow with his hands, so truly did his body, like that of Donne's Mistress Boulstred, think and remember and forebode.[49]

Once again, an ostensibly male genius's gift is associated with femininity, represented here by the figure of Mistress Boulstred. Lowell writes that Keats suffered from the disease of feeling too much, and that therefore "his health was injured by the failure of his book" (229). Keats thus resembles Lowell's Rousseau or Alcott's St. George in being a "victim of his own sensations," although the sensations Keats experienced were seen as morally far less unkempt.

Lowell's use here of the house as a metaphor for the bodies of "purely intellectual" natures, impervious (unlike Keats's) to emotion, is surprising given the extent to which figurations of Keats resemble those of the sentimental heroines of domestic fiction in their femininity and in their shuttling between tropes of disembodiment (ethereality) and embodiment (blushing, susceptibility to illness). But Lowell's interest lay in establishing an American tradition of high literary writing, a project that helped make Henry James into a leading novelist; he would hardly be likely to align Keats with phenomenally popular characters such as *Uncle Tom's Cabin*'s Little Eva. Instead, it is Alcott who develops in full the lines of confluence between female and male sentiment, between the sentimentalism of Eva and the sentimentalism of Rousseau. Stories such as "The Freak of a Genius," which involves the highly eroticized relationship of a male writer and his male muse, illustrate the generic and gendered flexibility of genius as a trope for authorship, a flexibility made possible by Alcott's mobilization of the queer formations of gender inherent in nineteenth-century models of genius and by her exploitation of the ease with which the heroic burning of a male poet may remind us of shy Beth's burning face of shame—and eventually of Beth's burning out from consumption and leaving a book behind.

CODA: HENRY AND LOUISA

Despite the many connections linking their families and friends, including a longstanding friendship between their fathers, Alcott and James appear to have had only the most scant personal acquaintance with one another. In the 1860s, James loomed on the side of Alcott's range of vision, his presence at home during the Civil War a contrast to his brother Garth ("Wilkie") Wilkinson's service as a Union soldier in the Fifty-fourth Massachusetts regiment. Wilkie and Louisa became acquainted after the former was sent home from the war with a serious wound. Sometime in 1865, Alcott was invited by Henry Sr. to dinner at the James' home in Cambridge; this was soon after she had published a "serious" novel, *Moods*. This occasion marked the only recorded meeting between Alcott and the younger James, who at twenty-three had just begun to publish fiction and criticism.

Alcott's record of her dinner at the James' residence in her journals shows her initially responding favorably to the young man, then—years later, her fame firmly established—revising this account. The first response to the occasion in her journal reads, "I went & was treated like the Queen of Sheba. Henry [Jr.] wrote a notice of 'Moods' for the North American & was very friendly, being a literary youth." While revisiting the entry at some unknown later date, however, she complained in some added notes, "he gave me advice as if he had been so as a girl. My curly crop made me look young tho 31."[50] The transition suggests that, sometime between the two entries, Alcott actually *read* the younger James's notice, which appeared in James Russell Lowell's *North American Review*.

"The two most striking facts with regard to 'Moods,'" James wrote, "are the author's ignorance of human nature, and her self-confidence in spite of this ignorance."[51] James ends the piece on a rather snotty note of encouragement: "With the exception of two or three celebrated names, we know not, indeed, to whom, in this country, we are to look for a novel above average" (195). But the full review reeks of an arrogance that likely had far less to do with

Alcott's youthful-looking "curly crop" than this characteristic note of self-blame suggests.

We have been discussing genius as a form of relation, and I would like briefly to imagine James and Alcott not as alienated strangers but as engaged in a kind of missed relationship. These public and private performative shamings are, indeed, hostile, but they also reinforce our sense of the deep connection each writer felt to the looming, yet identity-generative, sense of shame in modern cultural production and consumption. James's later review of *Eight Cousins* suggests that he recognized in Alcott some shared interest in theatricalizing sham(ing)—some shared bitchiness, or camp, or queer performativity. Now addressing Alcott as a hugely popular author, and clearly familiar with *Little Women,* he dubs her "the Thackeray, the Trollope of the nursery and the school-room . . . like Thackeray and Trollope, she is a satirist."[52] Although James expresses worry about the lessons children will learn from reading Alcott, nothing in the rest of the review suggests that this worries him significantly; rather, he seems a bit delighted by Alcott's insouciant treatment of so serious a matter as childrearing. To call the world's leading children's author a "satirist" strikes me as remarkably attuned to the ambivalence and humor of her work, and as a fairly extravagant display of that attunement—a red bow of sorts. Some specific items might be taken as evidence of the influence of Alcott's play with genius upon James's thinking (the plot of *Roderick Hudson* resembles "The Freak of a Genius," and "The Lesson of the Master" uses the name "St. George"), but the review suggests a broader possibility, beyond relations of "influence": that she embodied a form of queer performativity that existed alongside the Lowellian world, and that participated in yet mocked the great seriousness with which that world treated matters of aesthetic judgment such as genius. These textual dynamics may have helped fortify the presence of camp and queer humor in James's work, even as he strove to prove that the novel was a serious aesthetic form. In James's writing, however, queerness also becomes a more pointed, specific critique of assumptions concerning authorship, labor, and agency shaped by these categories.

CHAPTER 5

"It's the Treatment!" Queerness, Jewishness, and the Therapeutic Work of Genius in Henry James

The reparative role that genius played in Louisa May Alcott's work was grounded in her view of the term as relational, as a structure that rendered intimate relations between a sensually overburdened character and his or her partner productive of literary writing. Amid the tumult of a flagging career in the late 1880s, Henry James wrote his own version of this model, in which cultural production provides a setting and medium for same-sex interpersonal intimacy. But James's interest in this model of genius is caught up in the professional world of contemporary cultural labor in a broader manner than Alcott's. In *The Bostonians* (1886) and *The Tragic Muse* (1890), in particular, James portrayed genius's integration with the modern cultural marketplace and described that economy's new demands that genius *work* to produce the sort of self-realization that Alcott depicted as its affective value in her 1860s texts.

James's engagement with genius, lodged tightly in the institutions and politics of his contemporary moment, positions him as a critic of certain late nineteenth-century sciences. Cesare Lombroso, Frances Galton, Max Nordau, among others, developed a medicalized concept of the genius "type" as "highly gifted degenerate" (in Nordau's phrase)[1] to reinforce and legitimate racial and class hierarchies, anti-Semitism, and the pathologization of "deviant" behavior, particularly nonheterosexual sexuality.[2] Indeed, *The Bostonians* and *The Tragic Muse* position the literary as a site at which such scientific discourses of race and sexuality demonstrate their inability to account for a more opaque, self-constituting version of otherness. In these novels, genius is associated with forms of "difference" pathologized by Lombroso et al., particularly queer sexuality and Jewishness. But James places the genius characters in a therapeutic role; he or she liberates in others effective powers of self-expression, powers for which sexuality and aesthetics act as mutually constitutive media.[3] Geniuses get other people to acknowledge their own otherness and to progress toward becoming themselves. To perform this role, genius, in these novels, draws from the ethic of "variety" touted by James's brother William, among others, and from a growing tendency to universalize difference.

This view of James, of these novels, and of the relationship between the books emerges through a very particular reading of the texts, grounded in a category that until recently few James critics would go (least of all, ones who have taken genius as a straightforward term of evaluation): labor. These topics point toward a particularly vital and valuable aspect of James's queerness, which made genius a fascination on not only aesthetic but economic grounds. Indeed, James's discomfort with the emotional and financial returns of his own career at this time may well have opened his writing to considering ways that the cultural marketplace was diversifying and obscuring the forms of *agency* involved in the production of culture, especially forms that resisted assimilation to the idealized model of unalienated "free labor" to which James's friend William Dean Howells opposed the "superstition" of genius. *The Tragic Muse,* the novel with which James capped off the 1880s and prepared to devote himself to writing for the stage, suggests that James sees his own queerness and literary work as the basis of an insurmountable difference—difference of a form more structural, more resistant to universalization, and more prone to experiencing universalization as historical hurt.

Along with the Zola-influenced *The Princess Cassamassima* (1886), each of these novels was, for James, a disappointing failure after the success of *The Portrait of a Lady* (1881), his self-consciously constructed "masterpiece." *The Bostonians* and *The Tragic Muse* show James struggling to take up the position not just of great novelist, but of metacommentator on "the production, experience, and social vitality of 'culture' in its myriad and changing forms," as Sara Blair has described the primary focus of *The Bostonians.*[4] Taken together, these novels depict the category genius struggling to adjust to a revised, invigorated sense of what Gabriel Nash in

The Tragic Muse calls "the modernness of the age." The books portray that modernness, in an Anglo-American context, as challenging and reshaping the discernibility of genius by diversifying the forms of individual and institutional agency that make up the cultural field.[5] James portrays a range of agents in this struggle—artists, performers, statesmen, propertied women, professional men, activists, consumers, booking agents—all of whom grapple with integrating the category of genius with new understandings of difference; they depict the "unclassified condition," as Gabriel Nash calls it, confronting a modernity whose notions of difference, though grounded in the contemporary impulse toward classification, seek to defer its truth claims in favor of an overall ethic of diversity itself.[6]

In her book *The Uses of Variety* (2000), Carrie Tirado Brannen places William James at the origin of a modern liberal pluralism that Henry's novels mirror, enact, and scrutinize. Brannen writes of William, "Culture, for James, provides constancy and continuity at a time of flux and uncertainty. It also reinforces, in Arnoldian fashion, the values of liberalism, which Lionel Trilling has described as 'a sense of variousness and possibility,' two elements that are an 'intellectual and political necessity.'"[7] The "myriad and changing forms" of culture to which Blair refers index a cultural field newly representing itself *as* various, as offering the American bourgeoisie a cosmopolitan range of choices (in form and content) in the culture with which they have educated their children and filled their leisure time. Both *The Bostonians* and *The Tragic Muse* examine this metalevel of the category of culture, illuminating changes in the concept, playing themselves out in the contemporary moment. In the course of this process, James figures genius as embodying new concepts of difference and identity. James also fills the novels with an irony of which the politics are volatile and unpredictable, that are ultimately incoherent, and that almost certainly play a role in sparking the long history of critics' complaints that these texts are formally incoherent.[8] This irony is responsible for the "comic sense" of these novels (to borrow Richard Poirier's phrase), but it is also a textual medium in which to write, through genius, a politics of cultural labor that these novels associate with queerness and (in a more allusive way) Jewishness.

In the two novels in question, James examines social alterity through other arts than literature, and, in portraits of female performers, painters, and behind-the-scenes managers, explores cultural labor as an activity of erotically charged relations. He challenges some fundamental premises of William Dean Howells's understanding of artistic and intellectual labor as outlined in the "Editor's Study" columns Howells regularly wrote, during the same years, for *Harper's Monthly*.[9] While editing the magazine from 1886 to 1892, Howells used the column to delineate the principles of realism as an American literary genre.[10] Along the way, he portrayed genius as a misplaced form of value, a preoccupation that impeded the spread of his conviction that literature be considered a form of unalienated labor, on the originally antebellum "free labor" model.[11] Critics and readers who insisted on believing in the "superstition" of genius subscribed to an elitist ideal of "distinction" that went against the grain of the national culture and its contribution to world historical progress. Howells also suggested that critics used the term lazily without actually believing it, and challenged them to "severally lay their hands upon their waistcoats and swear that they think there is any such thing." He doubted that, with rigorous consideration, they would ultimately claim any difference between genius and "the Mastery which comes to any man according to the powers and diligence in any direction, conscious or unconscious, nature has given him." He pleaded, "Why not have an end of the superstition which has caused our race to go on so long writing and reading of the difference between talent and genius?" (649).[12]

Howells's attitude toward genius reflected his views on the cultural and national redemptiveness of work, principles he shared with privileged postbellum liberals who considered themselves the heirs of abolitionism.[13] As Alan Trachtenberg argues, "Realism represented [for Howells] nothing less than the extension of democracy into the precincts of fiction," and "genius" was antidemocratic not only in its Arnoldian conferral of "distinction" on its author, but also because it suggested that writers did not do "real work." In his critical polemics, Howells repeatedly compared the work of literary writing to that of craftspersons, "mechanics, farmers, day-laborers."[14] The author "is merely a working-man, and is under the rule that governs the working-man's life."[15] According to Trachtenberg, in Howells's criticism, authorship "appears as a solidarity of labor, a solidarity, moreover, which figures forth a broad community of producers strikingly like that of the antebellum free-labor doctrine."[16] From one intellectual abolitionist standpoint, of course, "free labor" ideals cast slavery as a denigration of a basic human right of an individual to realize the value of his or her labor, rather than to turn it over to a slave-owner or capitalist. This critique identified blackness with a body burdened by denigrated labor.

As David Roediger, Alexander Saxton, and others have shown, and as I discussed in chapter 3, the "free labor" ideal took shape in opposition not only to slavery but to blackness. It strengthened the tie between American whiteness and the belief that people of African origins, for either cultural or biological reasons, were not fully realized human beings because they lacked self-motivation to work. Henry James's writing, to be sure, did nothing to resist or revise this strain of white American liberalism when the work was published. But from the vantage point of more than a century's historical distance, it is possible to see these novels' portrayal of cultural labor as a counterstrain to the liberal logic that ultimately accounted for racial hierarchy in individualist rather than historical terms. James's key instrument in challenging free-labor liberalism is the notion of genius as marked specifically by his contemporary moment to carry associations of two forms of otherness: sex-gender "deviance" (as it would have been labeled "scientifically") and Jewishness.

The pairing is not simply coincidental. A number of critics have begun to examine seriously the historical congruence of the "invention" of homosexuality with a certain notion of Jewish identity; others have done extensive work on mutualities in the histories of racial and sexual discourses of the late nineteenth century.[17] The two categories became more proximate within an overall epistemology of difference during the 1880s. Both were "classified conditions" that, in certain configurations during this period, lost a significant degree of their corporeal emphasis. In neither case was this loss a complete or coherent transformation. But what Foucault identifies as the *discursive* basis of modern sexuality put a new emphasis on speech acts, psychological interiority, and confession, as the sites of sexual identity.[18] At the same time, racial discourse in the United States was undergoing tremendous shifts, as a result of the post-Reconstruction instantiation of the "color line" and a vast increase in the scale and demographics of immigration from Europe. As Matthew Frye Jacobson's work makes clear, these changes meant that *whiteness* itself became a category inclusive of "variety," in the

United States. As unprecedented numbers of Jewish immigrants, largely impoverished, entered the nation from Eastern Europe, a significant number of Jews (most of German ancestry) who had established secure cultural and economic lives in American cities became *white* in a broadly accepted sense (although the effects of this acceptance on anti-Semitism are highly debatable). Both trends were important influences on an increasing tendency to consign Jewishness and queerness to invisibility, to secrets of the human interior, whether bodily or mental.

In general, James's quirky attempt to write a comedy about the "woman business" makes *The Bostonians* less engaged with postwar cosmopolitan liberalism's universalized notions of difference than is *The Tragic Muse*. But together the novels coordinate an embrace of new notions of tolerance and variety—ones in which slavery and black-white relations in the United States do not figure, as *The Bostonians* makes especially salient.[19] In other words, in the United States this therapeutic ideal is significant not because it allows the reaction of white liberal guilt, but because it does *not* address black-white relations: guilt over slavery or Reconstruction is a red herring. At the same time, however, the novels' irony distances them from the vastly constrained pluralism of postbellum liberalism—and *The Tragic Muse* in particular suggests that James sees his own queerness and literary work as the basis of an insurmountable difference, difference of a form more structural, more resistant to universalization, and more prone to experiencing universalization as historical hurt.

Olive Chancellor's (Talent) Agency: *The Bostonians*

The Bostonians, the novel in which James famously returned his sights to the United States to take on the "Woman Question," nominates a series of characters for consideration as geniuses. The possibilities are myriad: Miss Birdseye, last vestige of "the heroic age of New England life"; Basil Ransom, the Mississippian Carlyle enthusiast whom the narrator calls "our hero";[20] Verena Tarrant, the rising star of the suffragist lecture circuit who has attracted the erotic attentions of both Basil and his Bostonian cousin; Olive Chancellor, a shy, genteel woman whom the novel famously calls "unmarried by every implication of her being." When Miss Birdseye first sees Basil, who has transplanted himself to the Northeast because of his bleak postbellum prospects in the South, the elderly suffragist and former abolitionist thinks to herself that he "looked like a genius" (28). When Verena Tarrant directly enters, "it floated before [Miss Birdseye] that she would probably be remarkable as a genius; her parentage was an implication of that. There was a genius for Miss Birdseye in every bush" (29). A largely satirical character, Miss Birdseye here stands for the lack of "discrimination" that Matthew Arnold associated with the United States, and James with the antebellum period in particular.[21] A bit later, the novel describes the physical suffering to which Miss Birdseye's artless home decorating subjects Olive. In Olive, the novel associates aesthetic judgment with observational canniness; unlike Miss Birdseye, Olive sees that Basil's heroism, as if drawn from the militant Anglo-Saxonist pages of Carlyle's *Heroes and Hero-Worship,* is a rapacious determination to defeat the "damnable feminization of the age" by force.[22] She recognizes what the novel itself portrays as Basil's desire: to capture Verena from Olive and take her back to the South as the spoils in a replayed Civil War, or in a twisted reenactment of the Fugitive Slave Law. At the end of the novel, when Basil and Verena leave hastily under the former's physical pressure, the description of their departure puns on the rhetoric of a national crisis only recently past: Verena's tears prompt the narrator to warn, "It is to be feared that, with the *union,* so far from brilliant, into which she was about to enter, these were not the last she was destined to shed" (435; my emphasis).

The contest between Olive and Basil to "win" Verena drives *The Bostonians,* and a significant portion of the criticism of the novel has suggested that to read the novel is to choose sides in this contest. Yet the irresolute nonclosure of Jamesian narrative overdetermines these arguments: this decidedly untriumphant "union" between Verena and Basil, during which Basil physically seizes the girl and puts a cloak over her face, coincides with Olive's mounting the Boston Music Hall stage, from which Verena had been about to lecture to the largest audience of her career, to face an angry (but for the moment "respectful") crowd. We have no idea whether Olive delivers the lecture, or tells the audience how to get their money back, or freezes in silence. But there is certainly a note of triumph, and a conferral of authority, when the novel leaves Olive, a queer figure, still *inside* a modern institution of culture and still discursively, physically, and mentally involved in its operations and social relations.[23] Indeed, the novel leaves Olive inside without suggesting she has been trapped there as a result of Basil's apparent triumph and self-liberation; in fact, at the end of the novel, Olive is exactly where her work in the "myriad and changing forms" of culture has got her. Throughout the book, because she cannot counter Basil's efforts with the kind of force he employs climactically at the end, she resorts instead to accruing power by managing the dispersed forms of agency available in the modern cultural marketplace. She tries to make Verena's unique qualities as a "genius"—what the novel calls her "gift"—as fully mediated by the institutional mediums of contemporary culture as possible. She attempts to make Verena increasingly famous and increasingly available to a mass public of strangers. She herself assumes the institutional role involved in coordinating these forms of agency, that of the professional agent.

The "power" that William Dean Howells attributed to genius as an antidemocratic category appears here and in *The Tragic Muse* as highly eroticized relationships between cultural producers and their most intimate associates.[24] *The Bostonians* summons some of this erotic energy from racial, commercial, and cultural rhetorics associated with the antebellum era, despite its devotion to satirizing that period's nostalgic idealization by suffragists like Miss Birdseye ("It would have been a nice question whether, in her heart of hearts, for the sake of this excitement, she did not sometimes wish the blacks back in bondage" [24]). The pun in the novel's final sentence about Basil and Verena's "union" is one prominent example of this, as is the sense James conveys of Basil's absolute difference from the New Englanders when the book refers to his voice early on as "African." Indeed, the irony of describing the proslavery Basil as African echoes the fact that Olive, Miss Birdseye's heir in activism, essentially *purchases* Verena from her father, paying him off to grant permission for the girl to move in with her. Slavery's centrality in antebellum culture seeps into the novel in surprising places, such as the image of Verena in performance when both Basil and Olive first see her, at Miss Birdseye's apartment, when she is still performing under the apparent mesmeric influence of her "transcendental bohemian" father Selah Tarrant (a character who recalls Bronson Alcott, Louisa's father). This liminal racialization is a factor in how both Basil and Olive understand their desire for the girl. Olive's sense that the girl "seemed to belong to some queer gipsy-land or transcendental bohemia" (74) supplements the manner in which Basil views her a bit earlier in the same scene:

> The value of her performance was yet to be proved, but she was certainly very pale, white as women are who have that red shade of hair; they look as if the blood had gone into it. There was, however, something rich in the fairness of this young lady; she was strong and supple, there was colour in her lips and eyes, and her tresses, gathered into a complicated coil, seemed to glow with the brightness of her nature. She had curious, radiant, liquid eyes (their smile was a sort of reflection, like the glisten of a gem), and though she was not tall, she appeared to spring up, and carried her head as if it reached rather high. Ransom would have thought she looked like an Oriental, if it were not that Orientals are dark; and if she had only had a goat she would have resembled Esmerelda, though he had but a vague recollection of who Esmerelda had been.[25]

Verena's orientalized, racially liminal femininity makes whiteness an embodied quality—a color present in, or as, the skin, rather than a lack of racial specificity. We have seen versions of this before: in Jenny Lind, for example, and in the "fancy girl" of William Wells Brown's *Narrative.* Indeed, the passage is especially reminiscent of Brown's writing when it suspends the question of "the value of her performance," recalling the way that physical beauty manifested as whiteness deferred the signs of market value in the fancy girl.[26]

The erotic pull of Verena as performance-spectacle draws the attention of both Basil and Olive in these racialized ways, but with some notable differences. The off-white quality that drives Basil's desire to make Verena his possession asserts itself with more force to Olive as a delicious inscrutability of heritage, a quality that increases the girl's resemblance to antebellum literary heroines such as Poe's Ligeia and Hawthorne's Miriam. Instead, Olive looks at Verena through a more modern lens, less tied to racial notions of tradition, a view that does not suspend the "value of her performance" from its appraisal:

> It was notorious that great beauties, great geniuses, great characters, take their own times and places for coming into the world, leaving the gaping spectators to make them "fit in," and holding

> from far-off ancestors, or even, perhaps, straight from the divine generosity, much more than from their ugly or stupid progenitors. They were incalculable phenomena, anyway, as Selah would have said. Verena, for Olive, was the very type and model of the "gifted being"; her qualities had not been bought and paid for; they were like some brilliant birthday-present, left at the door by an unknown messenger, to be delightful forever as an inexhaustible legacy, and amusing forever from the obscurity of its source. They were superabundantly crude as yet—happily for Olive, who promised herself, as we know, to train and polish them—but they were as genuine as fruit and flowers, as the glow of the fire or the plash of water. For her scrutinizing friend Verena had the disposition of the artist, the spirit to which all charming forms come easily and naturally. It required an effort at first to imagine an artist so untaught, so mistaught, so poor in experience; but then it required an effort also to imagine people like the old Tarrants, or a life so full as her life had been of ugly things. (109)

Amid an in-crowd of Bostonian women turned into "gaping spectators," Olive's "scrutinizing" impression of Verena constructs the girl as a "great genius" by asserting her originality as independent of her familial origins. Unlike Basil's, Olive's erotic attraction to Verena links her physical particularities to "the disposition of the artist." This configuration of her exceptionality allows Olive to extract the girl from the more traditionally racial logic of identity conferred by "ugly and stupid progenitors." Deferring the familial and ancestral influence, Olive imagines the girl's exceptional quality as cultural, as an essentially individualized difference that in turn expresses itself *as* difference. But to see Verena this way, Olive must, as James depicts the process, exert an effort to understand and then *forget* "people like the old Tarrants," former antislavery activists who lack not only an identity-defining purpose but what Pierre Bourdieu (in what this passage reveals to be an echo of James) called the "aesthetic disposition" definitive for bourgeois subjectivity.[27] As a result, Olive can construct a narrative of *rescue* around the young, racialized heroine in spite of the passing of abolitionism and with it the forms of agency, personal and political, that it once offered to educated, bourgeois, white women from New England (such as Miss Birdseye).[28] This is an ambiguous moment in the novel's political unconscious: it simultaneously triggers an amnesiac view of antebellum race politics *and* conjures the spectacle of the "tragic mulatta."

Although the fact is not immediately apparent, this imagery also imbues Verena with a specific form of commercial value for Olive, for this early scene's spectacularity soon leads Olive to exercise the privilege of spectatorship at a "slave auction," and to essentially purchase (or at least rent) Verena from her father. But of course this is not literally a slave auction; it is a gathering of culturally and economically entitled Bostonian women; my point is not that there is no difference between the two, nor that the theatricality this scene shares with, say, the multiple slave auction scenes in William Wells Brown's *Clotel* inevitably submits those on display to some generic (and ultimately, I think, not very analytically useful) process of "commodification." A more important point of comparison resides in the way such scenes' theatricality portrays, and ironizes, an eroticized fantasy of rescue from the commodity market. Both Brown and James are more interested in portraying such dynamics than in lodging a general condemnation of "commodification" or "objectification." Though an odd pairing, the two authors share an ironic impatience with the supposition that particular ideals (female beauty, genius) can be kept "pure" and isolated from commerce.

In *Clotel,* the wealthy young white man who purchases the protagonist seeks to fulfill his fantasy by installing her in a domestic space free from the tensions of his real home. In *The Bostonians,* Olive, whom F. R. Leavis called "representative of the earnest refinement of Boston culture," brings Verena to share her home, having liberated the younger woman from what Olive considers the vulgarity of her parents, their Cambridge home, and the cheap lecture circuit on which they have made Verena perform.[29] Yet Olive's attraction to Verena differs from Basil's (or Horatio's to Clotel) in that Olive does not disavow the "value of [Verena's] performance." Although Olive essentially sets Verena up in her home as a kept woman, she ultimately uses the domestic space to cultivate the girl as a *public* figure, a celebrity genius in the contemporary cultural marketplace. And as this narrative proceeds, Olive gradually becomes less Verena's teacher and more her manager and agent. In other words, Olive's rescue mission ultimately brings both women further into the modern capitalist market in culture. And she is depicted as acting shrewdly and tactically; marketing Verena to larger and larger audiences (including a large New York women's cultural organization and, ultimately, the Boston Music Hall) makes the girl both more dependent on Olive and less accessible to Basil.

The novel's depiction of this process shows Olive negotiating what Mark Seltzer has called the "melodramas of uncertain agency" of late nineteenth-century capitalism in the United States.[30] As she proceeds with her rescue narrative by acting the Arnoldian Higgins to Verena's Eliza Doolittle, she is simultaneously learning the complex skills of producing value through the labor of management, a cultural position associated with the exceptional instincts of a celebrity like P. T. Barnum. Olive's competition with Basil drives her to succeed in this process, from which she learns that making Verena more of a *commodity* in the modern cultural marketplace actually makes her less of an *object* for Basil's taking: into heterosexuality, into the South. The "uncertain agency" of this marketplace gradually becomes, in Olive's view, the best shelter for her object of desire.

The first step in this work is educating Verena in order to bring her genius into synch with modernity. During this process, culture becomes the medium of the women's relationship in a manner that cultivates, rather than sublimates, eroticism. The novel aligns Olive's pedagogical labor with her erotic pleasure as it describes the year the two spend hunkered down in Olive's apartment cultivating Verena's artistic "disposition." In effect, Olive organizes a home school in au courant cultural feminism. The two spend their days listening to Miss Birdseye tell stories about the abolition struggle or about landmark events of antebellum culture and genius, such as "Emerson and Tremont Temple." They read books about great historical women. They spend their evenings attending programs of music by Bach and Beethoven at the Boston Music Hall, where the novel eventually reaches its climax. In anticipation of the novel's ending, when Olive mounts the Music Hall stage in Verena's stead, *Olive* occupies the position of performer during this period of instrucion. The imagery of this pedagogical process is highly eroticized and corporeal, suggesting genital manipulation and penetration: "She was able to exhibit [the history of female suffering] to Verena with the greatest authority and accuracy, to lead her up and down, in and out, through all the darkest and most tortuous passages" (174).[31] Such "passages" simultaneously suggest vaginal caresses and the increasing immersion of Olive and her protégé/talent—the commodity form of performer in the culture of *agents*—in larger and more diffuse networks of cultural production and consumption.

Thus, in this stage of the Olive-Verena relationship, James portrays not simply Verena's training in contemporary standards of culture, but the queer erotics made available in both public and private spaces by that process and by what Blair called the "myriad and changing forms" of culture. This sexual intimacy also serves to figure Olive's agent-like managing of Verena, as genius figure, through the "tortuous passages" that make up the institutional networks of these many, varied forms. As time passes, Olive's economic and erotic investments in the girl become increasingly linked. Verena's cultivation makes her an increasingly valuable commodity in the marketplace of culture. She performs in increasingly larger venues, until Olive ultimately decides to embrace this value head-on by booking a performance at the Music Hall at an event promoted via mass-produced merchandise bearing Verena's image: posters, photographs, documents featuring a "sketch of her life" (415). Through the lens of the novel's queer-romance plot, we can see Olive employing the exchange economy as part of her strategy for "keeping" Verena; the more Verena is mass-reproduced, the more difficult it becomes for Basil to possess her with a single act of agency—and, in fact, late in the novel he curses his inability to "buy up the stock" of Verena kitsch in the neighborhood of the Music Hall. Despite the emphasis that critics have traditionally placed on Olive's shyness and recalcitrance, her agency (in both senses of the term) is clear to Basil: "Verena was not in the least present to him in connexion with this exhibition of enterprise and puffery; what he saw was Olive, struggling and yielding, making every sacrifice for the sake of the largest hearing, and conforming herself to a great popular system" (415–16).[32]

Olive succeeds in the novel to the degree that she embraces genius as a currency in the cultural market rather than a category of conservative resistance to it.[33] Portrayed as desperately unfulfilled at the beginning of the novel, longing for both sympathy and martyrdom, she realizes her dreams by becoming Verena's manager—by performing cultural labor of a sort associated in the present-day mass entertainment industry with the role of *producer.* This designation is an odd one, since the producer, like the agent, does not do the specific work called *culture*; instead, she negotiates its commercial and physical situation, playing a role easily susceptible to charges of parasitism. Thus Olive, bent on martyrdom, fulfills her wish in some sense by aligning herself with Jewishness—at least in the sense readily available to James's readers in the figure of "the Jew" that Catherine Gallagher and Jonathan Freedman have described as resonant for late-nineteenth-century Anglo-American writers' representations of conflicted understandings of the value of cultural labor.[34] Indeed, the narrative implies that Olive has *contracted* (in the term's simultaneous epidemiological and capitalist connotations) the *condition* of Jewishness from her work with Verena, thus alluding to associations among Jews, genius, and disease in contemporary scientific and medical discourse.[35] The eroticism surrounding these dynamics also conjures the specter of sexually transmitted disease, a fear that Sander Gilman has shown to permeate the late-century scientific discourses of both genius and anti-Semitism.

Olive thus becomes a test case for whether Jewishness, conventionally considered a "racial" quality, can rub off on a surface so *other* to it as a genteel gentile; she also becomes a test case of a *desire* to take on Jewishness. The combined sexual and "racial" salaciousness of Olive's actions is rendered with great directness by her sister, Mrs. Luna, who recognizes the constructions of queerness and Jewishness as they appear in the labor performed by the "agent."[36] That is, Mrs. Luna repeatedly jokes insinuatingly about Olive looking and acting like an agent in the business of culture, such as in this early exchange with her sister concerning Verena:

> "If I could take [Verena] to New York, I would take her farther," [Olive] remarked, hoping she was enigmatical.
>
> "You talk about *'taking'* her, as if you were a *lecture-agent*. Are you going into *that business*?" Mrs. Luna asked. (91; my emphases)

In an insinuating tone that is part anti-Semitic sneer, part homophobic leer, Mrs. Luna's response demonstrates a fine attunement to the way money, sex, and culture are culturally coimplicated, by playing on their simultaneous signification through the term "take," with its simultaneous suggestion of sexual seizure and box-office receipts. Despite Olive's self-protective concern to be "enigmatical" about her designs vis-à-vis Verena, her sister immediately perceives the symbiotic relationships of Olive's queer desire and cultural taste, and even anticipates what actually happens: Olive's entry into "that business," a phrase redolent of the protective dissociation provided by the vernacular euphemism *doing one's business.* Mrs. Luna attends (and makes possible that Basil attend) the second of Verena's performances described in the novel, at the meeting of the "Wednesday Club" in New York in the home of Mrs. Burrage, whose effete son, Henry, has become an instrument in Olive's attempt to divert Verena from Basil. When Basil remarks jealously how much attention Verena is showing Henry, Mrs. Luna replies by referring to her sister:

> You may say, as regards Mr. Burrage, that it's a queer taste in a gentleman; but there is no argument about that. It's a queer taste in a lady, too; for she is a lady, poor Olive. You can see that tonight. She is dressed like a book-agent, but she is more distinguished than any one here. Verena, beside her, looks like a walking advertisement. (249)

Mrs. Luna expressly associates the term "queer" with unconventional sexual object choices *and* "taste," a term itself carrying both aesthetic and sexual connotations. Mrs. Luna's foremost referent here is Verena, but the repeated phrase "queer taste in a [gentleman/lady]" also resonates with the suggestion of Olive's and Henry's own queer tastes. Mrs. Luna uses the evidence before her so perceptively as to foretell the denouement, the eventual immersion of Verena in mass publicity by Olive, her "agent."[37] And notably, the "book agent" is portrayed by Mrs. Luna as a liminal figure, not as abject as the "advertisement" embodied in Verena, thus in a sense foretelling Olive's triumph.[38]

James's portrayal of Verena performing in New York, having studied and traveled with Olive, opens the novel's framework to representing larger networks of cultural consumption in the form of this Wednesday Club, a routine gathering of women with moneyed husbands, described succinctly by Mrs. Luna: "They form an association for meeting at each other's houses, every week, and having some performance, or some paper read, or some subject explained" (247). When Basil enters Mrs. Burrage's, he is transformed into the object of this female cultural gaze, in a manner that, like his view of Verena at Miss Birdseye's, is erotically racialized: "He didn't know how much his head looked over the heads of others, or that his brown complexion, fuliginous eye, and straight black hair, the leonine fall of which I mentioned in the first pages of this narrative, gave him that relief that, in the best society, has the great advantage of *suggesting a topic*" (239; my italics). He finds himself subject to much the same racializing gaze as that to which he submitted Verena during her performance at Miss Birdseye's. In that gaze lurked the legacy of the slave market and the fancy girl, the fantasy realm of antebellum racial commidification of humanness; in the new milieu, however, the purpose of the gaze is ostensibly to collect and produce *topics* out of persons—to produce additional meetings of the Club, and thus provide additional occasions for female homosociality in which culture is the medium of intimacy. Indeed, the canny Mrs. Luna jokes with Basil that the Club "wouldn't easily let him go, they would make him entertain them, induce him to give a lecture—on the 'Lights and Shadows of Southern Life,' or the 'Social Peculiarities of Mississippi.'" Underlying the joke is the not so subtle suggestion that what these women really want from Basil is access to Southern blackness—the blackness that they, in their cultural sophistication, recognize in Basil's appearance when he enters. We may imagine that what they ultimately desire is that Basil act as their "agent," their *Olive,* for providing romantic and/or erotic images of African Americans. Indeed, this seems James's version of the female-female erotics of abolition nostalgia evident in a text like Alcott's incomplete novel *Diana and Persis*—particularly in the 1870s (when James's novel is set) with the passing of the cultural field associated with women like Miss Birdseye, the "heroic age" which regularly produced images of suffering slaves. These New York women bring the provinces of serious culture, in the modern, Arnoldian sense, into a female homosocial domestic space reconfigured, from the inside out, into a salon. The Wednesday Club sponsors a do-it-yourself bohemianism lent ideological legitimacy by the principles of culture.

James's representation of the Wednesday Club suggests his attunement to the institutions of *middlebrow* culture, as Janice Radway defines it, "formed, . . . as a category, by processes of literary and cultural mixing whereby forms and values associated with one form of culture were wed to forms and values usually connected with another."[39] And if there is a strong sense in which Olive acts as a kind of lesbian Svengali in her work with Verena, it also makes sense to see her along the lines Jonathan Freedman has associated with du Maurier's Svengali, as the projection of the conflicts attending the middlebrow subject's need to access serious culture through the commodity market.[40] As we see through

Mrs. Luna, the women of the Wednesday Club depend on Olive, yet disdain the necessity of dealings with "book-agents." Indeed, James constructs a surprisingly long conversation between two anonymous club members that embodies both sides of Freedman's anxious middlebrow subject; one woman makes clear the club's pervasive anxiety about producing a sufficient number of "topics" for their meetings, while the other disparages the effort altogether:

> "Are you a member?" one of the ladies said to the other. "I didn't know you had joined."
>
> "Oh, I haven't; nothing would induce me."
>
> "That's not fair; you have all the fun and none of the responsibility."
>
> "Oh, the fun—the fun!" exclaimed the second lady.
>
> "You needn't abuse us, or I will never invite you," said the first.
>
> "Well, I thought it was meant to be improving; that's all I mean; very good for the mind. Now, this woman tonight; isn't she from Boston?"
>
> "Yes, I believe they have brought her on, just for this."
>
> "Well, you must be pretty desperate, when you have got to go to Boston for your entertainment."
>
> "Well, there's a similar society there, and I never heard of their sending to New York."
>
> "Of course not, they think they have got everything. But doesn't it make your life a burden, thinking what you can possibly have?"
>
> "Oh dear, no. I am going to have Professor Gougenheim—all about the Talmud. You must come."
>
> "Well, I'll come," said the second lady; "but nothing would induce me to be a regular member."
>
> Whatever the mystic circle might be, Ransom agreed with the second lady that regular membership must have terrors, and he admired her independence in such an artificial world. (239)

James presents these women as consumers in a postbellum market in both culture and cultural difference. This market no longer makes available for consumption the slave bodies with which they suspect Basil to have been intimate—perhaps sexually intimate, given his features. Now, however, the Wednesday Club members must settle, in Professor Gougenheim, for a version of racial difference in the process of transforming into *cultural* difference—a difference at least in part explicable *textually,* in the Talmud, rather than registered through physical signs.

More specifically, this segment of *The Bostonians* captures one version of a growing association between discourses of Jewishness and of genius, an association emergent on both sides of the Atlantic in several forms. Certainly the anti-Semitism driving the racial analysis of men like Lombroso and Nordau is present in some fashion in James's reference to Professor Gougenheim. Another widespread form of this association was the *belle Juive* figure, an association of Jewish femininity with a highly attuned sympathetic capacity, embodied in various cultural texts (including, as we shall soon see, Jame's *Tragic Muse*) and in the celebrity of actresses such as Rachel Felix and Sarah Bernhardt. But what *The Bostonians* represents here is yet another form of Jewish visibility in Anglo-American culture, one less tied to pathologies of the Jewish body: a figure of the Jew as middlebrow intellectual, as an adept cross-cultural translator whose work made ancient and modern Judaism salient for a mass audience imagined as middle-class, heterogenously gendered, and Anglo-Saxon.

The most prominent exemplar of such a figure in the 1880s was undoubtedly the poet and essayist Emma Lazarus, with whom both Henry and William James corresponded, and whom Henry visited in London shortly before her death at thirty-eight in 1887.[41] Lazarus embodies a cultural, textual conception of Jewishness with a number of representatives in institutions of the proto-middlebrow of the 1880s, particularly in New York, home of the Wednesday Club. The *Century,* the publication where *The Bostonians* was serialized, was the magazine most friendly to Lazarus and other Jewish intellectuals, such as the Englishman Israel Zangwill (himself a critic of Max Nordau and an avid reader of Henry James) and Abram Isaacs (City University of New York professor of ancient and modern Hebrew literature), whom I strongly suspect to be the model for Gougenheim.[42] Isaacs was editor of the journal the *Jewish Messenger* (the major venue for Lazarus's writing) and author of numerous books and essays, many reprinted in the *Century.* Isaacs's work also constructed him in the position of translator across difference, the sort of work we have seen both Olive and Basil asked to do in other contexts. In 1893 Issacs published, to commercial success, *Stories from the Rabbis,* a collection of magazine fiction in which he attempted to integrate Jewish lore with founding texts of modern Euro-American literature, with chapters like "The Faust of the Talmud" and "The Rip Van Winkle of the Talmud." Advertising copy for the book established its middlebrow credentials by boasting that, like *The Bostonians*' Gougenheim, Isaacs's volume would bring cultured leisure to the gentile masses: "Dr. Isaacs has gathered from the Talmud and Midrash a most entertaining collection of non-sectarian stories, and has re-told them in genial prose. This book is a capital companion for an hour's relaxation, and is also suited for reading purposes in schools and colleges."[43]

The image of the wives of propertied New York men studying the "Talmud and Midrash" lacks some of the eroticism evident in other stagings of culture we have been examining in James's novel. Yet, just as Mrs. Luna voices the possibility that Olive has in a sense "caught" Jewishness through the intimacy of her relationship with Verena, she suggests a similar possibility with respect to the women of the Wednesday Club. She notes the club's adherence to "sumptuary laws" limiting the extravagance of their meals together, and describes Olive and Verena's New York lodgings as "some extraordinary kind of New Jerusalem boarding-house, in Tenth Street" (247). With this allusion to the highly concentrated Jewish population of downtown Manhattan, the novel floats the scandalous suggestion that Jewishness is encroaching upon the bodies of the city's most culturally sophisticated white women when these bodies are most vulnerable, while they sleep and eat.[44] And although this implication does draw energy from a more pathologically conceived anti-Semitism, it also portrays the women as willful adventurers in these metropolitan contact zones.

As a number of important recent readings have shown, James's attitudes toward Jews were decidedly ambivalent, even incoherent.[45] What *The Bostonians* portrays as the sexual vulnerability of Anglo-Saxon womanhood to bodily invasion by Jewishness certainly echoes other conventional, racialized narratives of endangered, white, female virtue, such as the myth of the black male rapist or Edith Wharton's portryal of Lily Bart's sexual victimization by Sim Rosendale in *The House of Mirth*. But *The Bostonians*' broad preoccupation with the visibility of genius complicates its representation of this form of anti-Semitism. In the passage we have been examining, the members of the Wednesday Club convey this preoccupation, and, however satirically James depicts their efforts, the women are nevertheless engaged in the same activity as both Olive and James himself: the eroticized cultivation of genius. Their active attempts to mobilize cross-racial desire and even to seek out sexual-racial danger by encouraging participants to sleep on the Lower East Side are represented as one contemporary version of this process.

The ending of the novel floats the possibility that, with the loss of Verena, Olive becomes a public figure in her own right. This is, at least, one suggestion of the climactic pages that leave her standing on the stage upon which she and Verena had seen the works of the masters of European romantic music performed and where in James's lifetime such figures as Frederick Douglass, Wendell Phillips, Theodore Parker, and (as recently as 1882 and *after* the date on which Olive is portrayed mounting the stage) Oscar Wilde had spoken. It may also be that Olive goes mum, or that what she announces is the ticket refund policy. What we know for sure about Olive when the novel closes is that she has become an accomplished agent for the production of culture before a mass audience.[46]

Michael Davitt Bell writes that the question of whether James endorses Basil's or Olive's position, a question that has structured so much criticism of the novel, is "ultimately unanswerable, and it may even be meaningless."[47] But although Bell sees what he calls the novel's "ultimate incoherence" as James's misfire, one thing the book succeeds in *producing* is an Olive who is in a very modern sense emancipated. Emancipated from herself, that is: like a successful client in therapy, she has summoned the courage to transcend her self-imagined limitations. Notably, the novel does not represent the agent of Olive's liberation as either political activism or her individual will's transcendence of the mass. Rather, the agent is her freakish, spontaneous impulse at the end of the novel, the result of liberation from an enburdening self, made possible by the ongoing drama of her erotic attraction to Verena.

The denouement is also where Olive provides a sense of James's understanding of the value of cultural labor. The strength Olive shows in walking off toward the "unruly crowd" is the happiest form of semiclosure the novel offers. As she walks to the stage she is compared to Liberté and Hypatia, each a female martyr to physical violence, but, as it turns out, "it was not apparent that [the audience] were likely to throw chairs at her." Of course, we don't know how long this restraint lasts, but we are presented with the option of understanding this to be a happy conclusion in therapeutic terms: in the lay psychology vernacular of the twentieth century, Olive has "overcome the personal barrier" of shyness. The novel offers no hint of how to imagine her the following day, or even later that evening. But James would return shortly to the topic of genius's form within modern networks of culture in his next novel, *The Tragic Muse.*

Jamesians' readings of Olive's role in *The Bostonians* have recently become far more friendly than they were. Joseph Litvak and Hugh Stevens, both deeply informed by queer theory, grant Olive a particularly rich and complicated degree of epistemological and erotic weight.[48] For Litvak in particular, reading Olive seriously to a large extent means reading James *in her.* As Litvak points out, both *The Bostonians* and *The Tragic Muse* were written in the six years leading up to James's ill-fated attempt to remake himself as a professional playwright. Olive's ascending the stairs to the Music Hall stage thus becomes an allegory of James's own conflicted desire to display himself and his work in a new, more embodied, more visible medium. *The Tragic Muse* certainly advances this project. Indeed, in that novel, James's understanding of the current cultural dimensions of genius is invested with an intensely personal response to the new, universalizing notions of difference that we saw *The Bostonians* track in the culture at large.

Queer "I" for the Straight Guy: The Tragic Muse

In the first scene of *The Tragic Muse,* the Dormer family squabble about whether the art they are seeing at the Paris Salon will stunt the development of their teenage daughter. Nick, eldest son and heir to the parliamentary career of the family's recently deceased patriarch, wearily exclaims, "Mother, don't play the British matron!" while the girl herself, Biddy, cites aestheticist doctrine: "It's not the subject, it's the treatment!"[49] As the novel proceeds, virtually all of its characters confront cultural labors as a locus of what the Dormer matriarch, Lady Agnes, calls "all kinds of disease and indecency," but only some find curative resources in this notion of aesthetic "treatment." In the novel as a whole, the characters struggle with their sense that degradation emanates from both the cutting edge of aesthetic innovation and the commercial arts, especially theater, which from some perspectives is becoming a realm akin to what we now call "entertainment."

The Dormers' argument is interrupted by the entrance of Gabriel Nash, with the young, untried actress Miriam Rooth and her mother in tow. An old school friend of Nick's, Nash announces almost immediately, "Ah, it was high time I should meet you—I see. I have an idea you need me" (719). Nash's greeting is characteristic of his direct, queerly seductive, performative rhetorical style. Nick's response—"Upon my word, I do!"—shows him deeply receptive to this seduction, as well as to the promise of liberation in diagnosis. He responds positively, that is, he responds to Nash's contention that he is sick and needs treatment.

Nash's manner has led a number of critics to associate him with Oscar Wilde, whose *Picture of Dorian Gray* bears resemblances to *The Tragic Muse.*[50] Nash is, indeed, the focal point of the James novel's queerness: like Olive with Verena, he cultivates Nick by establishing greater and greater personal intimacy with him; he appears in Nick's narrative as a figure of return, an uncanny reemergence of a male homosocial/erotic past; and he simply looks, sounds, and acts like the "type" of dandy-author embodied by Wilde (and various parodies of Wilde, such as Gilbert and Sullivan's Bunthorne) as a modern gay male icon. At the same time, reading Nash in this manner typically leads critics back to James's long series of ambivalent, sometimes cruel statements about Wilde, particularly during and after his sodomy trial. An unintended consequence of such readings has been to reinforce a view of James's queerness as partial in comparison to Wilde's. Without disavowing the violence of the juridical process to which Wilde was subjected, I think we can learn more about James's queerness, and historical formations of queerness in general, by suspending Wilde's presence as a lens for reading Gabriel Nash. In his recent study of queer male performance practices from James to Andy Warhol, Michael Moon asks the powerful heuristic question, "What if we took as a provisional starting point for our analysis [rather than Wilde] a figure such as Henry James, who had in many ways a much less readily legible relation to the emergence of homosexual identity in his lifetime?"[51] I think this can happen if we read Nash more broadly through associations between queerness and genius, associations that could include Olive Chancellor's relationship to Verena Tarrant despite the obvious fact that they are female characters.

If *The Bostonians* ends therapeutically, as a tale of personal liberation into the public display of difference, *The Tragic Muse* from the beginning sets up its most densely queer character as a medium for *others'* liberation—especially Nick Dormer's. The novel is deeply concerned with genius in two forms: as an embodied figure, in Nash's dandified mode and later in Miriam's Bernhardt-like sensation; and as an inner, individual, essential self-authenticity positioned as something to be rediscovered through a process of expression and self-knowledge. It is especially notable, in this light, that while Henry James was writing and serializing *The Tragic Muse,* William James was completing the ten-year process of composing his *Principles of Psychology,* the book that established him as the leading figure in the United States's contribution to Euro-American revisions of mind science. For in a sense, Henry's novel was his own version of William's book, both a treatise on what William called "healthy-mindedness" and an investigation of the cultural and historical frame in which such an ideal had come into being.[52]

The Tragic Muse constructs its discourse of therapeutic health with the claim of virtually every character in the novel to be anxious about the degradation of culture. This riff is repeated so many times, in so many ways, that it demands to be seen not so much as an opinion James is attempting to express fictionally, as a picture of this anxiety as a central mode of individual self-definition. The characters in this novel think and make choices on the basis of a threatening yet formative specter of being ashamed of one's relationship to culture. This "relationship to culture" is the crux of subjectivity, rather than simply the exercise of aesthetic *taste.* James's novel is constructing an explicitly post-Kantian framework in which aesthetic judgments and enunciations are made under the pressure of material, social circumstances;[53] this type of degradation is not a looming fear in Kant.

Yet the focus of the novel *is* (to use Biddy's terms) both "the subject" and "the treatment." It personalizes the historical moment's anxieties about the state of culture; although "anxiety" is not a major term in the novel, it is implicitly present, not in the metaphorical sense used so broadly by critics today, but in anticipation of the way clinical psychologists would soon discuss it as a "classified condition."

Nash's presence plays to this anxiety by shuttling between solid presence and in some ways equally palpable absence; indeed, Nash disappears from the unfolding of the plot for significant stretches of chapters. Thus Nick's view of

> the mystery [he] could never wholly dissociate from [Nash], the sense of the transient and occasional, the likeness to vapour or murmuring wind or shifting light. It was for instance a symbol of this unclassified condition, the lack of all position as a name in well-kept books, that Nick in fact had no idea where he lived, would not have known how to go and see him or send him a doctor if he had heard he was ill. (1229)

The passage equates not knowing someone with not knowing how to get a professional to name one's disease or "condition." Nick arrives at this point after the novel's long maintainence of Nash's ambiguity even from the beginning, when Nick stumbles through a description of Nash to Biddy as the author of "a sort of a novel."

In his first appearance, Nash establishes his skill as a diagnostician of the soul, an art he practices with "talk," the curative he later calls his "instrument": "Talk. I say the things that other people don't, that they can't, that they won't" (975). The novel's genius figures, Nash and Miriam, an aspiring actress whose partly Jewish background instantly becomes a focus, are both, in their way, performing artists, albeit in different venues; they arrive in the novel as embodiments of both the infection Lady Agnes fears and the "treatment" Biddy idealizes. Nash, in particular, renders this aestheticism, his *talk* cure, an effective treatment for the "crisis" he has correctly intuited in Nick: his desire to throw aside a political career inherited from his deceased father, as well as his eminent engagement to a beautiful and wealthy widow, Julia Dallow, from another politically entitled family, for the "artistic life" of a London portrait painter.

And indeed, Nick gives up his position as a representative man for a shot at realizing his aesthetic genius. That is, he leaves a career of representing constituents in Parliament for a career of representing individuals in the art of portrait painting. Moreover, his contact with Nash leads him to identify genius with the ability to express one's *self* both sexually and aesthetically. Divorcing his sexuality from his nationally entitled, preestablished engagement with Julia becomes an essential part of his attempt to realize his artistic genius.

Amid all this, culture becomes the medium of self-discovery. But attaining this end requires "treatment," as Biddy calls it with seeming innocence, because of the social pathology we also saw Alcott framing in the previous chapter—the self- and collectively diagnosed state of being "culturally sapped of instinct and feeling by cultural productions that catered to those below them in rank and education."[54] Nash offers Nick treatment, not cure—therapy, not remedy—for this situation. As Nick's "evil genius," he teaches his old friend a way to rewrite this script, a move away from the disciplinary individualism with which he is urged by his mother, conjuring the ghost of his father, to "go straight," and toward a therapeutic individualism that leads him to confess "I ought to be ashamed of myself, no doubt; for even my rubbish interests me." Although Nick is referring to his art, bad art in this novel takes on value as a kind of raw material upon which individuals might profitably *work,* that term significant as mental and manual labor as well as anticipating the notion of "working through" therapeutically. The novel represents a successful version of this process in its depiction of Nick Dormer's learning to trust what he calls his "sense of the artistic life" and acting on that sense by throwing aside his political career to become the painter he wishes to be and live out what Nash calls his "wonderful artistic nature."[55]

As Joseph Litvak suggests, James uses Miriam and, especially, Nash to depict labor he himself would like to perform as an artist and critic and/or that he sees the public as desiring from him. This aspect of the novel becomes particularly clear if one recalls *The Bostonians'* portrayal of the productive collision of artistic genius with modern forms of cultural publicity and management. These come into conflict in the end, when Nash disappears from the novel and Nick's painting of him fades. Miriam's Jewishness assimilates into the novel as a microcosmic performance of the Jewish culturalism of Professor Gougenheim and Abram Isaacs. But Nash's queerness is finally an insurmountable difference from everyone else in the novel: his queerness ultimately *is* the fact that he is insurmountably different. Indeed, the novel shifts its title's referent from an apparent association between Miriam and Rachel Felix, whose portrait as "The Tragic Muse" Miriam views backstage at the French National Theater, to *Nash* and, I will argue, to James himself as a kind of self-portrait of the artist as a queer man tragically implicated in keeping a straight world happy with conventions such as marriage and professionalism.

Nick's decision to give up Parliament to work as a painter comes about not merely because Nash encourages or inspires him but because he visits Nick in his studio and looks at his work while Julia is out of town at a country house party, mixing with influential political connections. Nash makes the studio a queer domestic-cultural space, akin to Olive's apartment in *The Bostonians,* an intervention that Nick appreciates both deeply affectively and in the language of value:

> It was the oddest thing how at present he found himself attributing value to Gabriel Nash—attributing to him, among attributions more confused, the dignity of judgement, the authority of intelligence. . . . He whistled now while he let his companion take time. He rubbed old panels with his sleeve and dabbed wet sponges on surfaces that had sunk. It was a long time since he had felt so gay, strange as such an assertion sounds in regard to a young man whose bridal day had at his urgent solicitation lately been fixed. He had stayed in town to be alone with his imagination, and suddenly, paradoxically, the sense of that result had arrived with Gabriel Nash. (973–74)

Nash gets "result[s]"; he creates "value" by enabling Nick to "be alone with his own imagination," to be intimate with *himself.* Elsewhere Nick considers Nash a "contemplative genius" who "seemed to take the words out of his mouth, to utter for him, better and more completely, the very things he was on the point of saying. Nash's saying them at such moments appeared to make them true" (992–93).

The novel's striking opposition between being "gay" and being engaged to be married is an instance of a kind of teasing queerbaiting it recurrently performs upon Nick, and which eventually generates a somewhat nasty ending. Although John Carlos Rowe calls *The Tragic Muse* a forerunner of the present-day gay-positive novel, I think it calls Nick "gay" only to shut down the possibility of this "gayness," leading him into a substantially different identity than the one through which he has always understood himself. The novel repeatedly tempts us to think Nick's experience will be transformative for his sexual identity, only to return to depicting his interaction with Nash as a vehicle for the former's discovery of an individuality for which there is no question of vexation by social regulation. A particularly charged illustration occurs in the hilariously screwball scene, arranged by Nash, when Nick paints Miriam's portrait in a vaguely described state of undress and Julia enters the studio, having decided to come back early from the family country house. Nick's very apparent lack of erotic interest in Miriam does not prevent Julia from saying to him bitterly, a bit later, "That's your innermost preference, that's your secret passion" (278). Especially when she exclaims, in this conversation, "I hate art, as you call it!" the novel coaxes us toward seeing Julia as responding homophobically to Nick's emergent gay identity. But the novel maintains the privilege of disavowal here, keeping in play the possibility that the "preference" really *is* "art." Similarly, when Nick tells his father's old friend Mr. Carteret that he plans to quit Parliament and paint, he takes up the rhetoric of coming out: "I'm not bad. But I'm different." But when Nick comes out as "different" he is coming out as himself. Indeed, the novel implies here that Nick makes a distinction between difference-as-individuality and difference-as-badness, maintaining deliberate uncertainty around how Nash figures for him on this spectrum.

Such scenes succinctly illustrate what makes the discourse of genius in *The Tragic Muse* therapeutic. In the world of this novel, to realize aesthetic freedom is to realize sexual freedom is to realize one's *preference(s)*. The more enlightened characters, among whom Julia eventually proves herself to belong, may not agree with Nick's choices, but they believe that it is *unhealthy* not to realize, yield to, one's genius—one's difference. To live in what the novel portrays as the state of self-ignorance is to be repressed in the manner of Peter Sherringham, the character whose persistent frustration over his attraction to Miriam Rooth and desire to immerse himself in the world of theater lead him to accept a diplomatic post in what James calls "the smallest of Latin American countries." James specifically portrays "freedom" as a life lived in Europe, unconstricted by the conventional symbolic capital of nation, family, and profession. Sexuality emerges across these bonds; it is, like art, a cosmopolitan ideal.

Nash is the primary agent effecting this therapeutic dimension of art in modernity, urging on Nick the "strong sane joys of the artistic life." In a strikingly straightforward process of transference,

Nash as genius becomes Nick's own genius. Nash's instrumental "talk" is written off by most of Nick's family, as well as by Peter, as the pose of a self-obsessed aesthete. But Nick sees Nash as a "contemplative genius," a working mind unrestrained and uncontained by the boundaries of behavior dictated by family and nation. The company of this genius leads Nick to separate his identity from his political career, his family's desires, his and their sense of the meaning of nation, their money, etc. The genius's company draws Nick, in other words, away from the ideals that William Dean Howells admired—the genius as great man, his greatness established in his transparency and simplicity. The view of genius James portrays through Nash and Nick is presented as ultimately impenetrable, an embrace of the state Nick happily finds himself in in the middle of the novel, fascinated by his "own rubbish." Nick learns through Nash to locate his identity in art and sexuality, realms imagined as uncoverable essences of the pure difference that *is* individuality.

The novel's therapeutic vein insists that part of modern variety *is* this "rubbish" as it manifests itself in spectacular cultural sensations such as Miriam Rooth's career, which by the middle of the novel has become extraordinarily successful despite her initial introduction by Nash as a kind of Barnumian freak. The novel follows her transformation toward a degree of public acclaim that, if not as great as Jenny Lind's or Trilby's, approaches that of Bernhardt. And James portrays an England nearly prepared to reckon with the specter of Jewishness in creating such a celebrity. Halfway through, Nash reverses his first assessment of the actress to construct a theory of the therapeutic virtue of vulgarity on a grand, cultural scale, calling Miriam "the great modern personage" and surprising her conservative admirer Peter Sherringham:

> As Sherringham had perceived, you never knew where to "have" Gabriel Nash; a truth exemplified in his unexpected delight at the prospect of Miriam's drawing forth the modernness of the age. You might have thought he would loathe that modernness; but he had a brilliant, amused, amusing vision of it, saw it as something huge and ornamentally vulgar. Its vulgarity would rise to the grand style, like that of a London railway station, and Miriam's publicity would be as big as the globe itself. (1091)

Nash predicts Miriam's rise and fall, "a drama more bustling than any she would put on the stage and a spectacle that would beat everything for scenery." She would eventually lose her talent, "still young and insatiate, but already coarse, hard and raddled, with nothing left to do and nothing left to do it with, the remaining years all before her and the raison d'être all behind. It would be curious and magnificent and grotesque."

This is a crucial moment, as it dramatizes Nash providing a definitive picture of genius in the context of "modernness." Nash is here articulating not only a theory of genius, but a theory of genius as a form of queer labor. Peter's response to this description of the "grand style" illustrates how the Howellsian view of genius, shaped by free labor principles, would likely respond to Nash: "You see her too much as a humbug and too little as a real producer. She has ideas—great ones; she loves the thing for itself. That may keep a woman serious." Nash's reply casts aside the "serious" and opens up a different sense of production:

> "Her greatest idea must always be to show herself; and fortunately she has a splendid self to show. I think of her absolutely as a real producer, but as a producer whose production is her own person. No 'person,' even as fine a one as hers, will stand that for more than an hour, so that humbuggery has very soon to lend a hand. However," Nash continued, "if she's a fine humbug it will do as well, and perfectly suit the time. We can all be saved by vulgarity; that's the solvent of all difficulties and the blessing of this delightful age. Let no man despair; a new hope has dawned." (1229)

To see Nash here as simply mocking Miriam (and by implication, Verena) is to miss the novel's portrayal, via Nash's view of Miriam, of a historical identification between queer men and actresses. Matthew Tinkcom has described this relational dynamic as inhering not so much in ego-constitutive psychic processes as in a recognition of the generally unrecognized *work* that actresses in particular do to present them*selves* both on and off stage.[56] Tinkcom focuses particularly on male homosexuals working in Hollywood studios in the 1930s, directors such as George Cukor and crew members involved in long sessions of make-up and wardrobe preparations for the film divas of the time. This focus resonates nicely with what we have seen of both Nash and Olive as managerial figures. In particular, it strikes a chord with Nash's proclivity to direct scenes like the Nick-Miriam-Julia studio encounter, a patently screwball episode that might be seen as anticipating Cukor's work.

One of Tinkcom's major interests is the labor of what he calls the "camp intellectual," whose work, performed collaboratively, consists in "translating the idioms of high-art modernism to mass forms."[57] Throughout *The Tragic Muse,* Nash distinguishes himself as a genius by playing this role, his distancing irony increasing the value of high culture to those who do not simply reject him, like Nick's mother and elder sister. Indeed, James uses Nash to articulate the contingency of labor itself within the "modernness" he describes. Through Nash, James begins to fashion a quasi-political argument about his own cultural and economic marginalization as an aesthetic "genius," on grounds shaped by modern notions of queerness and Jewishness. Jewishness, as Gallagher and Freedman make clear, is in one of its nineteenth-century Anglo-American forms defined in its conflict with a labor theory of value, via an aura of suspicion concerning precisely what work done by Jews *produces,* much as the modern notion of sexual "deviance" relies on questions about the (re)productivity of sexual practices. In *The Bostonians,* Olive Chancellor's queerness begins to look increasingly Jewish to the world as she becomes involved in work as genius's "agent"; this takes place in a cultural setting inclined to understand Jewishness as something textual, apprehensible, and inviting the immersion of outsiders. In *The Tragic Muse,* Jewishness is more explicitly thematized, and depicted as fluid. But over the course of the novel, its Jewish character, Miriam Rooth, becomes progressively *less* Jewish. That is, her Jewishness is less and less a topic, until a bizarre revisionary moment late in the book throws into question the very existence of this aspect of her identity. This ambiguity, deployed by the narrator in the form of opaque descriptions, such as referring to Miriam's nose as "somehow Jewish without the convex arch" (990), is, in fact, a fairly consistent aspect of Miriam's first-person self-presentation; in the preface to the novel James discusses his specific decision not to "go behind" Miriam as he did for the other two characters he considered "major," Nick and Peter.

A telling instance of the opacity of Miriam's Jewishness is her response when Peter Sherringham remarks that she is "of Rachel's tribe": "I don't care if I'm of her tribe artistically. I'm of the family of artists—*je me fiche* of any other!" (843). What "art" means is in flux in this world, and Miriam's suggestion here that artists constitute a kind of tribe is striking not only in that it claims a quasi-ethnic affiliation among artists akin to one modern understanding of Jewishness, but in that it makes that claim with reference to artists of any sort.[58] The remark helps emphasize the novel's sense of the historical present's "myriad" forms of cultural production, in diverse venues, whose availability for consumption is a central characteristic of what the novel calls modernness. For the word "artist," like the word "genius," is a generalized term of identity conveying expressiveness to be a more important aspect of individuality than any specific process of representation that one conducts as a career or vocation.[59]

Miriam's statement thus makes her status as genius and her vision of art coalesce to form a bridge between concepts of culture in its Arnoldian sense and in its anthropological, ethnographic sense. The two concepts become surprisingly indistinct in this depiction of artists as an elite, ethnicized category of persons expert at remaining true to their individuality by making great art. Miriam's embodiment of these key paradoxes becomes increasingly distinct as she fails to respond to Peter Sherringham's attempt to establish a relationship with her on the model of Olive's with Verena—the model, that is, of du Maurieresque erotic pedagogy. Peter's efforts repeatedly run up against the "queer jumble of taste," such as her "flashes of perception" at the Louvre, which erupt despite the fact that "she was on almost irreconcilable terms with the printed page" (857). Indeed, the novel implies that one would never call Peter a genius, that he is unable to be either queer or Jewish enough to traffic in the cultural conditions of modernness.

The phrase "queer jumble" embodies Miriam's genius as a range of paradoxes, mixtures, categories that, formerly opposed, are now performatively juxtaposed. Indeed, the novel repeatedly refers to her as a "mixture." To Peter, she demonstrates a "mixture of intelligence and puerility" (857): "Her mixture, as it spread itself before one, was a quickening spectacle: she was intelligent and clumsy—she was underbred and fine. She was certainly very various" (812). When James recorded his note for a character based on Rachel—"Ignorant. Illiterate. Rachel."—he apparently concurred with Peter's opinion that "the actor's talent was essentially a gift, a thing by itself, implanted, instinctive, accidental, equally unconnected with intellect and with virtue."[60] But over the course of the novel, descriptions of her "mixture" come to resemble the cultural and erotic energies that Michael Moon describes as embedded in the term "mixed" in James's autobiographical writings.[61] Miriam's "queer jumble" comes to resemble this amalgamation of erotic and cultural promiscuity through which Moon constructs an alternative male modernist genealogy of queerness, but which nonetheless characterizes her tactical appropriations of the work of Shakespeare, Rachel, Peter, and the oddly accommodating male friend whom, as the novel closes, she *does* marry: Basil Dashwood.[62]

Miriam's "mixture" also informs Peter's envious view of her capacity for self-expression, described by the narrator through Sherringham as the model of health sought by sufferers of nervous complaints. "With a hundred startled ideas about her wheeling through his mind," Peter is "for the first time and most vividly visited by a perception that ended by becoming frequent with him—that of the perfect presence of mind, unconfused, unhurried by emotion, that any artistic performance requires and that all, whatever the instrument, require in exactly the same degree" (934–35). Miriam's versatility, the ability to navigate variety, is portrayed as a state of mental soundness that Peter lacks. The novel lends Miriam's "mixture" an added twist, though, when it moves to deracialize it, revealing that Miriam is not in fact Jewish. Her racial difference collapses into the universalized difference that Nick announces, in his quasi-coming-out gesture, to his conservative uncle, Mr. Carteret.[63] In other words, Miriam attains a privileged assimilation into the contemporary discourse of difference—an opportunity never realizable, or articulable as a possibility, for the "mixed" or "mulatta" characters with whom she nevertheless shares a literary history.[64] It is important to see this aspect of the novel not so much as erasure as a change in the figurative status of Jewishness. From signifying a host of traits via the medium of racial typology (as Peter's remarks about her early on reflect), it becomes a generalized symbol, marking the paradoxic universality of difference.

This view of Jewishness is manifest in several contemporary texts originating in James's circle of friends and associates. In *Trilby,* for example, du Maurier's sympathetic character Little Billee is described as having:

> just a faint suggestion of some possible very remote Jewish ancestor—just a tinge of that strong, sturdy, irrepressible, indomitable, indelible blood which is of such priceless value in diluted homeopathic doses . . . Fortunately for the world, and especially for ourselves, most of us have in our veins at least a minim of

> that precious fluid, whether we show it or not. *Tant pis pour les autres!*[65]

The aging James Russell Lowell became increasingly preoccupied with Jews and Judaism, and wrote repeatedly about Jewishness as a universal trait. Its configuration along these lines anticipates a similar view of homosexuality evident in Freud's *Three Essays on Sexuality* and is given a poignant iteration for the genealogy of modern U.S. "multiculturalism" in a recent Margaret Cho stand-up performance film, when the comedian, imitating the highly accented English of her Korean immigrant mother, announces, "You know, I think *everybody little bit gay*."[66]

Although grounded in very different historical and cultural contexts, Cho's monologue is striking in its portrayal of gayness as the vehicle of an *ethnic* assimilation into the modern idea of difference. Indeed, the "tragic" aspect of *The Tragic Muse,* from the viewpoint of a liberal pluralist celebration of difference, is that the analogy between queerness and Jewishness does not hold up. As the novel moves toward its close, Nash's visibility fades as Miriam's increases. However, I want to read this as actually tightening Nash's hold on the novel by introducing a powerful sense of James's own sense of being irreducibly and unrecuperably different. Making this connection hinges on the growing ambivalence that Nick and Miriam exhibit toward Nash as the novel moves toward its end, and in the failed attempt by Nick to paint Nash's portrait late in the novel. This attempt marks Nick's return to a "straight" world; James rather bitterly shows him as presumptuously assuming that he can see Nash for who he is and render the results on canvas. The episode illustrates Nick's failure to understand Nash's revisionary understanding of "production" as a focus on large-scale processes of mediation. In a sense, the novel portrays the tragedy of Nick's failure to understand just how proto-Warholian James, through Nash, has become.

The end of *The Tragic Muse* has been criticized even by some of the book's most sympathetic readers for its apparent "exile" of Nash and simultaneous reuniting of Nick and Julia.[67] But tracking Nash as a camp intellectual worker suggests a very different reading of the novel's ending, of James's relationship to Nash and the novel, and of what James found provocative about the notion of genius at this historical moment. This view suggests, in fact, an identification between Nash and James that the preoccupation of most critics with Nash's resemblance to Wilde has led them to neglect, and a different way of understanding James's own queerness than in its comparative Wildeanness.[68] Nash's disappearance at the end of the novel—as well as the odd appearances and disappearances throughout the novel that critics often call his spectral or ghostlike qualities—may be viewed as the failure or inability of the other characters, the "straight" characters, to recognize his labor. In this view, Nash only appears when he is working for straight people. I mean "working" here to signify both his therapeutic function and the uses of this function for processes of capitalization—primarily cultural, but also economic ones: being a genius is the job that Nash does to produce capital for himself and others. Nick begins to sour on Nash at the end of the novel as he begins to fear that Nash will introduce him to his "coterie," the members of the Anonymous Club,—i.e., that he will have to meet Nash in a world with too much queerness, rather than just the right amount of queerness—a world in which there is no straightness to return to as the successful subject of therapy.

For what happens at the end of *The Tragic Muse* is not so much that Nash disappears but that everyone else does. The others disappear into prefabricated social narratives of bourgeois life—marriage, career, etc. These are narratives that therapy fixes, but only by shutting them down into the "nonnarratable," to borrow a term from D. A. Miller.[69] The novel does not end with Nick and Julia's marriage, but it does end with their reconciliation and a hint of the possibility that they will wed. This possibility is in fact a better closure for showing how successful Nash's therapy has been: Nick will now be able to make his own decision, not following the wishes of his mother or Mr. Carteret, but also not reactively rejecting their conventional assumptions. Something like this resolution takes place at the end of *The Bostonians,* on the surface: the soon-to-be married couple disappears, the wife's face having already vanished, as the queer figure embraces visibility. *Muse* inverts itself, putting the reader outside the novel with all its characters except Nash.

The Tragic Muse moves toward its closure in the last few chapters by suggesting that part of Nick's and Miriam's "treatments" has been to make them talk about work as innately good, in contrast to Nash's principles. When the two meet near the end as accomplished artists, for the first time since the portrait-painting scene, they complain of Nash's disdain for "the little prudences and compromises and simplifications of practice" (1225). Miriam, now a celebrity, confesses herself "sorry, awfully sorry and even rather angry, that I haven't before me a period of the same sort of unsociable pegging away that you have."

But Nash continues to act in ways that indicate his intimacy with Nick's own interiority, or, at least, the impression is that he perceives his friend's new ambivalence. For Nash begins preparations to send Nick off on his own, as *The Bostonians* did, far more abruptly, for Olive Chancellor at its ending. Nash visits Nick in his studio and proclaims, "It's very nice . . . your pictures and the whole thing . . . [y]our existence here, in this little remote independent corner of the great city. The disinterestedness of your attitude, the persistence of your effort, the piety, the beauty, in short the example, of the whole spectacle" (1230). Nick then proposes that Nash sit for a portrait, which causes Nash to respond with an uncharacteristically "blank" expression (1231). Nash's blankness signals the breach between the two men that punctuates the novel, and anticipates the outcome of Nick's attempt to paint Nash. Directly, Nash declares that, in fact, Julia will come to sit for Nick, and spins the monotonous nonnarratable future:

> Your differences with the beautiful lady will be patched up, and you'll each come round a little and meet the other halfway. Mrs. Dallow will swallow your profession if you'll swallow hers. She'll put up with the pallette if you'll put up with the country-house. It will be a very unusual one in which you won't find a good north room where you can paint. You'll go about with her and do all her friends, all the bishops and ambassadors, and you'll eat your cake and have it, and every one, beginning with your wife, will forget there is anything queer about you, and everything will be for the best in the best of worlds; so that, together—you and she—you'll become a great social institution, and every one will think she has a delightful husband; to say nothing of course of your having a delightful wife. Ah, my dear fellow, you turn pale, and with reason! (1232)

Here James portrays the formation of a "great social institution," Nick's and Julia's marriage, as eviscerating "differences." Nick's paleness answers Nash's blankness; neither sees the other anymore; hence the failure of Nick's portrait: Nash disappears before Nick finishes it, and what is left on the canvas seems to fade away.

But my main point here is that in a strong sense what fades is Nash's labor as a genius, as the agent of therapy; it fades with the fading of the other characters' ability to see it. Indeed, what the novel portrays as disappearing is the mental and emotional work done by people who don't marry, don't have children, don't do jobs broadly understood as work, for those who do (and thus use their own expenses of time and more material currency).[70] Put another way, this fading illuminates the materially different experiences overdetermined by a world universalizing and celebrating differences.

The politics of queer visibility in this novel have to do precisely with this work that Nash does, and which no one (including most of the novel's readers) seems to notice. The willfulness of this ignorance is embodied most forcefully by Nick Dormer's impulsive act, a few pages after what proves his and Nash's final parting: "The first thing Nick made out in the room, when he could distinguish, was Gabriel Nash's portrait, which immediately filled him with unreasoning resentment. He seized it and turned it about; he jammed it back in its corner, with its face against the wall" (1243). Rather than simply exiling Nash, the novel does the work of showing Nick do the work of turning Nash's portrait around to face the wall. James thus renders queerness in a manner different from what Michel Foucault called the "incitement to confess," the instrument of coercion used against Oscar Wilde and central to Foucault's conception of modern sexuality. The novel suggests for critics a way of talking about queerness without having to produce it through confession.

It may be objected that in focusing on labor I am desexualizing queer reading, so I should make it clear that I do not see this as a *more valid* way of pursuing a genealogy of queerness—simply one that opens up some new connections between texts and out to other issues. I have sought to open a connection between the genealogy of male queerness and the history of performing female geniuses, which occupies such a prominent status from the early nineteenth century (at least from de Stael) into what we saw of the critical reception to Jenny Lind and onward into modernism with such novels as Mary Austin's *A Woman of Genius* and Willa Cather's *Song of the Lark* and *Lucy Gayheart*. An area of female genius I have not had time to explore involves the female salon intellectuals, a genealogy extending at a minimum from Margaret Fuller to Gertrude Stein.

The labor of queer genius plays a crucial role in a "modernness" defined as disorganizing and alienating formerly unfragmented forms of individual agency. The social basis of difference/marginality/critical privilege—any of these names might be appropriate in different contexts—is covered over with a veneer of romance, which is essentially what the word genius is capable of doing. By "social basis," I mean that what these figures live as disenfranchisement, exclusion, bias—not getting marriage's benefits in financial as well as cultural capital, for instance (as we see in the attention Nash, in his final salvo to Nick, draws to the "country-house," which will almost inevitably have "a good north room where you can paint")—is rendered iconic as a culturally well-capitalized category. This is a tendency that, like many of this period, aligns homosexuality and Jewishness, as wit and intelligence become characteristics commonly celebrated and romanticized in the culture at large.[71]

Examining the way that work does or does not look has the counterintuitive effect of connecting the figure of genius with a broader range of modern cultural tropes that stand for people who, with widely varying consequences and under widely varying conditions, have seen their labor go unnoticed. We saw an analogous phenomenon earlier in the book, in William Wells Brown's depictions of fancy girls and the anxieties and recognitions they provided him. In fact, it increasingly seems to me that what we see when we look at genius can be a history of people who have suffered the burden of being seen and understood as not working (and *at least* in the case of the tragic mulatta, of neither working nor fitting into the economy neatly enough). I am not suggesting that Nash's experience of neglect and erasure really is the same as that of a person held captive in chattel slavery. But I do think this is a promisng avenue into thinking about the centrality of the relationship between labor and race in the United States.

It is also possible to read Nash's weariness at the end of the novel, in contrast to Miriam's success, as representing James's feeling that Jewish genius is finally integrable to the national symbolic field in a way that queer genius is not—as the real-life case of James's friend Emma Lazarus would indicate: the Statue of Liberty, completed in October 1886, bears her poem "The New Colossus." This integrable quality may even be the source of some of James's anti-Semitism, such as the section of *The American Scene* (the centerpiece of recent critical discussion of James's attitude toward Jews) in which he discusses immigrant Jews of the Lower East Side. The combination of rank anti-Semitic stereotypes and fascination with Yiddish urban culture that characterizes these rich passages makes better sense if we understand James as simultaneously recognizing the cultural vitality of diasporic Jewishness and feeling resentful toward it. One wonders in particular how James might have been sensitive to the relative ease with which the transplanted shtetls of lower Manhattan made visible forms of "traditional" family life, however refracted through lenses of racial and classed alterity.

Ultimately, genius is a useful term for examining cultural politics, rather than simply a mystificatory one, because of the insight the category provides into the politics of deciding what *counts* as labor, especially in the cultural area. The association between genius and Jewishness, and genius and sexuality, may well have originated as a quasi-racial alibi in relation to labor, connecting artistic production by people of color, women, and queers to a fantasy of labor so unalienated that one need not even exert one's will to do it: the energy is merely in the "blood." Similarly, as Brian Selsky has argued, genius would operate for practitioners of the avant garde as a kind of shelter from the criminological-juridicial rhetoric that accuses certain cultural producers—Gertrude Stein, Andy Warhol, or John Cage, for example—of "getting away with" something. In each of these cases, as Selsky points out, the artist's aesthetic marginality was bound up with the marginality of queer sexual identity.[72] I have tracked what I believe to be a history of responses to the anxious skepticism that such figures often inspire, and to the politics that often underlie them. More important, I have attempted to show how a long tradition of American cultural producers has diligently transvalued mass anxieties of this sort into the continuing provocations of genius.

Notes

Introduction

1. Pierre Macherey, *A Theory of Literary Production,* trans. Geoffrey Wall (London: Routledge and Kegan Paul, 1978), 68; Peter Kivy, *The Possessor and the Possessed: Handel, Mozart, Beethoven, and the Idea of Musical Genius* (New Haven, Conn.: Yale University Press, 2001); Harold Bloom, *Genius: A Mosaic of One Hundred Exemplary Creative Minds* (New York: Warner Books, 2002).

2. Cf. Perry Miller, writing in the mid-twentieth century: "It is a commonplace of literary history that the cult of genius came to a special flowering in the early nineteenth century. (We cannot possibly employ the word today with a like solemnity; half the time we use it as an insult.)" Miller, "Emersonian Genius and the American Democracy," *New England Quarterly* 26, no. 2 (1953): 30.

3. Immanuel Kant, "Fine Art Is the Art of Genius" from *Critique of Judgment,* trans. J. C. Meredith, in *Philosophical Writings,* ed. Ernst Behler (New York: Continuum/New German Library, 1999), 224.

4. Andrew Elfenbein, *Romantic Genius: The Prehistory of a Homosexual Role* (New York: Columbia University Press, 1999), and Barbara Will, *Gertrude Stein, Modernism, and the Problem of "Genius"* (Edinburgh: University of Edinburgh Press, 2000).

5. The history of the "culture concept" has been the site of some of the richest work in American studies in recent years, as the diversity of the following examples suggests: Michael Elliot, *The Culture Concept: Writing and Difference in the Age of Realism* (Minneapolis: University of Minnesota Press, 2002); Jonathan Freedman, *The Temple of Culture: Assimilation and Anti-Semitism in Literary Anglo-America* (New York: Oxford University Press, 2000); Susan Hegeman, *Patterns for America: Modernism and the Concept of Culture* (Princeton, N.J.: Princeton University Press, 1999); Mark Manganero, *Culture, 1922: The Emergence of a Concept* (Princeton, N.J.: Princeton University

Press, 2002); Charles Briggs and Richard Bauman, "'The Foundation of All Further Researches': Franz Boas, George Hunt, Native American Texts, and the Construction of Modernity," *American Quarterly* 51 (1999): 479–528; Nancy Bentley, *The Ethnography of Manners: Hawthorne, James, Wharton* (New York: Oxford University Press, 1995). More work remains to be done on both the aesthetic and the social scientific strains of this history; Elliot's book is of particular note because it extends the genealogy of the anthropological notion of culture as far back as the 1880s.

6. On the opposition between commerce and genius in Kant, see Jacques Derrida, "Economimesis," in *The Derrida Reader: Writing Performances,* ed. Julian Wolfreys (Lincoln: University of Nebraska Press, 1998).

7. Hegeman, "Haunted by Mass Culture," *American Literary History,* 12, no. 1 and 2 (Spring/Summer 2000): 309. My use of the term "modernity" here is meant to identify not concrete changes in reality so much as a self-conscious Euro-American understanding of certain changes as fundamentally transformational, an understanding that is itself historical. My thinking here is influenced by Bruno Latour, *We Have Never Been Modern,* trans. Catherine Porter (Cambridge, Mass.: Harvard University Press, 1993).

8. My larger point here is not that genius is a better focus than authorship, but that there is no need to oppose genius and authorship. Undoing this opposition may, I think, prove useful in addressing some of the problems McGill and Romero have raised with the category of the "author," particularly in historicist and ideological critique. According to McGill, "historicist" criticism "frequently invokes the author's life as a force field on which economic influences, understood as a variety of incitements and compulsions, are clearly inscribed." See McGill's *American Literature and the Culture of Reprinting, 1834–1853* (Philadelphia: University of Pennsylvania Press, 2002), 18. Similarly, Romero writes that in late-twentieth-century discussions of antebellum U.S. literature, "Literary value seems to depend upon the identification of idealized agents (authors or intellectuals) who stand outside the social and political ideologies of their time." See Romero's *Home Fronts: Domesticity and Its Critics in the Antebellum United States* (Durham, N.C.: Duke University Press, 1997), 5.

9. Pierre Bourdieu, *The Rules of Art: Genesis and Structure of the Literary Field,* trans. Susan Emanuel (Stanford, Calif.: Stanford University Press, 1992), 248.

10. On "free labor," see the classic text by Eric Foner, *Free Soil, Free Labor, Free Men: The Ideology of the Republican Party before the Civil War* (New York: Oxford University Press, 1970); for analysis of its overlapping ideologies of race and class, see David Roediger, *The Wages of Whiteness: Race and the Making of the American Working Class* (London: Verso, 1999). Roediger's most recent book contains a particularly rich, useful account of black abolitionists' interpretation of different employments of "free labor." See his *Colored White: Transcending the Racial Past* (Berkeley and Los Angeles: University of California Press, 2002).

11. Hofstadter, *Anti-Intellectualism in American Life* (New York: Vintage, 1963), 256.

12. Hofstadter, *The Paranoid Style in American Politics and Other Essays* (Cambridge, Mass.: Harvard University Press, 1996).

13. Howells, "Editor's Study," *Harper's New Monthly Magazine* 72, no. 430 (March 1886): 649.

14. Howells's view of genius here begins to coincide with aspects of the work of the American criminologist (and protégé of the famous Italian criminologist Cesare Lombroso) Arthur MacDonald, who describes an unrepentant man imprisoned for sex acts: "Instead of being repugnant to the accusation of sodomy, he maintained it was a mark of good taste, and that in general crime was permitted to some men, for they were free from the law." MacDonald then discusses what he sees as the deepening complicity between literary aesthetics and "deviant" sexual behavior: "Some of the letters and poems of Ceresa, Byron, and Foscolo show traces of the remorse and violence with which they tried to rid themselves of bad passions. Ceresa was a sodomite priest, who paints in vivid colors his struggle against evil. So Byron and Toscolo picture crime and adultery, but are irritated, if taken too literally." See MacDonald, *Criminology,* 2nd ed. (New York: Funk & Wagnalls, 1893), 118.

15. Henry James, *Novels, 1886–1890: The Princess Cassamassima, The Reverberator, The Tragic Muse* (New York: Library of America, 1989), 1229.

16. Armstrong and Tennenhouse, *The Imaginary Puritan: Literature, Intellectual Labor, and the Origins of Personal Life* (Berkeley and Los Angeles: University of California Press, 1992), 12; Bourdieu, *The Field of Cultural Production,* ed. Randall Johnson (New York: Columbia University Press, 1993), 35.

17. Or, as Mary Poovey has written in specific reference to the treatment of aesthetics in late-twentieth-century literary criticism, "A properly historical analysis would uncover not some truth of economics behind the self-justifications of aesthetics but the process by which the appearance of autonomous realms was generated from what was actually a continuum of human activity." See Poovey, "Aesthetics and Political Economy in the Eighteenth Century: The Place of Gender in the Social Constitution of Knowledge," in *Aesthetics and Ideology,* ed. George Levine (New Brunswick, N.J.: Rutgers University Press, 1994).

In addition to Bourdieu, the post-Marxist work of Michael Denning has been very productive for my thinking about genius as an object of study. Denning's revision of the labor theory of value into a "labor theory of culture" casts light on kinds of work that embody "the very resistance to becoming labor power . . . the contradictory realm of work in the shadow of value." In other words, his formulation is concerned with the appearance of labor in the theater of social relations. For instance, referring to "the promise of play, of unalienated labor," in "classical German aesthetics," Denning suggests asking: "How does labor get turned into beauty, particularly since we usually don't want to look at it? Performance is always tied to a strict economy of when and when not to show them that you're sweating. How do the rhythms of work become the rhythms of art?" See Denning, *Culture in the Age of Three Worlds* (London: Verso, 2004), 95–96.

18. Bourdieu, *Field of Cultural Production,* 36. Appadurai, introduction to *The Social Life of Things: Commodities in Cultural Perspective* (Cambridge: Cambridge University Press, 1986). On the production of belief in state power, see Michael Taussig, "State Fetishism," in *Border Fetishisms,* ed. Patricia Speyer (New York: Routledge, 1998).

19. Robert Weimann, "Text, Author-Function, and Appropriation in Modern Narrative: Toward a Sociology of Representation," *Critical Inquiry* 14 (Spring 1988): 440. Henry James's *The Tragic Muse* (1890) figures importantly in Weimann's argument, as it does in mine.

20. Charles Sellers describes this "revolution" as essentially the end of challenges to the hegemony of bourgeois capitalism. See *The Market Revolution: Jacksonian America, 1815–1846* (New York: Oxford University Press, 1991) 363. On the "print revolution" and the increasing school enrollments, see *Market Revolution,* 367–73.

21. See, for example, Ronald Zboray, *A Fictive People: Antebellum Economic Development and the American Reading Public* (New York: Oxford University Press, 1993).

22. See McGill, *American Literature and the Culture of Reprinting, 1834–1853,* and Jay Grossman, *Reconstituting the American Renaissance: Emerson, Whitman, and the Politics of Representation* (Durham, N.C.: Duke University Press, 2003).

23. Warner, *The Letters of the Republic: Publication and the Public Sphere in Eighteenth-Century America* (Cambridge, Mass.: Harvard University Press, 1990), 54.

24. Raymond Williams, *Culture and Society, 1780–1950* (New York: Columbia University Press, 1983), 300.

25. Michael Warner, "The Mass Public and the Mass Subject," in *Habermas and the Public Sphere,* ed. Craig Calhoun (Cambridge, Mass.: MIT Press, 1991), 385; Lauren Berlant, *The Anatomy of National Fantasy* (Chicago: University of Chicago Press, 1991); "National Brands/National Body," in *Comparative American Identities,* ed. Hortense Spillers (New York: Routledge, 1990); Ann Cvetkovich, *Mixed Feelings: Feminism, Sensationalism, and Victorian Mass Culture* (New Brunswick, N.J.: Rutgers University Press, 1992); Jonathan Elmer, *Reading at the Social Limit: Affect, Mass Culture, and Edgar Allan Poe* (Stanford, Calif.: Stanford University Press, 1995).

26. Robert Fanuzzi's *Abolition's Public Sphere* (Minneapolis: University of Minnesota Press, 2003) gets into some of these issues, but a full account of abolitionism's role in U.S. cultural history has yet to be written. This is particularly the case because of the continuing tendency of many Americanists to identify abolitionism and the antebellum era with national premodernity. See, for example, Louis Menand, *The Metaphysical Club: A Story of Ideas in America* (New York: Farrar, Strauss & Giroux, 2001).

27. See Kristen Silva Gruesz, *Ambassadors of Culture: The Transamerican Origins of Latino Writing* (Princeton, N.J.: Princeton University Press, 2002); Paul Giles, *Transatlantic Insurrections: British Culture and the Formation of American Literature, 1730–1860* (Philadelphia: University of Pennsylvania Press, 2001) and *Virtual Americas: Transnational Fictions and the Transatlantic Imaginary* (Durham, N.C.: Duke University Press, 2002); and David Shields, *Civil Tongues and Polite Letters in British America* (Chapel Hill: University of North Carolina Press, 1997). These books suggest the inadequacy of Sacvan Bercovitch's schematic opposition of American and European notions of genius. Shields's work is particularly notable for its treatment of aesthetics and gentility as a local, lived modality in the metropolitan centers of the proto-nation.

28. Sacvan Bercovitch, *The Puritan Origins of the American Self* (New Haven, Conn.: Yale University Press, 1972), 173.

29. See Phillip Nicoloff, *Emerson on Race and History* (New York: Columbia University Press, 1961), and James Chandler, "Representative Men, Spirits of the Age, and Other Romantic Types," in *Romantic Revolutions: Criticism and Theory,* ed. Kenneth R. Johnson, Gilbert Chaitin, Karen Hanson, and Herbert Marks (Bloomington: Indiana University Press, 1990); also David Lloyd and Paul Thomas on similar issues in *Culture and the State* (New York: Routledge, 1995).

30. From the work of David Eltis, as cited by Joan Dayan, "Romance and Race," in *The Columbia History of the American Novel,* ed. Emory Elliott (New York: Columbia University Press, 1991), 92. The relevant study is Eltis, *Economic Growth and the Ending of the Transatlantic Slave Trade* (New York: Oxford University Press, 1987).

31. Ralph Ellison, "Change the Joke and Slip the Yoke," from *Shadow and Act*; reprinted in *The Collected Essays of Ralph Ellison* (New York: Modern Library, 1995), 107–8.

32. This shift becomes clearer when we compare moments, separated by nearly half a century, in which William Wordsworth and Nathaniel Hawthorne portray the degradingness of the mass production of literature. In his 1800 preface to the second edition of *Lyrical Ballads,* Wordsworth writes, "The invaluable works of our elder writers, I had almost said the words of Shakespeare and Milton, are driven into neglect by frantic novels, sickly and stupid German tragedies, and deluges of idle and extravagant stories in verse" (see *Selected Poems and Prefaces,* ed. Jack Stillinger [Boston: Houghton Mifflin, 1965], 449). But Wordsworth's hostility lacks the sense permeating Hawthorne's famous comment indicting "damn'd women scribblers" that his books are competing for purchasers with the works of those excessively productive female authors.

33. See Bourdieu, *Field of Cultural Production* and *The Rules of Art.*

34. My sense of the historicity of sexuality is based on Michel Foucault's *History of Sexuality,* vol. 1, *An Introduction,* trans. Robert Hurley (New York: Vintage, 1978). An important recent study that proceeds in a manner that

parallels what I am describing here is Siobhan Somerville's *Queering the Color Line: Race and the Invention of Homosexuality* (Durham, N.C.: Duke University Press, 1998).

35. The "*Atlantic* group" is a phrase I borrow from Nancy Glazener, *Reading for Realism: The History of a U.S. Literary Institution, 1850–1910* (Durham, N.C.: Duke University Press, 1997). "Artistic and intellectual activities" is the phrase Raymond Williams uses to describe one strand in modern conceptions of *culture*; see *Keywords: A Vocabulary of Culture and Society* (New York: Oxford University Press, 1983) and *The Long Revolution* (Peterborough, Ont.: Broadview Press, 2001).

36. Henry James, *The American,* ed. William Spengemann (New York: Penguin Books, 1986), 50.

37. See Richard Brodhead, "Starting Out in the 1860s," in *Cultures of Letters: Scenes of Reading and Instruction in Nineteenth-Century America* (Chicago: University of Chicago Press, 1993).

38. *The Alternative Alcott,* ed. Elaine Showalter (New Brunswick: Rutgers University Press, 1988), 207.

39. Notably, Ralph Ellison calls this novel exceptional among classic late-nineteenth-century American novels for its depiction of the nation's "inversion of its moral values" in the period following the collapse of radical Reconstruction. See Ellison, "Stephen Crane and the Mainstream of American Fiction," in *Collected Essays,* 119.

40. Walter Benn Michaels sees in the early-twentieth-century United States "two important shifts in racial logic, one that emphasized not the inferiority of 'alien' races but their 'difference,' and a second that began to represent difference in cultural instead of political (and in addition to) racial terms." Michaels, *Our America: Nativism, Modernism, and Pluralism* (Durham, N.C.: Duke University Press, 1995), 11.

41. The phrase is Arjun Appadurai's in "Commodities and the Politics of Value," *The Social Life of Things.*

42. Freedman, *The Temple of Culture,* 43.

43. Ladbroke Black, *Some Queer People* (London: Sampson Low, n.d.) Thanks to Christina Zwarg for bringing this book to my attention several years ago. This line of my thinking was also deeply influenced by Brian Selsky's excellent essay on Gertrude Stein and Andy Warhol, "I Dream of Genius," in *Pop Out: Queer Warhol,* ed. Jennifer Doyle, Jonathan Flatley, and José Muñoz (Durham, N.C.: Duke University Press, 1995). Another important essay in a similar vein is Richard Poirier's "The Question of Genius," in his *The Renewal of Literature: Emersonian Reflections* (New York: Random House, 1987).

44. The book's final title nevertheless does allude to American popular music, a twist on "Trouble in Mind," the name of a traditional performed by a pantheon of artists including Big Bill Broonzy, Sister Rosetta Tharpe, Nina Simone, Janis Joplin, and Bob Dylan.

1. The Geography of Genius in Emerson, Fuller, and Douglass

1. Ralph Waldo Emerson, *Essays and Lectures* (New York: Library of America, 1983), 492. Further citations of Emerson's essays and lectures are generally from this volume and appear in the body of the text.

2. Michel de Certeau, *The Practice of Everyday Life,* trans. Steven Rendall (Berkeley and Los Angeles: University of California Press, 1984), xi.

3. Emersonian formulations in de Certeau such as the idea of reading as a form of "silent production" indicate a kinship between the two thinkers worthy of further analysis. The scholar who has made the most effective use of de Certeau in relation to the antebellum United States is Russ Castronovo, in *Fathering the Nation: American Genealogies of Slavery and Freedom* (Berkeley and Los Angeles: University of California Press, 1995).

4. A concomitant change is evident in the implication, for Emerson, of the simultaneously qualitative and quantitative category "great." In "History," from *Essays: First Series* (1841), he had assured "each man" that he was "greater than all the geography and all the government of the world." See *Essays and Lectures,* 239–40.

5. Figure from Thomas R. Hietala, *Manifest Design: Anxious Aggrandizement in Jacksonian America* (Ithaca, N.Y.: Cornell University Press, 1985), 1.

6. See Edward L. Ayers et al., *All Over the Map: Rethinking American Regions* (Baltimore, Md.: Johns Hopkins University Press, 1996).

7. Sources on "Young America" include Perry Miller, *The Raven and the Whale: The War of Words and Wits in the Era of Poe and Melville* (New York: Harcourt, Brace, 1956), and Edward L. Widmer, *Young America: The Flowering of Democracy in New York City* (New York: Oxford University Press, 1999). For an incisive reading of the group's nationalism, see Meredith McGill, "Poe, Literary Nationalism, and National Identity" in *The American Face of Edgar Allan Poe,* ed. Shawn Rosenheim and Stephen Rachman (Baltimore, Md.: Johns Hopkins University Press, 1995).

8. For a comprehensive account of the bifurcation of cultural production and labor within modern commercial capitalism, see David Lloyd and Paul Thomas, *Culture and the State* (New York: Routledge, 1995). As I noted in the introduction, my use of the category "culture" in this chapter is a necessary anachronism. My understanding of the term draws mainly from Raymond Williams's three-tiered account of the term in *The Long Revolution* (Peterborough, Ont.: Broadview Press, 2001 [1961]), as well as from Michael Denning's succinct account of the "modern" purpose of the term, across aesthetic and anthropological discourses, "to name those places where the commodity does not yet rule: the arts, leisure, and unproductive luxury consumption of revenues by the accumulators, and the ways of life of so-called primitive peoples." See Denning, *Culture in the Age of Three Worlds* (London: Verso, 2004), 79. On the politics of spatial rhetoric in general, see Neil Smith and Cindi Katz, "Grounding Metaphor: Towards a Spatialized Politics," in *Place and the*

Politics of Identity, ed. Michael Keith and Steve Pile (London and New York: Routledge, 1993), 67–83.

9. Particularly influential sources for my understanding of these matters are Richard Brodhead, *Cultures of Letters: Scenes of Reading and Instruction in Nineteenth Century America* (Chicago: University of Chicago Press, 1993), and Meredith McGill, *American Literature and the Culture of Reprinting, 1834–1853* (Philadelphia: University of Pennsylvania Press, 2003).

10. Studies useful for the history of the lyceum movement include Joan Shelley Rubin, *The Making of Middlebrow Culture* (Chapel Hill: University of North Carolina Press, 1992); James Perrin Warren, *Cultures of Eloquence: Oratory and Reform in Antebellum America* (University Park: Pennsylvania State University Press, 1999); Carl Bode, *The American Lyceum: Town Meeting of the Mind* (New York: Oxford University Press, 1956).

11. The sixty-thousand figure is from Frank W. Scott, "Newspapers, 1775–1860," in *The Cambridge History of English and American Literature in Eighteen Volumes,* vol. 16, ed. A. W. Ward et al. (New York: G. P. Putnam's Sons, 1907–1921), 35. Michael Schudson offers the one-million figure, although it is not precisely clear how he has come up with this estimate. See Schudson, *The Power of News* (Cambridge, Mass.: Harvard University Press, 1995), 44.

12. See, for example, Henry Louis Gates Jr., "Binary Oppositions in Chapter 1 of *Narrative of the Life of Frederick Douglass, an American Slave, Written by Himself,*" in *Critical Essays on Frederick Douglass,* ed. William L. Andrews (Boston: G. K. Hall, 1991), 83–84.

13. Douglass, *Narrative of the Life of Frederick Douglass, An American Slave, Written by Himself,* ed. William L. Andrews and William McFeely (New York: W. W. Norton, 1997), 18. Page numbers of further citations are from this edition and will appear in the body of the text. The passage in question is often referred to as the "sorrow songs" section of the book. Critics such as Henry Louis Gates Jr., W. J. T. Mitchell, Fred Moten, and Kimberly Benston have discussed it in some detail. See Benston, *Performing Blackness: Enactments of African-American Modernism* (London: Routledge, 2000); Gates, *The Signifying Monkey: A Theory of Afro-American Literary Criticism* (New York: Oxford University Press, 1988); W. J. T. Mitchell, "Narrative, Memory, and Slavery," in *Cultural Artifacts and the Production of Meaning: The Page, the Image, the Body* (Ann Arbor: University of Michigan Press, 1994); Fred Moten, *In the Break: The Aesthetics of the Black Radical Tradition* (Minneapolis: University of Minnesota Press, 2003).

14. Indeed, as Sterling Stuckey and other scholars have demonstrated, slave artisanship on the Southern plantation had a particularly powerful symbolic significance for the slave population at large, maintaining the presence of many African forms of technical knowledge and practice, and serving as a site at which slaves routinely taught white workers and overseers certain skills. See Sterling Stuckey, "'Ironic Tenacity': Frederick Douglass's Seizure of the Dialectic," in *Frederick Douglass: New Literary and Historical Essays,* ed. Eric J. Sundquist (Cambridge: Cambridge University Press, 1990), 23–46. For a fas-

cinating study of a similar dynamic around slave *agri*culture, see Judith A. Carney, *Black Rice: The African Origins of Rice Cultivation in the Americas* (Cambridge, Mass.: Harvard University Press, 2001).

15. Also see Paul Gilroy on the role of mobility for nineteenth-century black intellectuals, such as Martin Delany, in *The Black Atlantic: Modernity and Double Consciousness* (Cambridge, Mass.: Harvard University Press, 1995).

16. Kimberly Benston describes this space usefully as "A critical and contradictory arena, bounded by commerce but nurturing an economy of transgression, [a space that] destabilizes the unity of power without projecting some simple negating structure of counterpower." *Performing Blackness,* 295.

17. One might understand this passage as a critique of some of the guiding assumptions of "immediatist" abolition, a label applied to groups and individuals (including Douglass) associated with William Lloyd Garrison.

18. Douglass, *My Bondage and My Freedom,* 220; emphasis in original.

19. On this journey see the recent collection *Liberating Sojourn: Frederick Douglass and Transatlantic Reform,* ed. Alan J. Rice and Martin Crawford (Athens, Ga.: University of Georgia Press, 1999).

20. James McCune Smith, introduction to Frederick Douglass, *My Bondage and My Freedom,* ed. William L. Andrews (Urbana: University of Illinois Press, 1987), 14.

21. Margaret Fuller recounts this incident in the posthumously published *At Home and Abroad; or, Things and Thoughts in America and Europe* (New York: Tribune Association, 1869), 120.

22. Len Gougeon notes that Emerson did in 1852 "contribute a poem, 'Freedom,' to an antislavery gift book entitled *Autographs for Freedom,* which was sold to make money for Frederick Douglass's newly established antislavery newspaper." This does not tell us, of course, whether he had read Douglass or had merely paid attention to him as a public figure. See Gougeon, "Historical Background," *Emerson's Antislavery Writings,* ed. Len Gougeon and Joel Myerson (New Haven, Conn.: Yale University Press, 1995), xli.

23. Zwarg, "The Work of Trauma: Fuller, Douglass, and Emerson on the Border of Ridicule," *Studies in Romanticism* 41, no. 1 (Spring 2002): 65–88.

24. *The Journals of Ralph Waldo Emerson,* vol. 9, ed. Ralph H. Orth and Alfred R. Ferguson (Cambridge, Mass.: Belknap Press, Harvard University Press, 1971), 125.

25. *Journals of Ralph Waldo Emerson,* vol. 9, 83.

26. Robert Fanuzzi, "The Trouble with Douglass's Body," *American Transcendental Quarterly* 13, no. 1 (March 1999): 27–49.

27. Both Douglass and Brown, like many other African-American male cultural authorities, were repeatedly dogged by claims and insinuations that they had had sexual relations with white, female abolitionists, in both the United States and Britain. For a particularly interesting example of this in Douglass's case, see R. J. Blackett, *Building an Antislavery Wall: Black Americans in the Atlantic Abolitionist Movement, 1830–1860* (Baton Rouge: Louisiana State University Press, 1983).

28. An example of this, in a book that on the whole I have found very useful, is Jonathan Elmer's contrast between this image and the liquid eyes of Poe's "Ligeia" in *Reading at the Social Limit: Poe, Affect, and Mass Culture* (Stanford, Calif.: Stanford University Press, 1995). Although Christopher Newfield works largely with later Emerson texts, his point that "Emerson's sense of consummation derives from feeling permeated by alien fluids" resonates with my sense of his increasing association of cultural labor with physicality. See *The Emerson Effect: Individualism and Submission in America* (Chicago: University of Chicago Press, 1996), 118.

29. See Charles H. Walcott, "Address on the Origin and Growth of the Concord Lyceum," in *The Massachusetts Lyceum during the American Renaissance: Materials for the Study of the Oral Tradition in American Letters: Emerson, Thoreau, Hawthorne, and Other New England Lecturers,* ed. Kenneth Walter Cameron (Hartford, Conn.: Transcendental Books, 1969), 30.

30. Mary Kupjec Cayton, "The Making of an American Prophet: Emerson, His Audiences, and the Rise of the Culture Industry in Nineteenth-Century America," *Ralph Waldo Emerson: A Collection of Critical Essays,* ed. Lawrence Buell, New Century Views (Englewood, N.J.: Prentice Hall, 1993), 98.

31. The lyceum, then, was a cultural space in which figures who were attributed intellectual and cultural authority were taken up along the same lines as in the emerging modern category of "celebrity." We explore this phenomenon in more depth in the next chapter.

32. *Journals of Ralph Waldo Emerson,* vol. 9, 272.

33. See Cayton, "The Making of an American Prophet"; Donald M. Scott, "The Popular Lecture and the Creation of a Public in Mid-Nineteenth-Century America," *Journal of American History* 66 (1980): 791–809; Carl Bode, *The American Lyceum.*

34. Just before coming to the *Tribune,* Fuller had published her best-known work, *Woman in the Nineteenth Century* (1844), in which she disserted upon sexual difference as a phenomenon shaped by cultural, historical, and philosophical contexts. This book reflected the scholarliness with which she had gained her reputation among the Transcendentalists, and the New England intellectual world more generally. With *Summer on the Lakes* (1843), she produced a work of travel writing that was to a significant degree an early ethnography of native American culture in Wisconsin and Minnesota.

35. Judith Mattson Bean and Joel Myerson, introduction to *Margaret Fuller, Critic: Writings from the New-York Tribune, 1844–1846,* ed. Bean and Myerson (New York: Columbia University Press, 2000), xxx.

36. Repr. in *The Letters of Margaret Fuller,* vol. 4, *1845–1847,* ed. Robert N. Hudspeth (Ithaca, N.Y.: Cornell University Press, 1987), 39; and in *Memoirs* 2: 164. The letter is undated.

37. She also reviewed (positively) Herman Melville's first novel, *Typee.*

38. She had mentioned Douglass in a still earlier article, a review of the abolitionist yearbook the *Liberty Bell,* which included a piece by Douglass. She called the contributions by Douglass and other "men of color," "the most unan-

swerable arguments in favor of the *capacities* of the African race. Their claims need no argument." *Margaret Fuller, Critic,* 29, and *Tribune,* January 7, 1845.

39. Zwarg, "The Work of Trauma: Fuller, Douglass, and Emerson on the Border of Ridicule," *Studies in Romanticism* 41, no. 1 (Spring 2002), 65–88.

40. Buckley, "Culture, Class, and Place in Antebellum New York," in *Power, Culture, and Place: Essays on New York City,* ed. John Hull Mollenkopf (New York: Russell Sage Foundation, 1988), 25.

41. Kristen Silva Gruesz, *Ambassadors of Culture: The Transamerican Origins of Latino Writing* (Princeton, N.J.: Princeton University Press, 2002), 10.

42. Raymond Willisams, *The Long Revolution* (Peterborough, Ont.: Broadview Press, 2001), 57.

43. Ross Posnock, *Color and Culture: Black Writers and the Making of the Modern Intellectual* (Cambridge, Mass.: Harvard University Press, 2000), 297–98n3.

44. As a female, and indeed feminist, literary figure, her relationship to Douglass and antislavery differed strongly from the more well-known affective, imaginary, and rhetorical connections that Karen Sanchez-Eppler's scholarship has so usefully analyzed. See Sanchez-Eppler, *Touching Liberty: Abolition, Feminism, and the Politics of the Body* (Berkeley and Los Angeles: University of California Press, 1993).

45. Margaret Fuller, "Victory," *New-York Tribune,* May 21, 1846, 1, repr. in *Margaret Fuller, Critic.* For a particularly cogent, transnationally framed critique of slavery and colonialism, see Fuller's piece for the *Tribune* titled and dated "First of August, 1845," repr. in ibid., 183.

46. See Zwarg, "The Work of Trauma," for provocative speculations about the erotics of Fuller's relation to Douglass.

47. Margaret Fuller, "Review of Narrative of Frederick Douglass," *New-York Tribune,* June 10, 1845, 1; emphasis added.

48. Fuller, review of *Narrative,* 1. The paragraph continues: "It is to be remarked in the writings both of Soulié and Dumas, full of faults, but glowing with plastic life and fertile in invention. The same torrid energy and saccharine fulness may be felt in the writings of this Douglass, though his life, being one of action or resistance, has been less favorable to *such* powers than one of a more joyous flow might have been." Fuller cites Alexander Kinmont and "the late Dr. Channing" as Anglo-American intellectuals who hold these views, derived generally from the writings of Herder, with which Fuller was familiar from her studies in German literature and philosophy.

49. Fuller, "Entertainments of the Past Winter," *Dial* 3, no. 1 (1842): 52. Quoted in Eric Lott, *Love and Theft: Blackface Minstrelsy and the American Working Class* (New York: Oxford University Press, 1993), 16.

50. For a very differently framed reading of the review, see Stephen Mailloux, "Misreading as Historical Act: Cultural Rhetoric, Bible Politics, and Fuller's 1845 Review of Douglass's Narrative," in *Readers in History: Nineteenth-Century American Literature and the Contexts of Response,* ed. James L. Macher (Baltimore, Md.: Johns Hopkins University, 1993), 3–31.

51. In a sense, here Douglass's work does speak to Fuller along lines similar to those described by Sanchez-Eppler, as a metaphor for social constrictions and pressures on female bodies—a problematic sympathy, collapsing differences of racial formation, space, time, and so on.

52. Margaret Fuller, "Review of *Napoleon and His Marshals* by J. T. Headley," *New-York Tribune,* June 18, 1846, 1.

53. Fuller, "Review of *Napoleon,*" 1; emphases added. Later in the review, Fuller labels this "partial" criticism, a term that finds a provocative echo in Russ Castronovo's reading of W. E. B. DuBois in Castonovo's essay on Enlightenment liberalism and the politics of interdisciplinarity, "Within the Veil of Interdisciplinary Knowledge? Jefferson, DuBois, and the Negation of Politics," *New Literary History* 31, no. 4 (2000): 781–804.

54. Ann Douglas, *The Feminization of American Culture* (New York: Avon Books, 1978).

55. Such was certainly the case when Fuller was living in New England and conducted a famous series of "Conversations" with women. But this reputation continued after she entered the world of journalism; see, for example, Horace Greeley, *Recollections of a Busy Life: Including Reminiscenses of American Politics and Politicians* (New York, 1869).

56. *Margaret Fuller, Critic,* 227.

2. Cosmopolitan Whiteness

1. Peter G. Buckley, "Culture, Class, and Place in Antebellum New York," *Power, Culture, and Place: Essays on New York City,* ed. John Hull Mollenkopf (New York: Russell Sage Foundation, 1988), 37.

2. On this history, see Mark N. Grant, *Maestros of the Pen: A History of Classical Music Criticism in America* (Boston: Northeastern University Press, 1998). On Dwight specifically, see Michael Broyles, *"Music of the Highest Class": Elitism and Populism in Antebellum Boston* (New Haven, Conn.: Yale University Press, 1992), and Ora Saloman, *Beethoven's Symphonies and J. S. Dwight: The Birth of American Music Criticism* (Boston: Northeastern University Press, 1995).

3. *Tribune,* September 12, 1850, 1.

4. Lawrence Levine, *Highbrow/Lowbrow: The Emergence of Cultural Hierarchy in Nineteenth-Century America* (Cambridge, Mass.: Harvard University Press, 1988), 9.

5. Raymond Williams, *The Long Revolution* (Peterborough, Ont.: Broadview Press, 2001), 57.

6. The details of Lind's tour have been described extensively in scholarship on P. T. Barnum, who arranged the visit and managed it during the first few months of appearances. Yet the emphasis on Lind as a chapter in Barnum's biography has obscured the seriousness with which her performances

were taken and the tour's broader significance for historicizing practices of cultural consumption in the nineteenth-century United States. Period documents recounting the history of the tour include Willis, *Memoranda of the Life of Jenny Lind* (Philadelphia: Robert E. Peterson, 1851); Charles Rosenberg, *Jenny Lind in America* (New York: Stringer & Townsend, 1851); P. T. Barnum, *Struggles and Triumphs; or, The Life of P. T. Barnum, Written by Himself* (New York: Knopf, 1927). More recent analyses of the tour include: John Dizikes, *Opera in America: A Cultural History* (New Haven, Conn.: Yale University Press, 1996); Sherry Lee Linkon, "Reading Lind Mania: Print Culture and the Nineteenth-Century Construction of American Audiences," *Book History* 1, no. 1 (1998): 94–106; Lowell Gallagher, "Jenny Lind and the Voice of America," *En Travesti: Women, Gender Subversion, Opera,* ed. Corinne E. Blackmer and Patricia Juliana Smith (New York: Columbia University Press, 1995), 190–215; W. Porter Ware and Thaddeus C. Lockard Jr., *P. T. Barnum Presents Jenny Lind: The American Tour of the Swedish Nightingale* (Baton Rouge: Louisiana State University Press, 1980); Bluford Adams, *E Pluribus Barnum: The Great Showman and the Making of U.S. Popular Culture* (Minneapolis: University of Minnesota Press, 1997). Of particular note is the book *Jenny Lind* by the literary critic and historian Edward Wagenknecht, who wrote books about Henry James, Harriet Beecher Stowe, and Willa Cather, among other American authors. See Wagenknecht, *Jenny Lind* (Boston and New York: Houghton Mifflin, 1931).

7. Peter Buckley writes: "This period encompassed the highest decennial rate of urbanization ever experienced by an American city: an almost ninefold increase in population, from a town containing 120,000 people to a metropolitan area of over one million. New York established and maintained both mercantile and manufacturing supremacy over its rivals, Baltimore, Philadelphia, and Boston." In "Culture, Class, and Place," 25.

8. See Levine, *Highbrow/Lowbrow,* 64–68. Also see John Kasson, *Rudeness and Civility: Manners in Nineteenth-Century Urban America* (New York: Noonday Press, 1991).

9. Peter Buckley reads Barnum's entertainment projects and Frederick Law Olmstead's Central Park as two different ways of addressing this "need."

10. The historical context of their work calls for situating these critics' reception of Lind within what Meredith McGill calls "the resistance a republican theory of authorship can offer to the forward march of possessive individualism." McGill, "The Matter of the Text: Commerce, Print Culture, and the Authority of the State in American Copyright Law," *American Literary History* 9, no. 1 (Spring 1997): 24. On eighteenth-century republicanism, see Michael Warner, *The Letters of the Republic: Publication and the Public Sphere in Eighteenth-Century America* (Cambridge, Mass.: Harvard University Press, 1990). On the persistence and transformation of eighteenth-century notions of publicity, see Jay Grossman, *Reconstituting the American Renaissance: Emerson, Whitman, and the Politics of Representation* (Durham, N.C.:

Duke University, 2003); and Glenn Hendler, *Public Sentiments: Structures of Feeling in Nineteenth-Century American Literature* (Chapel Hill: University of North Carolina Press, 2001).

11. Eric Lott, *Love and Theft: Blackface Minstrelsy and the American Working Class* (New York: Oxford University Press, 1993), 98.

12. Levine, *Highbrow/Lowbrow,* 120. The Dwight quotation is from *Dwight's Journal of Music,* October 4, 1873, 102.

13. *Tribune,* September 9, 1850, 1.

14. *Tribune,* September 12, 1850, 1.

15. For an extended reading along these lines, see Lowell Gallagher, "Jenny Lind and the Voice of America."

16. Reginald Horsman identifies an emergent interest in Scandinavia and Norse tradition among Northeastern intellectuals in the 1840s as one element of the emergence of "Anglo-Saxonism" on a large scale in the United States. This interest was fortified by Thomas Carlyle's inclusion of a chapter on Norse gods in "The Hero as Divinity" in *Heroes and Hero-Worship* (1841), a book read widely by erudite Americans and influential on Emerson's *Representative Men.* But it was given a particularly nationalist spin by the increasing interest in the Viking exploration of North America, and the possibility, entertained by many, that Norse navigators had sailed as far south as what was now New England. John Greenleaf Whittier and Henry Wadsworth Longfellow were among the writers most taken with Scandinavian history and literature, but James Russell Lowell in 1855 transformed this fascination into a historical fantasy in verse, "The Voyage to Vinland," in which Leif Ericson sails as far down the coast of North America as Boston Harbor. Popular Swedish novelist (and abolition supporter) Frederika Bremer, touring the United States, introduced Lind and Longfellow, who met three more times; Longfellow also attended several of her Boston concerts. See Andrew Hilen, *Longfellow and Scandinavia* (New Haven, Conn.: Yale University Press, 1947), and Horsman, *Race and Manifest Destiny,* 180–81. See also Erik Ingvar Thurin, *The American Discovery of the Norse: An Episode in Nineteenth-Century American Literature* (Lewisburg, Penn.: Bucknell University Press, 1999).

17. Richard Dyer, *White* (London and New York: Routledge, 1997), 45.

18. Much of my sense of the ideological configuration of these publications is drawn from Alexander Saxton, *The White Republic: Class Politics and Mass Culture in the Nineteenth-Century United States* (London: Verso, 1990).

19. Lawrence Levine uses part of this passage to argue that the New York press's coverage of Lind's first concerts, including one of Dwight's later articles, constitute an early sign of a historical pattern by which "the ideology of culture assumed ethnic and racial dimensions" (*Highbrow/Lowbrow,* 219). Levine describes this passage as anticipating the racial politics underlying the split between "high brow" and "low brow" culture, a rhetoric for describing cultural production articulated more fully later in the century.

20. *Tribune,* September 18, 1850, 1.

21. Matthew Frye Jacobson, *Whiteness of a Different Color: European Im-*

migrants and the Alchemy of Race (Cambridge, Mass.: Harvard University Press, 1998), 26.

22. See Grant, *Maestros of the Pen.*

23. Most likely, the article was written by the *Herald*'s editor, James Gordon Bennett, who wrote an editorial about Lind the day before her first Castle Garden concert, from which P. T. Barnum quotes at length in his autobiography, *Struggles and Triumphs.*

24. Until recently, Willis has been treated as something of an oddity in the antebellum literary world, despite his prolific production of writing (mostly travel writing and essays) and his editorial oversight of serials such as the New York *Evening Mirror* and the *Home Journal.* Thomas Baker's recent book-length study provides an interesting account of his career, and is particularly good on Willis's involvement in a scandal with Edwin Forrest, the actor and one of the main players in the Astor Place Opera House conflict. Unaccountably, however, Baker does not mention Willis's fascination with Lind, or his writing on her. See Thomas Baker, *Sentiment and Celebrity: Nathaniel Parker Willis and the Trials of Literary Fame* (New York: Oxford University Press, 1999). For other compelling analyses of Willis, see Hendler, *Public Sentiments,* and in particular two essays by Sandra Tomc: "An Idle Industry: Nathaniel Parker Willis and the Workings of Literary Leisure," *American Quarterly* 49, no. 4 (1997): 780–805; and "Restyling an Old World: Nathaniel Parker Willis and Metropolitan Fashion in the Antebellum United States," *Representations* 85 (Winter 2004): 98–124.

25. Quoted in Elisa Tamarkin, "Black Anglophilia; or, The Sociability of Antislavery," *American Literary History* 14, no. 3 (2002): 459.

26. *Home Journal* article excerpted in Nathaniel P. Willis, *Memoranda of the Life of Jenny Lind,* 182. Also see Willis's comments on Lind's tour improving the nation's taste in *Famous Persons and Places* (Auburn, N.Y.: Alden, Beardsley & Co., 1854), 408.

27. His emphasis. Reprinted in Willis, *The Rag-Bag: A Collection of Ephemera* (New York: Charles Scribner, 1855), 45.

28. It was also an extraordinary book in a material sense, engraved by J. W. Orr and illustrated by Thomas Prichard Rossiter.

29. Parke Godwin, preface to Johann von Goethe, *Autobiography of Goethe: Truth and Poetry; From My Own Life,* ed. Godwin, trans. Godwin, John H. Hopkins, Charles A. Dana, John Sullivan Dwight (New York: Wiley and Putnam, 1846), ix.

30. On Fourierism in the United States, see Carl Guarneri, *The Utopian Alternative: Fourierism in Nineteenth-Century America* (Ithaca, N.Y.: Cornell University Press, 1991).

31. John R. Wennersten, "Parke Godwin, Utopian Socialism, and the Politics of Antislavery," *New York Historical Society Quarterly* 60, no. 3/4 (July/October 1976): 107–27.

32. Foner, "The Causes of the American Civil War: Recent Interpretations and New Directions," in *Politics and Ideology in the Age of the Civil War*

(Oxford: Oxford University Press, 1980), 24. See also George Fredrickson, *The Inner Civil War: Northern Intellectuals and the Crisis of the Union* (New York: Harper and Row, 1965).

33. Historian Susan-Mary Grant argues that, as the antebellum period proceeded, Americans from North and South became "more interested in inventing a myth of *uncommon* descent" than in "constructing a unifying myth of common origins and descent." For many Northerners, "The ideas of freedom, liberty, and republicanism were part of a national creation myth, which became a northern creation myth." See Grant, *North over South: Northern Nationalism and American Identity in the Antebellum Era* (Lawrence: University of Kansas Press, 2000), 58.

34. On American writers' interest in these events, see Larry Reynolds, *European Revolutions and the American Literary Renaissance* (New Haven, Conn.: Yale University Press, 1988).

35. Michel de Certeau, *The Practice of Everyday Life,* trans. Steven Rendall (Berkeley and Los Angeles: University of California Press, 1984).

36. See Nicholas E. Tawa, *High-Minded and Low-Down: Music in the Lives of Americans, 1800–1861* (Boston: Northeastern University Press, 2000).

37. "A Complaint on Behalf of Native Composers," *Dwight's Journal of Music* 5, no. 12 (1854): 94.

38. Ibid.

39. *Dwight's Journal of Music,* November 4, 1856, 56.

40. Theodore Parker, "The American Scholar," reprinted in *American Literature, American Culture,* ed. Gordon Hutner (New York: Oxford University Press, 1999), 81.

41. "National Music," *Dwight's Journal of Music* 6, no. 18 (February 3, 1855): 140.

42. Ibid.

43. See Horkheimer and Adorno, *The Dialectic of Enlightenment,* trans. John Cumming (New York: Seabury Press, 1972).

44. See Christopher Newfield, *The Emerson Effect: Individualism and Submission in America* (Chicago: University of Chicago Press, 199), 100–105.

45. "Jenny Lind's First Concert in New York—Triumphant Success and Tremendous Excitement in Castle Garden," *New York Herald,* September 12, 1850, 1.

46. Ryan, *Women in Public: Between Banners and Ballots, 1825–1880* (Baltimore, Md.: Johns Hopkins University Press, 1990), 79–80.

47. For a parallel point concerning literature published in 1850, see Sacvan Bercovitch, *The Office of the Scarlet Letter* (Baltimore, Md.: Johns Hopkins University Press, 1991).

48. This sort of language parallels the contemporaneous calls, made by Willis and others from at least the 1840s, for the construction of a major park area in the city.

49. "City Items—Jenny Lind's Third Concert—Another and Greater Triumph," *Tribune,* September 18, 1850, 1.

50. *Tribune,* September 23, 1850, 1; my italics.

51. Tuckerman, *Essays, Biographical and Critical; or, Studies of Character* (Boston: Phillips, 1857), 231.

52. See Neil Hertz, "The Experience of Blockage in the Literature of the Sublime," in his *The End of the Line: Essays on Psychoanalysis and the Sublime* (New York: Columbia University Press, 1985).

53. For example, Faye Dudden's book on nineteenth-century American actresses discusses the cultural association of female performers with non-normative sexuality as simply oppressive. See Dudden, *Women in the American Theatre: Actresses and Audiences, 1790–1870* (New Haven, Conn.: Yale University Press, 1994). I also disagree with Bluford Adams's assessment of Lind as "the foremost domestic 'angel' in the United States before Harriet Beecher Stowe's Little Eva" (*E Pluribus Barnum,* 41).

54. Wordsworth, preface to the second edition of *Lyrical Ballads,* in *Selected Poems and Prefaces of William Wordsworth,* ed. Jack Stillinger (Boston: Houghton Mifflin, 1965).

55. Willis, *Memoranda of the Life of Jenny Lind,* 140.

56. If Italian opera was considered more rarified than Lind's performances, it was also associated with aristocratic dissipation. Indeed, middle-class complaints from this time about the behavior of the "upper ten" at public events resemble those about the working class: bodily unruliness of various sorts, lack of focused attention. Lind made opera a middle-class art because she managed to make it strike a compromise between body and mind, feeling and intellect. She modeled this position of moderation in her singing, and inspired her audience to replicate it. For more on the class dimensions of opera audiences, see Richard Butsch, *The Making of American Audiences: From Stage to Television, 1750–1990* (Cambridge: Cambridge University Press, 2000), and John Dizikes, *Opera in America.*

57. The erotics of Lind's appeal to a middle-class public make up part of the analysis of her in Dizikes, *Opera in America.*

58. *Tribune,* September 27, 1850, 1.

59. Berlant, *The Anatomy of National Fantasy: Hawthorne, Utopia, and Everyday Life* (Chicago: University of Chicago Press, 1991), 27. On these dynamics and the Statue of Liberty, see also Marina Warner, *Monuments and Maidens: The Allegory of the Female Form* (London: Weidenfeld and Nicolson, 1985), chapter 1.

60. *United States Democratic Review* 28, no. 151 (January 1851): 80. This poem is also further evidence of the cross-party appeal of Lind.

61. Michel Foucault traces the emergence of this category in *History of Sexuality,* vol. 1, trans. Robert Hurley (New York: Vintage, 1978).

62. "Come and hear her! Sell your old clothes, dispose of your antiquated boats, distribute your hats, hypothecate your jewelry, come on the canal, work your passage, walk, take up a collection to pay expenses, raise money on a mortgage, sell 'Tom' into perpetual slavery, dispose of 'Mose' to the highest

bidder, stop smoking for a year . . . and then come hear Jenny Lind." Reprinted in *Detroit Free Press,* November 14, 1850, online at http://chnm.gmu.edu/lostmuseum/lm/198/ (November 1, 2004).

63. See Robert W. Fogel and Stanley L. Engermann, *Time on the Cross: The Economics of American Negro Slavery* (Boston: Little, Brown, 1974).

64. Some observers, like the New York *Herald,* immediately interpreted Genin's outlay as its own publicity stunt: "Genin calculated that this auction would be attended by a reporter from the Herald, and that if he bought the first choice ticket, his name and establishment would be recorded, and would come before a hundred times as many readers as it could by any other means. We understand he is about to follow up this idea on the night of the concert, and that he will sit in the front of the audience with an immense hat suspended over his head. Truly it is a Yankee notion. The ticket is worth $1000 to him." *New York Herald,* September 7, 1850. An interesting reading of this aspect of Barnum's career appears in Elmer, *Reading at the Social Limit.*

65. See Peter Stallybrass, "The Value of Culture and the Disavowal of Things (draft version)," http://eserver.org/emc/1-1/stallybrass.html (November 1, 2004).

66. Brown, *A Sense of Things: The Object Matter of American Literature* (Chicago: University of Chicago Press, 2003), 30.

67. Douglass, *My Bondage and My Freedom,* in *Autobiographies* (New York: Library of America, 2001), 220.

3. Stages of Genius

1. C. L. R. James, *American Civilization* (Oxford: Blackwell, 1993).

2. Edmund Quincy to Caroline Weston, July 2, 1847, quoted in William Edward Farrison, *William Wells Brown: Author, Reformer, Lecturer* (Chicago: University of Chicago Press, 1969), 113.

3. See Karl Marx, *Capital: A Critique of Political Economy,* vol. 1, trans. Ben Fowkes (Harmondsworth, England: Penguin, 1976), 125–28.

4. Larry Gara, "Professional Fugitives in the Abolition Movement," *Abolitionism and Issues of Race and Gender,* ed. John McKivigan (New York: Garland, 1999).

5. Quoted in R. J. Blackett, *Building an Antislavery Wall: Black Americans in the Atlantic Abolitionist Movement, 1830–1860* (Baton Rouge: Louisiana State University Press, 1983), 107.

6. Quotation is from *Narrative of William W. Brown,* reprinted in *Slave Narratives,* ed. William L. Andrews and Henry L. Gates Jr. (New York: Library of America College Editions, 2001), 377. Further citations are from this edition and will appear parenthetically in the body of the text.

7. Farrison's *William Wells Brown* remains an invaluable resource for anyone interested in Brown's career and writings. A good collection of background materials and a good chronology of Brown's life appears in *Clotel; or, The President's Daughter,* ed. Robert S. Levine (Boston and New York: Bedford/St. Martin's, 2000), 29–43.

8. Brawley, *Early Negro American Writers* (Chapel Hill: University of North Carolina Press, 1935), 168.

9. Indeed, Paul Giles has brought new attention to the limitations of this understanding of both Franklin and Thomas Jefferson. See *Transatlantic Insurrections: British Culture and the Formation of American Literature, 1730–1860* (Philadelphia: University of Pennsylvania Press, 2001). See also Gordon Wood, *The Americanization of Benjamin Franklin* (New York: Penguin Books, 2004).

10. William Wells Brown, *Clotel; or, The President's Daughter,* in *Three Classic African-American Novels,* ed. William L. Andrews (New York: Mentor, 1990), 105–6.

11. Quoted in Farrison, *William Wells Brown,* 143.

12. Sources important for my understanding of the fancy girl include Monique Guillory, "Some Enchanted Evening on the Auction Block: The Cultural Legacy of the New Orleans Quadroon Balls" (Ph.D. dissertation, New York University, 1999); Eugene Genovese, *Roll, Jordan, Roll: The World the Slaves Made* (New York: Pantheon, 1974); Walter Johnson, *Soul by Soul: Inside the Antebellum Slave Market* (Cambridge, Mass.: Harvard University Press, 1999); and Edward E. Baptist, "'Cuffy,' 'Fancy Maids,' and 'One-Eyed Men': Rape, Commodification, the Domestic Slave Trade in the United States," *American Historical Review* 106, no. 5 (2001): 1619–50.

13. Michael Newbury has explored this congruence from a different in angle in his book *Figuring Authorship in Antebellum America* (Stanford, Calif.: Stanford University Press, 1997).

14. Hilton Als, preface to William Wells Brown, *Clotel; or, The President's Daughter* (New York: Modern Library, 2000), xix. Als's emergence as a commentator on *Clotel* also suggests a new way of seeing Brown's novel as part of a tradition of queer black U.S. writers, perhaps particularly suggesting a surprising kinship with James Baldwin. See also the last section of this chapter.

15. On the "tragic mulatta" and surplus value, see Carla L. Peterson, "Capitalism, Black (Under)development, and African-American Literature in the 1850s," *American Literary History* 4 (Winter 1992): 559–83.

16. There is certainly an implication here that white faces have a value that black faces do not, even that they *have* faces while dark-skinned slaves do not, a reading following lines that have led a number of critics to be deeply critical of Brown's racial politics—though such criticism has been compellingly challenged more recently by Ann duCille. See duCille, *The Coupling Convention: Sex, Text, and Tradition in Black Women's Fiction* (New York: Oxford University Press, 1993), and her more recent essay, "'Where in the World Is William Wells Brown?' Thomas Jefferson, Sally Hemings, and the DNA of African-American Literary History," *American Literary History* 12, no. 3 (2000): 443–62. Of course, the blacking of the faces itself suggests that slaves are racialized through a variety of "regimes of value" that have only tangentially to do with "natural" skin color. But a more significant aspect of this

scene's destabilization of racial categorization arises in its portrayal of the girl's compromised whiteness, with its concomitant suggestion that her work is primarily sexual, as enabling her participation in an economy of *knowledge*.

17. See Sedgwick, *The Epistemology of the Closet* (Berkeley and Los Angeles: University of California Press, 1990), 45.

18. My theoretical and historical understanding of these issues is especially indebted to Jean-Christophe Agnew, *Worlds Apart: The Market and the Theater in Anglo-American Thought, 1550–1750* (Cambridge: Cambridge University Press, 1986); Pierre Bourdieu, *Outline of a Theory of Practice,* trans. Richard Nice (Cambridge: Cambridge University Press, 1977); and *The Field of Cultural Production,* ed. Randall Johnson (New York: Columbia University Press, 1993). For an influential study of analogous issues in antebellum U.S. culture, see Karen Haltunnen, *Confidence Men and Painted Women: A Study of Middle-Class Culture in America, 1830–1870* (New Haven, Conn.: Yale University Press, 1982).

19. See Johnson, *Soul by Soul,* 199–202, and "The White Slave Trader, and the Politics of Racial Determination in the 1850s South," *Journal of American History* (June 2000), http://www.historycooperative.org/journals/jah/87.1/johnson.htm. Also see Joseph Roach, *Cities of the Dead: Circum-Atlantic Performance* (New York: Columbia University Press, 1996), 213–17.

20. "FANCY [as opposed to imagination] has no other counters to play with, but fixities and definites. The Fancy is indeed no other than a mode of Memory emancipated from the order of time and space; and blended with, and modified by that empirical phenomenon of the will, which we express by the word CHOICE. But equally with the ordinary memory it must receive all its materials ready made from the law of association." Samuel Taylor Coleridge, *Biographia Literaria; or, Biographical Sketches of My Literary Life and Opinions* (London: Everyman's Library, 1965), 167.

21. It is possible to see Brown as an author making tactical use of the intimate links in antebellum discourses of sexuality and economics that Michael Moon illuminates in his study of Walt Whitman and anti-onanism. See Moon, *Disseminating Whitman: Revision and Corporeality in "Leaves of Grass"* (Cambridge, Mass.: Harvard University Press, 1990). For Brown, like Whitman, is in many ways a writer of radical *form.* Particularly in *Clotel,* his texuality presents itself as undisciplined, governed partially at best by some of the most basic assumptions of his era's literary culture about originality, genre, continuity, and address. If Brown, while working as a waiter, could in some ways identify with the "beautiful slave-girl" because he, like her, administered to the pleasures of whites with surplus wealth, as an author he kindled some of the analogous meanings of "fancy" from Romantic aesthetic theory. Fancy in fact describes the impression made by much of Brown's writing—a career in which he recycled, borrowed, cited, and neglected to cite in a fashion that has been often condemned, occasionally described along lines of postmodern critique, but which also links him, oddly, to Thomas Jefferson, who faced multiple charges of plagiarism during his life, including accusations involving the Declaration of Independence (see coda of this chapter).

22. I am drawing here, as in the previous chapter, on Richard Dyer's description of the simultaneous abstract and embodied meanings of whiteness. See Dyer, *White* (London: Routledge, 1997), 38–40.

23. It should be noted that this relationship between whiteness and value seems to have been highly contingent on context. Henry Bibb, for instance, writes of whiteness as a quality that lowered male slaves' value on the market because it meant they had a greater chance of mounting a successful flight. See *Narrative of the Life and Adventures of Henry Bibb, an American Slave, Written by Himself, with an Introduction by Lucius C. Matlack,* in *Slave Narratives,* ed. Andrews and Gates, 425–63. Bibb's narrative was published in 1849.

24. Farrison, *William Wells Brown,* 29.

25. On theater and the market, see Agnew: "Aestheticism and economism effectively cartelized the social world by dividing cultural exchange and market exchange into separate disciplinary jurisdictions. As a consequence, the juncture of these two aspects of life vanished from view, and the deep and unacceptable division *within* market culture reemerged as the deep but eminently acceptable division *between* the market and culture." *Worlds Apart,* 6–7.

26. Johnson, *Soul by Soul,* 164.

27. See Paul Gilmore, *The Genuine Article: Race, Mass Culture, and American Literary Manhood* (Durham, N.C.: Duke University Press, 2001), 43–46, for an interesting reading of antebellum minstrelsy as a context for this scene.

28. "Knowledge producing project" is a phrase I borrow from Mary Poovey, *A History of the Modern Fact: Problems of Knowledge in the Sciences of Wealth and Society* (Chicago: University of Chicago Press, 1998).

29. Baudelaire, quoted in Peter Stallybrass and Allon White, *The Politics and Poetics of Transgression* (Ithaca, N.Y.: Cornell University Press, 1986), 137. Benjamin describes the prostitute as "image" of "pure commodity: as fetish" in *Reflections: Essays, Aphorisms, Autobiographical Writings,* trans. Edmund Jephcott (New York: Schoken Books, 1986), 157. Brown's (and Willis's) addition to the circuit of connections among Poe, Baudelaire, and Benjamin certainly deserves more consideration. This would necessarily involve looking at Brown's antislavery panorama, given Benjamin's extensive comments on the form in *The Arcades Project,* trans. Howard Eiland and Kevin McLaughlin (Cambridge, Mass.: Belknap Press, Harvard University Press, 1999).

30. Catherine Gallagher, "George Eliot and *Daniel Deronda*: The Prostitute and the Jewish Question," *The New Historicism Reader,* ed. H. Aram Veeser (New York: Routledge, 1993), 124–40.

31. Tamarkin, "Black Anglophilia; or, The Sociability of Antislavery," *American Literary History* 14, no. 3: 459–60.

32. Derrida, "Economimesis," in *The Derrida Reader: Writing Performances,* ed. Julian Wolfreys (Lincoln: University of Nebraska Press, 1998), 267.

33. See previous chapter.

34. *Sketches,* 312.

35. Jacobs at one point describes being happy to see a former slave acquaintance "on Northern soil—though I no longer called it *free* soil"; more directly,

she writes, "I was, in fact, a slave in New York, as subject to slave laws as I had been in a Slave State." See Harriet Jacobs, *Incidents in the Life of a Slave Girl* (New York: Schomburg Library/Oxford University Press, 1988), 289–90.

36. The classic source on this is Eric Foner's *Free Soil, Free Labor, Free Men: The Ideology of the Republican Party before the Civil War* (New York: Oxford University Press, 1970). David Roediger trenchantly portrays the racial politics of antebellum white working-class conceptions of labor in *The Wages of Whiteness: Race and the Making of the American Working Class,* rev. ed. (London: Verso, 1999).

37. See Sandra Tomc, "An Idle Industry: Nathaniel Parker Willis and the Workings of Literary Leisure," *American Quarterly* 49, no. 4 (1997): 780–805. Tomc's argument is a likely explanation for why Willis is generally absent from, or only tangentially present in, scholarly studies of antebellum authorship.

38. Robert Reid-Pharr, *Conjugal Union: The Body, the House, and the Black American* (New York: Oxford University Press, 1999). Positioning both Willis and Brown this way suggests an alternate genealogy for queer American writing than the one typically constructed around Whitman and Melville, mostly by means of a flexible yet finite notion of Americanness. This genealogy of queer cosmopolitan genius would also reinvigorate studies of earlier writers, such as Washington Irving and John Neal, and provide a way of extending the insights of recent work such as Michael Warner's essay on Irving and bachelorhood, "Irving's Posterity," *ELH* 67 (Fall 2000): 773–79. The point of making such connections ought not to be to renationalize this literature, though—it might instead open up work on women's writing to a more international context.

39. Quoted in Baker, *Sentiment and Celebrity: Nathaniel Parker Willis and the Trials of Literary Fame* (New York: Oxford University Press), 131. Oliver Wendell Holmes made the most cited comparison between Willis and Wilde, calling the former "something between a remembrance of the Count D'Orsay and an anticipation of Oscar Wilde." Quoted in Tomc, "Restyling an Old World: Nathaniel Parker Willis and Metropolitan Fashion in the Antebellum United States," *Representations* 85 (Winter 2004): 103.

40. Compare this to Emerson's own writing on the demands real space places on the bodies of geniuses, discussed in chapter 1.

41. See Baker, *Sentiment and Celebrity,* for a useful overview of Willis's attitudes toward and relationships with women.

42. More specifically, the central role of *fancy* in what Willis presented as his approach to aesthetics suggests congruity between Brown's interest in the New York man of letters and the "beautiful slave girl" or "fancy girl" of his *Narrative.* Notably, Edgar Allan Poe's essay on Willis centers on *fancy*: "the marked idiosyncrasy of the prose style of Mr. Willis—that the charm which was wrought for it so vast and so well-merited a popularity—is traceable, in the last result, to the brilliant FANCY with which it perpetually scintillates or glows." Poe, *Essays and Reviews* (New York: Library of America, 1984), 1126. Originally printed in *Broadway Journal,* January 18, 1845.

43. See Farrison, *William Wells Brown,* 169. On Willis, see Baker, *Sentiment and Celebrity.*

44. Roediger, *Colored White: Transcending the Racial Past* (Berkeley and Los Angeles: University of California Press, 2002), 106.

45. On this topic, see also Karen Sanchez-Eppler, *Touching Liberty: Abolition, Feminism, and the Politics of the Body* (Berkeley and Los Angeles: University of California Press, 1993).

46. Quoted in Farrison, *William Wells Brown,* 207.

47. Quoted in Josephine Brown, *Biography of an American Bondman,* reprinted in *Two Biographies by African-American Women,* ed. Henry L. Gates (New York: Oxford University Press/Schomburg Library of Nineteenth-Century Black Women Writers, 1991), 85.

48. Willis, *Hurry-graphs; or, Sketches of Scenery, Celebrities, and Society, Taken from Life* (New York: Charles Scribner, 1851), 101.

49. Brown writes with particular detail and enthusiasm about the Thames Tunnel (cf. 254).

50. As Douglass would do in *My Bondage and My Freedom,* Brown recounts a humiliating incident of racism directed toward him on the steamer he takes in his voyage from the United States.

51. On London as a literary center in the African and Asian diasporas, see Sukhdev Sandhu, *London Calling: How Black and Asian Writers Imagined a City* (London: Harper Collins, 2003).

52. Benjamin, *Arcades Project,* 7.

53. Jenkins's performance and his African background suggest that if he is indeed a fictional character, as I strongly suspect, he is substantially based on the famous black actor Ira Aldridge. Aldridge was born in the United States but lived in Britain for most of his life. His father was, apparently, an African prince who came to the West but later returned to his homeland.

54. Compare Frederick Douglass's discussion of "the heads of A. Crummel, Henry H. Garnett, Sam'l R. Ward, Chas. Lenox Remond" in "The Claims of the Negro Ethnologically Considered," reprinted in *A House Divided : The Antebellum Slavery Debates in America, 1776–1865,* ed. Mason I. Lowance Jr. (Princeton, N.J.: Princeton University Press, 2003). Brown's passage describing Jenkins in relation to other individual great black men reanimates elements of the language of Edmund Quincy's letter to Caroline Weston, in which Quincy described Brown as "more valuable than" Douglass. Indeed, the scene's setting in a theater literalizes what in the letter was more symbolic drama of value and exchange.

55. For a very interesting discussion of *Clotel,* pedagogy, and the Jefferson-Hemmings affair, see duCille, "Where in the World Is William Wells Brown?" DuCille's essay actually registers surprise that *Clotel* is not taught more and not taken more seriously, particularly in light of the publicity around Jefferson and Hemmings. She constructs an incisive argument concerning the novel's lukewarm reception by some late-twentieth-century African-American intellectuals. She also provides an eloquent account of teaching the text in an undergraduate classroom in the midst of the Jefferson-Hemmings controversy.

56. Jay Fliegelman, *Declaring Independence: Jefferson, Natural Language, and the Culture of Performance* (Stanford, Calif.: Stanford University Press, 1993). Another vital piece of recent scholarship on eighteenth-century rhetorics of male sentimentalism is Julie Ellison, *Cato's Tears and the Making of Anglo-American Emotion* (Chicago: University of Chicago Press, 1999).

57. Giles, *Transatlantic Insurrections,* 114.

58. Gates discusses the importance of Jefferson to a series of nineteenth-century African-American intellectuals, beginning with David Walker. See his *The Trials of Phillis Wheatley: America's First Black Poet and Her Encounters with the Founding Fathers* (New York: Basic Civitas Books, 2003).

59. On this issue see Hazel V. Carby, *Race Men* (Cambridge, Mass.: Harvard University Press, 1998).

4. Genius Burns

1. Ellison, *Collected Essays of Ralph Ellison* (New York: Modern Library, 1995), 104.

2. Saidiya V. Hartman, *Scenes of Subjection: Terror, Slavery, and Self-Making in Nineteenth-Century America* (New York: Oxford University Press, 1997), 116.

3. The meaning of this term is an ongoing matter of contestation and transformation, particularly with its decreasing visibility in radical activism and its entrance into mass entertainment culture via television programs such as *Queer Eye for the Straight Guy* and *Queer as Folk.* My basic use of the term reflects Eve Kosofsky Sedgwick's description of it as naming "the open mesh of possibilities, gaps, overlaps, dissonances, and resonances, lapses and excesses of meaning when the constituent elements of anyone's gender, of anyone's sexuality aren't made or can't be made to signify monolithically." Sedgwick, *Tendencies* (Durham, N.C.: Duke University Press, 1993), 5. See also Michael Warner, introduction to *Fear of a Queer Planet: Queer Politics and Social Theory* (Minneapolis: University of Minnesota Press, 1993).

4. In his *Cultures of Letters* and *The School of Hawthorne* (New York: Oxford University Press, 1986).

5. The four extant chapters of *Diana and Persis,* which was based on Alcott sister May's experience as a painter in Europe and given up upon May's death, are reprinted in *The Alternative Alcott,* ed. Elaine Showalter (New Brunswick, N.J.: Rutgers University Press, 1988). Around the time Alcott mentions *Genius,* she was also exploring the possibility of writing a novel based on her father's life; it is unclear to me whether these two projects were one and the same.

6. Louisa May Alcott, *Little Women* (Harmondsworth, England: Penguin Books, 1989), 131. Further quotations from this novel will be cited parenthetically in the text.

7. Lawrence Levine, *Highbrow/Lowbrow: The Emergence of Cultural Hierarchy in Nineteenth-Century America* (Cambridge, Mass.: Harvard University Press, 1988).

8. *Journals of Louisa May Alcott,* ed. Joel Myerson, Daniel Shealy, Madeline Stern (Boston: Little, Brown, 1989), 98. On Lowell's wartime and postwar reconciliationism, see Martin Duberman, *James Russell Lowell* (Boston: Houghton Mifflin, 1966), 275–76.

9. The term is Nancy Glazener's, from *Reading for Realism: The History of a U.S. Literary Institution, 1850–1910* (Durham, N.C.: Duke University Press, 1997).

10. *Journals of Louisa May Alcott,* 85. On Alcott and Brontë, see Christine Doyle, *Louisa May Alcott and Charlotte Brontë: Transatlantic Translations* (Knoxville: University of Tennessee Press, 2000), which notes that Alcott's "vortex" model of authorship was shared with or drawn from Brontë's.

11. Joel Myerson, Daniel Shealy, and Madeline Stern, eds., *The Selected Letters of Louisa May Alcott* (Boston: Little, Brown, 1987), 321. On Fuller's effort to embrace the position of genius, see Ann Douglas, *The Feminization of American Culture* (New York: Avon Books, 1978). Perhaps equally important for Alcott was a textual relationship indirectly introduced to her by Emerson: the correspondence between the German authors Bettina von Arnim and Goethe as portrayed in von Arnim's epistolary novel, *Goethe's Correspondence with a Child.* Published in 1835 and first translated into English by the author two years later, von Arnim's book was discovered by the fifteen-year-old Alcott during a visit to Emerson's library. The text, highly popular in the United States, represents the rapturous state, for von Arnim, of being a reader of Goethe more than it reflects on the content of his writings or on the young woman's relationship with the older man. It uses von Arnim's contact with the writer and his books only as the starting point for fanciful flights of narrative, memoir, and aesthetic philosophy. Von Arnim's claim that the correspondence took place when she was twelve (she was actually twenty-two) only added to the outlandish impression the book made, especially on American and English readers, at least some of whom were suspicious about the letters' authenticity. Also adding to the sensationalism surrounding the book was the apparently accurate story that von Arnim had learned English solely to translate the book and had succeeded in doing so in a remarkably brief period of time.

Von Arnim seems a particularly fruitful model for the structure of genius that we find in Alcott, particularly because of the erotically charged devotion portrayed in her book on Goethe and her later book on the poet Günderode, which Margaret Fuller translated into English in 1842. Both volumes blend the genres of collected letters, memoir, novel, and essay; both are presented as inspired by a state of rapture or possession engendered by the more well-known, more conventionally authorial, figure. Both *Günderode* and *Goethe's Correspondence with a Child*—which also include rapturous letters to Günderode and to Goethe's mother—seem to disconnect von Arnim's entire relation to genius from heterosexuality or cross-sex fertility. Christina Zwarg has argued that Emerson and Fuller's relationship was in part modeled on von Arnim's *Günderode,* and that Fuller derived from the correspondence "a complete confusion and ultimate displacement of familiar gender roles as well as some traditional genre considerations." See Zwarg, *Feminist Conversations: Fuller, Emerson, and the Play of Reading* (Ithaca, N.Y.: Cornell University Press, 1995), 89. Von Arnim's book, or books, may well have offered Alcott, too, a template for imagining a sexually charged pairing that rearranged traditional gender and erotic roles and produced literary writing.

12. In her exhaustively researched *Novels, Readers, and Reviewers,* Nina Baym finds that among female fiction writers at midcentury, "only three were discussed in American magazines as though they were eligible to be thought of as examples of genius: George Sand, Harriet Beecher Stowe, and Charlotte Brontë." See Baym, *Novels, Readers and Reviewers* (Ithaca, N.Y.: Cornell University Press, 1984), 255.

13. In addition to the other examples here, see the chapter "The Sunny Side" in *An Old-Fashioned Girl* (1870).

14. These apparently divergent energies are not incoherent; taken together, they contribute to the overall sense in Alcott's fiction that people are (as we might put it today) *addicted* to each other. There are very few scenes in her fiction that feature a character alone. In the first scene of *A Modern Mephistopheles* (1877), a character is depicted alone, but on the verge of committing suicide by stuffing a manuscript into his pockets and sitting down next to a raging fireplace. He is rescued, and the book's narrative is allowed to take form.

15. Eve Kosofsky Sedgwick, "Shame, Theatricality, Queer Performativity: Henry James's *The Art of the Novel,*" in *Touching Feeling: Affect, Pedagogy, Performativity* (Durham, N.C.: Duke University Press, 2003), 35–66. (Page numbers of further citations will appear in the body of the text.) Elizabeth Barnes provides a reading of Alcott and *Little Men,* in particular, that resonates with Sedgwick compellingly in its depiction of scenes of humiliation as formative for subjectivity. See "The Whipping-Boy of Love," *Journal X* 2, no. 1 (Autumn 1997). At http://www.olemiss.edu/depts/english/pubs/jx/jx2_1_barnes.html (November 1, 2004).

16. Yet critical work on *Little Women* has not been sufficiently attuned to Alcott's wit to make much of "Literary Lessons" as a hilariously double-edged parody of what Janet Wolff has called a "common idea of a social type" of artist, "The author/artist/composer as social outcast, starving in a garret." Alcott's text seems to both romanticize and ironize this "universal definition" of the artist as genius. Her text issues a critique of the cultural hierarchy emerging around her, one that resists assessment as oppositional, as articulated from outside the tradition. Ambivalence is one way to read Alcott's approach here; another apt term might be *camp,* now long established as a queer performance practice. Camp practices recast the relationship of parody and reverence as nonoppositional. Moreover, they position their performer-author as both subject and object of satire's sharpness. Wolff, *The Social Production of Art* (New York: St. Martin's Press, 1981), 11.

17. On this, also see my reading of Alcott's story "Psyche's Art" in the introduction.

18. Quoted in Octavia Davis's introduction to Alcott, *A Modern Mephistopheles,* vi.

19. Quoted in Elizabeth Young, *Disarming the Nation: Women's Writing and the American Civil War* (Chicago: University of Chicago Press, 1997), 77.

20. Armstrong, "Who's Afraid of the Cultural Turn?" *differences: Journal of Feminist Cultural Studies* 12, no. 1 (2001): 25.

21. Freedman, *Temple of Culture: Assimilation and Anti-Semitism in Literary Anglo-America* (New York: Oxford University Press, 2000), 43.

22. Thomas Wentworth Higginson, "A Plea for Culture," *Atlantic Monthly* 19, no. 111 (January 1867): 31.

23. Many of these are evident in Arnold's *Culture and Anarchy* (1869); Spencer is William James's object of critique in the latter's essay "Great Men, Great Thoughts, and Their Environment," *Atlantic Monthly* 46, no. 276 (October 1880): 449–70.

24. Lowell's essay begins by recounting a litany of complaints about Rousseau by noted writers, including Samuel Johnson's to Boswell: "Three or four nations have expelled him, and it is a shame that he is protected in this country. Rousseau, sir, is a very bad man. I would sooner sign a sentence for his transportation, than that of any felon who has gone from the Old Bailey these many years. Yes, I should like to have him work in the plantations." Lowell's after-comment underlines the referent of Johnson's "plantations" as those of the American South: "*We* were the plantations then, and Rousseau was destined to work there in another and much more wonderful fashion than the gruff old Ursa Major imagined." James Russell Lowell, "Rousseau and the Sentimentalists," *North American Review* 105, no. 216 (July 1865): 244. Further citations appear in the body of the text.

25. The Lowell essay also anticipates Marshall Berman's treatment of Rousseau as the pivotal figure of Western modernity in *All That Is Solid Melts into Air: The Experience of Modernity* (New York: Simon & Schuster, 1982).

26. Lowell, "Rousseau and the Sentimentalists," 257.

27. Recall, though, that George Sand served as the French minister of propaganda during the Second Republic (1848–1852).

28. The year after Lowell left the editorship of the *Atlantic,* Andrew White's essay "Jefferson and Slavery" appeared therein, constructing a series of connections between Southernness, the culture of slavery, and a troubled psychological model of genius that in many ways parallels Lowell's depiction of Rousseau. Here, as with Rousseau, genius provides a shield from moral (and, in this case, in the postbellum United States, political) condemnation, transvaluing suspicion into symbolic capital in terms suited to both reconciliationism and contemporary ideals of culture. The essay attempted to rescue the Virginian Jefferson's reputation by arguing that he was a staunch critic of slavery. White bases his claims in specific letters and documents, but at its broadest, his thesis is that Jefferson was an intellectual, that his learnedness made it impossible for him to support slavery, and that owning slaves reflected his intellectual complexity. This view of Jefferson as shunned by the nation for being too smart is something of an American bromide; Richard Hofstadter writes that around the time he ran for the presidency, Jefferson was subject to charges of being a "closet philosopher." Such a phrase also echoes the

long-standing rumors surrounding the secrets of his sex life. Although this claim was made before a wide public only rarely during the nineteenth century, it clearly formed the undertone of the many shifting accounts of Jefferson's character and importance.

White's essay then sublimates this notion of a libertine Jefferson into a portrayal of him as a risk-taking intellectual. Discussing the "indirect influences on his early culture," White notes that "the reform literature of that time was coming almost entirely from France. Active, earnest men everywhere were grasping the theories and phrases of Voltaire and Rousseau and Montesquieu, to wield them against every tyranny. Terrible weapons these—often searing and scarring frightfully those who brandished them—yet there was not one chance in a thousand that any man who had once made any considerable number of these ideas his own could ever support slavery" (31). White's basis for this point, however, is not analysis of these French writings, but their place in a hastily sketched intellectual genealogy that travels through New England abolition and culminates with Matthew Arnold: "Whoever, at that time, studied the 'Contrat Social,' or the defense of Jean Calas, whatever other sins he might commit, was no more likely to advocate systematic oppression than are they who now read with reverence Dr. Arnold and Charles Kingsley; and whoever, at that time, read earnestly 'The Spirit of the Laws' was as sure to fight slavery as any man who today reveres Channing or Theodore Parker" (31). The essay thus not only implies that, if Jefferson were alive today, he would be an Arnoldian; it assimilates reverence for Arnold with a history of antislavery activism. White advises the *Atlantic*'s readers to allay any shame or embarrassment over the sense emanating from Jefferson, or Jefferson's patrician Southern identity; it does so specifically by encouraging them to take an intellectual risk of the sort that brings together this line of thinkers. The value of subjecting oneself to this sort of risk drives the essay Lowell himself published a few years later on one of the "terrible weapons" that Jefferson wielded: Jean-Jacques Rousseau. Citations are from Andrew White, "Jefferson and Slavery," *Atlantic Monthly* 9, no. 51 (January 1862): 29–40. Hofstadter discusses attacks on Jefferson's philosophical bent in *Anti-intellectualism in American Life* (New York: Random House, 1962), 146–151.

29. See Matthew Frye Jacobson, *Whiteness of a Different Color: European Immigrants and the Alchemy of Race* (Cambridge, Mass.: Harvard University Press, 1998), chapter 2.

30. Biographies of Alcott and her family include: Madeleine Stern, *Louisa May Alcott* (Norman: University of Oklahoma Press, 1950); Madelon Bedell, *The Alcotts: Biography of a Family* (New York: C. N. Potter, 1980); and Martha Saxton, *Louisa May: A Modern Biography of Louisa May Alcott* (Boston: Houghton Mifflin, 1978).

31. Louisa May Alcott, "The Freak of a Genius," in *Behind the Mask: Complete Thrillers,* ed. Madeline Stern (Boston: Northeastern University Press, 1993), 431. Further quotations from this story are from this edition and cited parenthetically in the text.

32. It is fascinating to note the remarkable similarity between this story and Henry James's "The Lesson of the Master" (1892), another narrative of suspicion centering on a genius figure that traces a man's initiation into authorship despite his apparent betrayal by his former genius icon. In that tale the empty genius is also named St. George, although he is the older and more staid of the two writers who are the story's principal characters.

33. The names Alcott uses for the women are both provocative. May, the name given to the vapid younger sister, is of course the real name of Amy March, the youngest Alcott girl. The source of Margaret's name may be the Faust tale, which would further suggest the phantom presence of Goethe; it also seems likely that Alcott is here alluding to Margaret Fuller as well. Alcott would also, in *Little Women,* give the name Margaret to her older sister, Anna.

34. Michel Foucault, *History of Sexuality,* vol. 1: *An Introduction,* trans. Robert Hurley (New York: Vintage, 1978), 71.

35. *Dictionary of American Slang,* ed. Robert Chapman with Barbara Kifer (Boston: HarperCollins, 1995).

36. On the coarticulation of nonnormative sexualities and "addictive" behaviors, see Eve Kosofsky Sedgwick, "Epidemics of the Will," in her *Tendencies* (Durham, N.C.: Duke University Press, 1993).

37. The logic, that is, that Alcott repressed her "true" feelings in her sentimental work and released them in her pseudonymous thrillers.

38. *The Journals of Louisa May Alcott,* 99.

39. Examples of burning in the March/Plumfield novels are so numerous as almost to require no mention, but I cannot resist noting two of the most striking in *Little Men*: the sacrifice-ritual involving the burning of favorite toys for the "Naughty Kitty-Mouse," and the near burning down of the Plumfield schoolhouse by Jo's wild stand-in Dan.

40. For a compelling analysis of the blush in the nineteenth-century novel, see Mary Ann O'Farrell, *Telling Complexions: The Nineteenth-Century English Novel and the Blush* (Durham, N.C.: Duke University Press, 1997).

41. Brodhead, *Cultures of Letters,* 91.

42. Jo's initial venture into sensation fiction, in a contest arranged by the "Spread Eagle" storypaper, is also conceived on Beth's behalf. Jo enters the contest with the aim of using the prize money to send the ailing Beth to a seaside resort. She wins, and overcomes Beth's deprecations of the idea of spending the money on a vacation: "Ah, but you shall go, I've set my heart on it; that's what I tried for, and that's why I succeeded. I never get on when I think of myself alone, so it will help me to work for you, don't you see?" (268–69). After a spell of sensation writing, Jo finishes her manuscript and reaffirms her claim to "never get on" when she thinks of herself alone, by submitting the work to the family for advice and criticism.

43. We might also remind ourselves of the association in Alcott's mind between her sister Elizabeth and her master/muse Emerson, who developed a particularly intimate relationship with the youngest Alcott in the last months of her life and who served as a pall-bearer at her funeral.

44. Compare Edgar Allan Poe, *Marginalia* (Charlottesville: University Press of Virginia, 1981), 81: "Keats died of a criticism."

45. On the importance of Milnes's biography in establishing Keats's American reputation, see Hyder Edward Rollins, *Keats's Reputation in America to 1848* (Cambridge. Mass.: Harvard University Press, 1946), 94–101.

46. Joseph Severn, "On the Vicissitudes of Keats's Fame," *Atlantic Monthly,* April 1863, 26.

47. James Russell Lowell, "Keats," *Lowell's Works I: Literary Essays* (Boston: Houghton Mifflin, 1898), 218.

48. Quoted without attribution in Rollins, *Keats's Reputation,* 80. See also Leon Chai, *The Romantic Foundations of the American Renaissance* (Ithaca, N.Y.: Cornell University Press, 1987).

49. Lowell, "Keats," 229

50. *Journals of Louisa May Alcott,* 139, 147n13.

51. James, *Literary Criticism,* vol. 1: *Essays on Literature, American Writers, British Writers* (New York: Library of America, 1984), 194.

52. James, *Literary Criticism,* 195.

5. "It's the Treatment!"

1. Max Nordau, *Degeneration* (New York: D. Appleton, 1895), 24. No translator is listed.

2. Sander Gilman's scholarship is an invaluable source on these authors; see especially *Freud, Race, and Gender* (Princeton, N.J.: Princeton University Press, 1993), *The Jew's Body* (New York: Routledge, 1991); and *Smart Jews: The Construction of the Image of Jewish Superior Intelligence* (Lincoln: University of Nebraska Press, 1996).

3. On the notion of the "therapeutic" in the late-nineteenth-century United States, see Carrie Tirado Bramen, *The Uses of Variety: Modern Americanism and the Quest for National Distinctiveness* (Cambridge, Mass.: Harvard University Press, 2001); T. J. Jackson Lears, *No Place of Grace: Anti-Modernism and the Transformation of American Culture* (New York: Pantheon, 1981). On the history of psychotherapy in the United States, see Eric Caplan, *Mind Games: American Culture and the Birth of Psychotherapy* (Berkeley and Los Angeles: University of California Press, 1998).

4. Blair, "Realism, Culture, and the Place of the Literary in *The Bostonians,*" *The Cambridge Companion to Henry James,* ed. Jonathan Freedman (Cambridge: Cambridge University Press, 1998), 152.

5. See, for example, Bill Brown's reading of *The Red Badge of Courage* as exemplifying "a decontextualizing strategy" that was "the first stage in rehistoricizing the Civil War as an event not in the nation's internecine past but in its unifying, imperializing future" (Brown, *The Material Unconscious: American Amusement, Stephen Crane, and the Economies of Play* [Cambridge, Mass.: Harvard University Press, 1996], 158).

6. An important recent work of scholarship on this impulse toward classi-

fication is Jennifer Terry, *An American Obsession: Science, Medicine, and Homosexuality in Modern Society* (Chicago: University of Chicago Press, 1999).

7. Carrie Tirado Bramen, *The Uses of Variety: Modern Americanism and the Quest for Distinctiveness* (Cambridge, Mass.: Harvard University Press, 2002), 54. She quotes from Lionel Trilling, *The Liberal Imagination* (New York: Doubleday Anchor, 1953), 8–10.

8. For a relatively recent example, see Michael Davitt Bell's comments on *The Bostonians* in *The Problem of American Realism* (Chicago: University of Chicago Press, 1993).

9. Like Henry James himself, the American cultural history of this period has almost always been treated as the preface to a more fully developed modernism of the early twentieth century. In much of the most sophisticated work of the past three decades, we learn of an age of generic "anxiety" due to the loss and fragmentation of authority and authenticity, brought about by expansive capitalism, the elimination of the gold standard, heavy immigration, urbanization, and other forms of social, spatial, and symbolic displacement. Such accounts, some of which Carrie Tirado Bramen has referred to as "pathologizing," not only tend to reproduce some of the most hegemonic terms through which the era attempted to understand itself, but also implicitly construct its recent past as a time of simple, organic existence, a premodernity whose sectional conflict is paradoxically seen as a form of symbolic union, a time when Americans knew what they were fighting for. As we saw in the previous chapter, however, the genealogy of the category "genius," with its cogency as a gauge of ideas about race and nation (and labor), illuminates the lasting effects and continuing presence of cultural notions entrenched in discourse during the antebellum period, when slavery and racial conflict were foremost problems in attempts to conceive of a coherent national culture. In this chapter, I look at how the discourse of genius creates some historical dissonances in the narrative of modernization that some cultural authorities were trying to produce at the time, and which some have uncritically reconstituted in our own.

10. These writings may well mark an especially influential, early instance of the critical practice of using prophylactic "scare quotes" around the word *genius,* as so often today (and as is manifest in many other twentieth-century invocations of the term, such as Theodore Dreiser's 1915 novel *The "Genius."* Howells did not literally understand genius as a disease, and he wrote a strong condemnation of Nordau's *Degeneration* in *Scribner's* in 1895, but this practice nevertheless suggests a desire to keep oneself safe from the threat of infection by the category.

11. Without treating Howells's writings on the topic directly, Daniel Borus makes the critique of genius a defining feature of realism in his *Writing Realism: Howells, James, Norris, and the Mass Market* (Chapel Hill: University of North Carolina Press, 1989), 36–37.

12. Howells wrote partly in response to the "romantic revivalism" of critics like Edmund C. Stedman, a Wall Street broker, with whom he jousted in

public over the issue of genius. On the late-nineteenth-century U.S. "romantic revival," see Nancy Glazener, *Reading for Realism: The History of a U.S. Literary Institution, 1850–1910* (Durham, N.C.: Duke University Press, 1997). Howells bestowed high praise on the recently published *Personal Memoirs of Ulysses S. Grant,* calling it "a great piece of literature, because great literature is nothing more nor less than the clear expression of minds that have something great in them, whether religion, or beauty, or deep experience. . . . All the conditions here, then, are favorable to supposing a case of 'genius.' Yet who would trifle with that great heir of fame, that plain, grand, manly soul, by speaking of 'genius' and him together?" William Dean Howells, "Editor's Study," *Harper's* 72, no. 430 (March 1886): 649.

13. See Nancy Cohen, *The Reconstruction of American Liberalism, 1865–1914* (Chapel Hill: University of North Carolina Press, 2002), 63–66.

14. W. D. Howells, "The Man of Letters as a Man of Business," *Literature and Life* (New York and London: Harper and Brothers, 1902), 34.

15. In "Man of Letters," quoted in Trachtenberg, *The Incorporation of America: Culture and Society in the Gilded Age* (New York: Hill and Wang), 196.

16. Trachtenberg, *Incorporation of America,* 196. Amy Kaplan suggests that much the same was true of Howells's view of the activity of reading: "As a cultural force, realism turns reading into work, an act which unites its practitioners not through the worship of high art or the transport to imaginary worlds but through the mutual recognition of a common identity rooted in the productive sphere." Kaplan, *The Social Construction of American Realism* (Chicago: University of Chicago Press, 1988), 17.

17. Important sources on congruent understandings of homosexuality and Jewishness around the time include: Daniel Boyarin, *Unheroic Conduct: The Rise of Heterosexuality and the Invention of the Jewish Man*; Sander Gilman, *The Case of Sigmund Freud: Medicine and Identity at the Fin-de-Siècle* (Baltimore, Md.: Johns Hopkins University Press, 1993); Daniel Itzkovitz, "Passing Like Me," *South Atlantic Quarterly* 98 (1999): 36–57.

18. This, of course, is the historical process traced in Michel Foucault, *The History of Sexuality,* vol. 1: *An Introduction,* trans. Robert Hurley (New York: Vintage, 1978).

19. *The Bostonians* performs this excision most explicitly when it twice demurs rendering characters' *dialect,* either Basil Ransom's Mississippi accent or the conversation of African Americans in a New York boarding house. On this issue, see Walter Benn Michaels, "Local Color," *MLN* 113 (1998): 734–56.

20. Henry James, *The Bostonians* ([1886] Oxford: Oxford University Press, 1998), 173. Further page numbers will be cited in the body of the text.

21. See Arnold, *Civilization in the United States: First and Last Impressions of America* (Boston: DeWolfe, Fiske, 1888). Over the course of his career, James was consistently derisive of literary culture in the antebellum United States, a view he described in his short critical study *Hawthorne* (1878) and maintained as late as his memoir *Notes of a Son and Brother* (1914).

22. The degree to which James identified his character with Carlyle is reinforced by his November 3, 1884, letter to Grace Norton, in which he discussed reading Froude's recently published biography with the same sort of fascinated ambivalence with which he treats Basil: "Decidedly Carlyle was a brute, a man of jealous, grudging, sinister, contemptuous, ungenerous, most invidious soul; and one who, with all his violence of feeling, felt like, as a whole, most incompletely (calls Keats a 'dead dog,' 'venal of hell,' etc., sneers at 'art' in a way which shows that all *that* salutary world was closed to him). But what a genius, painter, humourist, what a literary figure, what a faculty of expression . . . I am convinced that he will be a curiosity for future people rather than a teacher." *Henry James: Letters,* vol. 3, *1883–1895,* ed. Leon Edel (Cambridge, Mass.: Belknap Press, Harvard University Press, 1980), 55.

23. *Queer,* however, is a more appropriate term than *lesbian* in this regard. Olive's individual psychology of desire, or the status of what we could anachronistically call her sexual identity, is not so much the center of epistemological wealth as a vehicle in the novel's overall depiction of modern culture and its forms as creating spaces conducive to generating illicit, nonnormative forms of desire in women.

24. This is the model of genius in James's earlier novel, *Roderick Hudson.* See chapter 4. Also, on genius as a figure of homoerotic desire in this novel, see Wendy Graham, *Henry James's Thwarted Love* (Stanford, Calif.: Stanford University Press, 1999).

25. The Esmerelda connection in the description of Verena is especially salient because Hugo's character from *Hunchback of Notre Dame* occupies a position (both in Ransom's mind and more generally) in some liminal space between literary textuality and some larger public mythology, and in this way she parallels one of James's central concerns with Verena and Miriam—the relationship between mass culture and a literary culture still defining itself by disavowing its status as a component of mass culture. We've seen in previous chapters how hugely popular novelists like Hugo and Dumas have figured relations between genius and public fame, as in Margaret Fuller's comparison of Frederick Douglass to Dumas.

26. As seen through (James's description of) Basil's eyes, she also resembles Virginian Edgar Allan Poe's description of his heroine Ligeia, whom Joan Dayan has portrayed as an allusion to the "tragic mulatta" figure as well. Specifically, Poe's narrator orientalizes Ligeia by calling her "Hebraic," and the plot turns in a large measure on the liquidity of her eyes, which reappear as free-floating tears after her death. See Joan Dayan, "Amorous Bondage: Poe, Ladies, and Slaves," in *Subjects and Citizens: Nation, Race, and Gender from "Oronooko" to Anita Hill,* ed. Michael Moon and Cathy N. Davidson (Durham, N.C.: Duke University Press, 1995), 109–44. See also Harriet Beecher Stowe's discussion of the similarities between Africans, "the Hebrews of old and Oriental nations of the present," in her *Key to Uncle Tom's Cabin.* Hortense Spillers discusses this in her essay "Changing the Letter: The Yokes, the Jokes of Discourse, or Mrs. Stowe, Mr. Reed," in *Black and White*

in Color: Essays on American Literature and Culture (Chicago: University of Chicago Press, 2003), 177–78. Another predecessor for Verena (also an allusion of *Tragic Muse*'s Miriam Rooth) is Miriam of Nathaniel Hawthorne's *The Marble Faun* (1860).

27. Bourdieu develops his notion of the "aesthetic disposition" in several works, mainly in *Distinction: A Social Critique of the Judgement of Taste,* trans. Richard Nice (Cambridge, Mass.: Harvard University Press, 1987), but also in *The Rules of Art: Genesis and Structure of the Literary Field,* trans. Susan Emanuel (Stanford, Calif.: Stanford University Press, 1992), and the essays collected as *The Field of Cultural Production,* ed. Randal Johnson (New York: Columbia University Press, 1993).

28. Miriam Rooth, the actress who functions as the center of *The Tragic Muse,* is a refinement of this figure. Specifically described as "more than half a Jewess," she captivates her audiences by means of her seductive beauty and voice. James's choice to name this character Miriam suggests that Hawthorne's *The Marble Faun* was an important pretext for both of these heroines. In both novels, James mimics what Nancy Bentley calls the indeterminate "hidden racial significance" of Hawthorne's character, established through suggestions that she may be Jewish, African-American, Egyptian, English, German, and/or Italian. Bentley argues that the point of this promise of racial meaning is *not* to relinquish its indeterminate referentiality: "Miriam is not a member of any particular race so much as an emblem *of* race or, what amounts to the same thing, an emblem of racial difference—of race *as* difference—a contentless, unspecified alterity. . . . Like the figure of the tragic mulatta that she is rumored to be, Miriam embodies an invisible, undetectable identity that nevertheless determines her social fate. . . . [She] recalls the ideas of Romantic thinkers such as Herder, who conceived of race as a spiritual, supra-individual identity that is the essential 'genius' of a people, a notion of race that would become the basis of the anthropological ideal of culture."

Bentley's reading of Hawthorne suggests that James, too, figures his heroines of "form" as owing their aesthetic value to mysterious, indeterminate, but clearly racial qualities. See Bentley, *The Ethnography of Manners: Hawthorne, James, Wharton* (New York: Oxford University Press, 1995), 34, 36. It's also possible to read a particularly American connotation of Jewishness in the deferral of Verena's ancestry to antiquity—the Puritan symbolic use of Judaism discussed by Bercovitch in *Puritan Origins of the American Self.*

For a related reading of "ethnology" in James's novel *The American,* see Matthew Frye Jacobson, *Whiteness of a Different Color: European Immigrants and the Alchemy of Race* (Cambridge, Mass.: Harvard University Press, 1998) 168–69.

29. F. R. Leavis, *The Great Tradition: George Eliot, Henry James, Joseph Conrad* (London: Chatto and Windus, 1948), 134.

30. Mark Seltzer, *Bodies and Machines* (New York: Routledge, 1992), 21.

31. On the specifics of these erotics: it is perhaps possible to see Olive's

interest in Verena's voice, rather than an interest in the air passages of her throat, as an interest in her finely formed but untrained *tongue*.

32. Indeed, Basil's keen vision invites a comparison of the Olive-Verena relationship with the relationship of Kent and St. George in Alcott's "The Freak of a Genius." Like Kent, Olive begins the novel looking for a beautiful prosthetic body to carry out her ideas, but she gradually (and at the end abruptly) sheds this body.

33. The novel's exemplary figure of the latter would be Carlyle.

34. See Gallagher, "George Eliot and *Daniel Deronda*: The Prostitute and the Jewish Question," *The New Historicism Reader,* ed. H. Aram Veeser (New York: Routledge, 1993), 124–40; and Freedman, *Temple of Culture*.

35. It is worth noting that *producers* name a form of cultural labor both culturally and historically associated with Jews and Jewishness in the United States—in Mel Brooks's film and musical, for example, or in figures like Phil Spector and Samuel Goldwyn. This association plays out as part of the long-running anti-Semitic association of Jews with the mass entertainment industry.

36. See Nancy Glazener, *Reading for Realism,* on the origins of the literary agent in this era. Also, Olive's assumption of this role brings her into proximity with theater managers, one of whom we see at the end of the novel. But there is an interesting analogy to Olive in the theater manager of Wilde's *Dorian Gray,* the swarthy Jew who knows his Shakespeare.

37. Mrs. Luna recognizes in this figure of the agent the cultural laborer who arranges the material conditions in which geniuses can exercise their "gift"—who can, in other words, provide the conditions in which the term "gift" can exercise its long-held position, powerfully privileged in the principles of modern Western aesthetics, as outside the "interested" concerns of economic matters. But she also registers and makes use of the disrepute and suspicion with which it is safe to assume most people will look on this figure. And she does so in a way that again recalls, in a refracted form, William Dean Howells's conception of genius as a parasitical shadow figure threatening to pervert the true figure of greatness.

38. Indeed, Olive's proximity to these contemporary cultural figurations of Jewishness takes shape along lines James conceived in a conversation with George du Maurier in the mid-1880s that eventually led to du Maurier's invention of the powerfully anti-Semitic character Svengali in the novel *Trilby*. What I mean to suggest, in other words, is that James may have used that conversation as fodder for writing Olive as a queer or lesbian Svengali, managing Verena's career for her erotic satisfaction in much the same way Svengali manages that of the good-natured British girl Trilby. In his entry of March 25, 1889, James says the initial conversation between the two men had taken place "a year or two ago . . . but it had passed from my mind." It may be stretching my argument to say that this conversation would have influenced James's composition of *The Bostonians,* but it seems quite possible that

James could have misremembered the timing of the conversation or, if the conversation took place after the book came out, that it could have had some relation to a novel he had recently completed. See *The Complete Notebooks of Henry James,* ed. Leon Edel and Lyall H. Powers (New York: Oxford University Press, 1987), 51–52.

39. Janice Radway, *A Feeling for Books: The Book-of-the-Month Club, Literary Taste, and Middle-Class Desire* (Chapel Hill: University of North Carolina Press, 1997), 152.

40. Freedman reads Svengali as embodying this "persistent expression of the simultaneous idealization and abjection of 'culture'" that he calls "the mark of the middlebrow." Freedman, *The Temple of Culture: Assimilation and Anti-Semitism in Literary Anglo-America* (New York: Oxford University Press, 2000), 10.

41. For accounts of the relationship between James and Lazarus, see Carole Kessner, "The Emma Lazarus–Henry James Connection: Eight Letters," *American Literary History* 3, no. 1 (Spring 1991): 46–62; and Alan G. James, "The Master and the Laureate of the Jews: The Brief Friendship of Henry James and Emma Lazarus," *Henry James Review* 21 (2000): 27–42. A good source on Lazarus in the context of American nationalism, Zionism, and "Jewish modernity" is Ranen Omer-Sherman, *Diaspora and Zionism in Jewish American Literature: Lazarus, Syrkin, Reznikoff, Roth* (Hanover and London: Brandeis University Press, 2002). James, in fact, is known to have called on Lazarus while she was visiting London in the spring of 1886, shortly before she learned that she had contracted the cancer from which she would die the following year. In the tradition of *la belle Juive,* Lazarus's gentile readers tended to understand her less as a writer than as a singer or performer, an artist of presence, as in John J. Whittier's comment just after her death: "With no lack of rhythmic sweetness, she has often the rugged strength and verbal audacity of Browning. Since Miriam sang of deliverance and triumph by the Red Sea, the Semitic race has had no braver singer." Indeed, Miriam would be the name James chose for the character with which he revisited the topic of the performing female genius.

42. This is despite the fact that James is clearly drawing on the eminence of the philanthropic Guggenheim family.

43. Abram S. Isaacs, *Stories from the Rabbis* (New York: Charles Webster, 1893). The ad appears in *Century* 45, no. 6 (April 1893).

44. The inclusion of Professor Gougenheim in James's "very American tale" also suggests, albeit satirically, that New York is a more culturally modern city than Boston, less constricted by its associations with abolitionism and antebellum reform in general; Howells's own move from Boston to New York, the basis of the plot of *A Hazard of New Fortunes* (1890), reflected this trend as well; the novel included a background moment similar to the *Bostonians*' mention of Prof. Gougenheim when Basil March dines at a bohemian downtown restaurant filled with "young literary men and artists [and] . . . Hebrews and Cubans" (71). In his July 1886 "Editor's Study," Howells praised

the novel *Mrs. Peixada,* by Sidney Luska, the pseudonym of Henry Harland, a gentile, who wrote a series of novels about what Howells called "Beekman Place interiors, with the eating and smoking that goes on in them, and those Beekman Place figures of naturalized German Jews" (taken from *Selected Literary Criticism*).

45. See, for example, Sara Blair, *Henry James and the Writing of Race and Nation* (Cambridge: Cambridge University Press 1996); Michael Moon, *A Small Boy and Others: Imitation and Initiaion in American Culture from Henry James to Andy Warhol* (Durham, N.C.: Duke University Press, 1998); Ross Posnock, *The Trials of Curiosity: Henry James, William James, and the Challenge of Modernity* (New York: Oxford University Press, 1991).

46. Joseph Litvak associates Olive with "a particular kind of *genius loci,* where the place in question is an improbable, inert-looking semiotic residue in the narrative machinery, a residue that even the more astute critics have not begun to notice, much less activate." Litvak asks "what imaginative relations [Olive's pain] makes possible . . . between the gay author and the lesbian character" (223), and suggests that we might see Olive's ongoing potential at the end of the novel as James's dissatisfaction not just with heterosexuality but with the novel as a genre—as enacting his ongoing fascination with theatricality. This view comports with the ongoing concerns with public performance in *The Tragic Muse,* for which James made his first notes as he was writing *The Bostonians.* It also makes Olive a figure who anticipates James's own turn to writing for the stage in the years following *Muse.* That Olive is headed toward the stage suggests James's identification with this female character as she heads bravely off toward what Litvak calls "the very social-sexual vulgarity she professes to 'despise.'" Litvak, *Caught in the Act: Theatricality in the Nineteenth-Century British Novel* (Berkeley and Los Angeles: University of California Press, 1990), 307.

47. Bell, *The Problem of American Realism,* 91.

48. See Litvak, *Caught in the Act,* and Stevens, *Henry James and Sexuality* (Cambridge: Cambridge University Press, 1998).

49. Henry James, *Novels, 1886–1890* (New York: Library of America, 1989), 710. Further citations will appear in the body of the text.

50. See, for example, Jonathan Freedman, *Professions of Taste: Henry James and British Aestheticism* (Stanford, Calif.: Stanford University Press, 1990), and Eric Haralson, "Elusive Queer Comrade."

51. Moon, *A Small Boy and Others,* 2.

52. It also makes sense then that despite the mixed reputation of the novel today, *The Tragic Muse* was hailed by Howells and William James as Henry's triumph. In an 1890 letter to his brother, William wrote: "At last you've done it and make no mistake. The Tragic Muse caps the climax. It is a most original, wonderful, delightful and admirable production." See *The Correspondence of William James,* vol. 2, *William and Henry, 1885–1896,* ed. Ignas K. Skrupselis and Elizabeth M. Berkeley (Charlottesville: University Press of Virginia, 1993), 142. To Howells, he wrote, "The year which shall have

witnessed the apparition of your Hazard of N. F. of Harry's Tragic Muse, and of *my* Psychology, will indeed be a memorable one in American literature!" William was referring to Howells's novel *A Hazard of New Fortunes.* See *The Correspondence of William James,* vol. 7, *1890–1894,* 88. Although William's tone is not wholly serious, his declaration to Howells that *The Tragic Muse* is an eminent *American* novel is provocative. His contextualization of the novel within the history of American literature provides some historical grounding for claims made by some of the most compelling recent readings of the novel, particularly those in Sara Blair, *Henry James and the Writing of Race and Nation* (Cambridge: Cambridge University Press, 1996), and John Carlos Rowe, *The Other Henry James* (Durham, N.C.: Duke University Press, 1997). Rowe argues that *Muse* has been neglected by Jamesians because it problematizes presumptions about James's anglophilia because it is actually a satire of Britishness. Blair has suggested a different reading of *The Tragic Muse,* which, she writes, "can be said variously to exploit and expend the symbolic capital of a figuratively American freedom of filiation, reordinating the meaning of whiteness in various sites of contested modernity" (13). Blair sees the novel as instrumental in an attempt by James to articulate a kind of moderate cosmopolitanism, working to refine the Anglo-Saxonism of Euro-American culture while embracing the contributions of certain forms of ethnicity, such as Jewishness.

53. I should note that this view of Kant is highly mediated by history; for a detailed study of Kant's writings in historical perspective, see Howard Caygill, *The Art of Judgement* (Oxford: Basil Blackwell, 1986).

54. Nancy Armstrong, "Who's Afraid of the Cultural Turn?" *differences* 12, no. 1 (2001): 25.

55. In his enthusiastic notice in the "Editor's Study," Howells praised the novel effusively as a "more than a novel," a text that could have been produced only by "an American of Henry James's modernity." He used the topic of James's "baggy monster" (as James referred to the novel in his preface to the revised edition) to describe the ills of reading novels in the United States, which he saw as superficially concerned with closure and moral clarity. His favorite characters were Nash and Miriam, whom he found eminently realistic "types." See Howells, "Editor's Study," *Harper's New Monthly Magazine* 81 (September 1890), reprinted in Kevin Hayes, ed., *Henry James: The Contemporary Reviews* (Cambridge: Cambridge University Press, 1996), 234.

56. Matthew Tinkcom, *Working Like a Homosexual: Camp, Capital, Cinema* (Durham, N.C.: Duke University Press, 2002).

57. Tinkcom, *Working Like a Homosexual,* 41.

58. As the work of scholars such as Bentley and Michael Elliot shows, the line also captures the contemporary currency of ethnographic definitions of culture. See Bentley, *The Ethnography of Manners;* and Elliott, *The Culture Concept: Writing and Difference in the Age of Realism* (Minneapolis: University of Minnesota Press, 2002).

59. In this view of the contemporary cultural field, literature is not guar-

anteed cultural preeminence, and in fact genius works against such an assumption. Peter Sherringham, whom the novel burdens with the role of foil in many matters, defends literature as the essential art when he insists to Miriam that she must learn Milton and Wordsworth, and come to understand Shakespeare as a poet as well as a dramatist.

60. *The Complete Notebooks of Henry James,* 28.

61. See Moon, *A Small Boy and Others.*

62. Notably, in Alcott's *Little Women,* "Mr. Dashwood" is the name of the cigar-chewing editor of the *Weekly Volcano* to whom Jo March takes her sensation stories in hope of publishing them. "Basil," of course, is self-appropriated from *The Bostonians* (and was also the name of Howells's protagonist in *A Hazard of New Fortunes*).

63. The recurrent use of forms of the word *mix* also reflects the idealization of variety that Carrie Tirado Bramen associates with turn-of-the century U.S. liberal intellectuals, particularly William James, in *The Uses of Variety.*

64. This is also a convention of *la belle Juive* narratives, similar to the ending of Halevy's opera, *La Juive.*

65. George du Maurier, *Trilby* (Oxford: Oxford University Press, 1998), 6–7. Late in his life, James Russell Lowell articulated a similar form of philo-Semitism, sometimes expressed amid vitriolic anti-Semitism. See for example the last few pages of *The Letters of James Russell Lowell,* vol. 1, ed. Charles Eliot Norton (New York: Harper, 1894).

66. *Notorious C. H. O.,* dir. Lorene Machado (2002).

67. See, for example, the readings by Haralson in *Henry James and Queer Modernity* (Cambridge: Cambridge University Press, 2003); Rowe in *The Other Henry James;* and Christopher Lane in his *The Burdens of Intimacy: Psychoanalysis and Victorian Masculinity* (Chicago: University of Chicago Press, 1999).

68. This in itself is significant, for it suggests a way that James in this novel may contribute to the diversification of genealogies of queer culture, a project evident in Michael Moon's resituation of James's work in his book *A Small Boy and Others.* This would make possible a queer studies less strictly dependent on the arrest and trial of Wilde—i.e., on a moment of highly publicized pathologization and punishment (in Moon's *A Small Boy and Others*).

69. D. A. Miller, *Narrative and Its Discontents* (Princeton, N.J.: Princeton University Press, 1981).

70. In an unpublished letter to Grace Norton, James complains of the "impedimenta" that accompany Howells when the latter visited London in 1882. See Michael Anesko, *Letters, Fictions, Lives: Henry James and William Dean Howells* (New York: Oxford University Press), 176.

71. On these issues more broadly, see Daniel Boyarin, Daniel Itzkovitz, and Ann Pellegrini, eds., *Queer Theory and the Jewish Question* (New York: Columbia University Press, 2003).

72. Brian Selsky, "I Dream of Genius," in *Pop Out: Queer Warhol,* ed. Jennifer Doyle, Jonathan Flatley, and José Muñoz (Durham, N.C.: Duke University Press, 1995).

Index

GUSTAVUS STADLER is associate professor of English at Haverford College. He lives in Haverford, Pennsylvania, and New York City.